Youth Culture and Private Space

GW00493482

Youth Culture and Private Space

Siân Lincoln
Senior Lecturer in Media Studies, Liverpool John Moores University, UK

First published 2012 by
PALGRAVE MACMILLAN

Palgrave Macmillan in the UK is an imprint of Macmillan Publishers Limited,
registered in England, company number 785998, of Houndmills, Basingstoke,
Hampshire RG21 6XS.

Palgrave Macmillan in the US is a division of St Martin's Press LLC,
175 Fifth Avenue, New York, NY 10010.

Palgrave Macmillan is the global academic imprint of the above companies
and has companies and representatives throughout the world.

Palgrave® and Macmillan® are registered trademarks in the United States,
the United Kingdom, Europe and other countries.

ISBN 978-1-349-31332-7   ISBN 978-1-137-03108-2 (eBook)
DOI 10.1057/9781137031082

This book is printed on paper suitable for recycling and made from fully
managed and sustained forest sources. Logging, pulping and manufacturing
processes are expected to conform to the environmental regulations of the
country of origin.

A catalogue record for this book is available from the British Library.

A catalog record for this book is available from the Library of Congress.

10   9   8   7   6   5   4   3   2   1
21 20 19 18 17 16 15 14 13 12

For Carys
My sister and my best friend

Contents

List of Figures

Foreword

Issues of space and place have been core to the study of youth culture since the formative work of the CCCS on post-war working class 'subcultures'. Problematically, however, much of that work, in keeping with its emphasis on 'spectacular youth', has focused on young people's appropriation of public space and place as arenas for displays of style-coded resistance. Only very rarely has there been any acknowledgement of youth's relationship to private space or, indeed, the connections between the private and public spheres of youth cultural practice. McRobbie and Garber's mid-1970s study of teen girls' use of bedroom space in the domestic sphere of the family home was an innovative moment in this respect, presenting a very different account to the majority of youth cultural studies which tended to focus on predominantly male, street-based examples of style-centred youth cultures. By contrast, McRobbie and Garber's work demonstrated another aspect of youth cultural activity in which patriarchal authority and gender roles forced a particular set of relationships to space among teenage working-class and lower-middle-class girls. Excluded from the more public, male-based forms of youth cultural activity, these teenage girls were instead forced to utilise the private, domestic spaces available to them, typically the bedroom, for their own symbolic rituals of stylistic and musical practice. Innovative as this study was, however, it remained relatively unique in its insight for many years; a central aspect of McRobbie and Garber's argument, that the academic gaze remained transfixed on male-based and publicly spectacular youth cultures, was reinforced as youth cultural research continued to produce scholarship broadly situated within that vein. But at the same time, McRobbie and Garber's work began to look increasingly dated, its key arguments effectively summing up a period of pre-digital late twentieth-century history in which the bedroom could more easily be represented as a hermeneutically separate space free from the blurring of the public and private that would become evident as the latter were increasingly impacted by new media technologies.

Youth Culture and Private Space is thus a very important book in many ways. Most crucially it offers an in-depth account of an area of youth cultural practice that has been decidedly overlooked since the study of youth culture became a bona fide aspect of academic research. Drawing on very high quality ethnographic data, the book offers a sophisticated analysis of young people's appropriation and use of private space in the family home in an era where both gendered dimensions of identity have begun to shift and reliance on digital media technologies is increasingly the norm. Highly significant here is Lincoln's concept of 'zoning' which she uses as a means of explicating the various means to which contemporary youth, both female and male, use and understand 'private' space with reference to the level of interface between the 'public' and the 'private' afforded by digital media. As Lincoln masterfully demonstrates, the connections between private and public space are continually rearticulated by young people with the effect that the contemporary young person's bedroom takes on inherently multi-functional qualities, being at once an individualised space for relaxation, study or recreation and a place for collective gatherings often associated with the preparation for a 'night out' or a space to chill out in following a night on the town. Through the connectedness offered through new media technologies, the zonings that Lincoln identifies in the youth bedroom space acquire complex dynamics of their own as young people use the internet and iPhone as a means of keeping in touch with friends, sourcing information for their school and academic studies, or downloading music to listen to individually or collectively.

Critically important too is Lincoln's overall reconceptualisation of space and place as this pertains to the cultural practices of young people and the relationships they build with each other. All too often the language of youth cultural studies assumes a crude equation of youth's spatial politics with dimensions of resistance that overlook the ordinary everyday lives of youth. In *Youth Culture and Private Space*, this over-emphasis on space appropriation as 'resistance' is readdressed and rebalanced, giving equal – and long overdue – attention to the more mundane ways in which private space is utilised by young people. In *Youth Culture and Private Space* Lincoln has produced a very important book; highly original in its approach this is a study that is set to make a major impact on youth studies and provide the foundations for a major new area of research in the sphere of contemporary youth culture.

Andy Bennett
Griffith Centre for Cultural Research
Griffith University

Acknowledgements

First and foremost I would like to thank my editors at Palgrave Macmillan, who have been exceptional in their managing of this project and always forthcoming and generous with their advice, comments and feedback. I would particularly like to thank Emily Salz who encouraged me to submit a proposal for this project in the first place, Cristabel Scaife who took me smoothly through the commissioning stage and Felicity Plester, who was so patient and attentive during the final stages of submitting the manuscript. I would also like to thank Catherine Mitchell, who advised me throughout on many aspects of the book's production.

The image used on the cover was shot by the photographer Carey Gough, whom I met through our mutual interest in teen spaces. I am so grateful to her for not only allowing me to use the image on the front cover, but for shooting it especially. Thanks so much.

A number of colleagues have inspired, encouraged and supported me along the way. Most notably I would like to thank Rob MacDonald at Teesside University, who taught me as an undergraduate between 1994 and 1997. If I had not taken his youth cultures module I would probably have never have been inspired to write this book. Thanks also to Andy Bennett at Griffith University, who examined my PhD thesis in 2003, has been hugely supportive of my work ever since and who kindly wrote the foreword to this book. I would also like to thank Graham McBeath, my colleague during my time at the University of Northampton, who is an extraordinary academic and who helped me through some really tough times. Thank you also to my colleagues in the Media and Cultural Studies department at Liverpool John Moores University: Nickianne Moody, Steve Spittle, Clare Horrocks and Joanne Knowles, who supported me throughout.

Much of the research for this book was undertaken during my postgraduate studies at Manchester Metropolitan University, where I gained my MA and my PhD. Studying there was a great experience and I was very privileged to be supervised by Tim Dant, Katie Milestone and the late Derek Wynne. I also made some great friends there too, namely Mareike Barmeyer, Joanne Massey and Fiona Hutton. Much of the research conducted in Liverpool during the later stages of the project was supported by the Liverpool John Moores UoA66 capability fund, from which I received financial assistance to undertake aspects of the fieldwork.

A number of people have been kind enough to read drafts of various chapters and I would particularly like to thank Nedim Hassan and Peter Hopkins. I would also like to thank David Oswald for helping me with the images and Craig Thompson for transcribing a number of the interviews.

There are a number of friends (too many to mention here, but you know who you are and thanks to each and every one of you) whom I am sure are now fed up with asking me the question 'so, how's the book going?'. I would particularly like to thank the following people for repeatedly asking me this question and keeping up the momentum: Annie Gosling, Steve Spittle, Gary Needham, Frank Halligan, Rupa Huq, Angela Gentille, Derren Gilhooley, Paul Hodkinson, Ben Light, Marie Griffiths, Susie Tamplin, Becky Finnegan, Alison Moore, Judi Turner-Gill and Sophia Maine. I would also like to thank Janan Fifield, who took me under his wing during my time in Northampton, and Jonathan Brook and his family, who were always very supportive. Kathleen Phythian helped me immensely through the final stages of writing this book, making me see that I could do it – thanks so much, Kathleen. I would also like to thank Colin Fallows for his great friendship and wonderful and inspiring conversations.

Paula Noble and Fiona O'Mahony have been incredibly supportive for a number of years. Both are great friends who have never failed to be there and with whom I've had some really good times. Thank you.

My family has supported me in a number of ways over the years, so thank you to Mum and Dad, Carys, Alex, James and Scarlett and also to the Tzioumakis family. Mum, you get a special mention for helping on so many occasions to look after Roman in the first few months of his life so that I could work on the book – thank you so much!

I would like to give thanks to all of my research participants. If they hadn't allowed me privileged access to their bedrooms and provided me with such insightful accounts into their worlds, I would not have been able to complete this book. I would also like to thank all those people who put me in touch with participants in the first place which made access to my research sites so much easier.

Finally, I would like to thank my partner Yannis Tzioumakis, without whom I would never have got through this. During the final stages of writing this book we welcomed our son Roman into the world. With your unfailing patience, encouragement, love and support, I was able to finish this project as well as be a mum. Thank you so much.

Introduction

I don't know, it's just something about bedrooms ...
they become part of you. (Erin, 18 years old)

I want you to sit back, close your eyes, relax and get ready for a little trip down memory lane. Take yourself back to your teenage years and try to remember what your bedroom looked like when you were at this age. Think about its size and its shape, the colours, the things in it, the posters up on the walls, the music you played, what the room smelt like. Think about what you used to do in there and who with, the things you did but were not really supposed to and with what consequence. Whether you are an adult and this exercise takes you decades back or a young person either still living in the family home, or having only recently moved out, I bet you can remember some of those details pretty well. You see, whenever anyone asks me what my research interests are, and I tell them, they might initially let out a rather nervous laugh but, invariably, this is followed up with some story or another that recounts memories of their bedrooms when they were young. Sometimes friends and colleagues who are now parents themselves will tell me about their children's bedrooms or indeed young people themselves will describe that space to me. It is a space about which we seem to have a lot to say.

So why should this be the case? What is so special about what is essentially a room in a house, usually owned by your parents? First, for those young people who have a bedroom,[1] this is often one of the first spaces over which they have some sense of ownership. This sense is achieved in a number of ways, for example through the room's decoration, through the material objects and items within it that personalise the space or through its regulation. Many young people share a

1

bedroom with their siblings but often, even in these circumstances, the corner of the room that they occupy is marked out as their own and is regulated as such.

Second, as they move through their adolescent years young people begin to demand or crave 'space' of their own (Larson, 1995), where they can have some privacy and where they can be away from their families, siblings and peers (or connect with them at their leisure, for example, through new technologies) As Evie, 16 years old, said: '[it was] just the best thing that happened when I managed to get a room to myself and I think it's incredibly important to have it to yourself because, you know, sometimes the family is overwhelming ...' In their bedrooms young people can escape, if temporarily, from the problems and issues associated with growing up, puberty and the changing of their bodies and emotions; they can have some time alone or they can hang out with their friends; they can do homework or find ways to avoid it; engage in activities such as smoking, drinking, drug taking or sex (whether their parents know or approve or not); lose themselves in mediated worlds of music, games or social networking for hours on end. A young person's bedroom can be a hub of activity.

Third, it is a space over which young people are able to 'mark out' their identities. As one of my participants claimed in showing me his room, 'I've stamped my personality all over it', or as another said, 'this is *my* space!' As I shall explore in this book, this is a space over which young people work hard to make it their own, to represent who they are at a particular age in their lives, what they have become and what they have left behind. Each and every bedroom that I have visited, while in many ways utterly predictable, has also been unique and, after getting to know my participants, it was clear that each individual bedroom represents their respective personalities, interests and hobbies, their social, cultural, everyday lives, whatever the extent of their use of the space.

Fourth, this is a space that is by no means 'static'. Young people constantly move in and out of their bedrooms, for example as a prequel or a sequel to the activities of the day or night. It is a space within which they might dwell for extended periods of their leisure time and within which they may change the landscape of the world around them – be it through the moving around of things, objects and items in that space or through the opening up of virtual worlds and media 'zones' that function as 'bedrooms' beyond the traditional borders and interpretations of the actual room. Irrespective of the extent to which a bedroom is used by its owner or whether it assumes a secondary position compared to spaces outside the home, the bedroom is an integral space in their lives and one that is constantly changing, alongside the young person who uses it. For these reasons, as well as for many others, this is why young people have a lot to say about their rooms.

My bedroom(s)

I was a teenager who spent a lot of my time in my bedroom, and a lot of time working on what my bedroom looked like. I remember making various demands of my father, who subsequently became an expert in painting a sun bursting from behind an array of clouds on my bedroom wall (a demand in my bedroom when we lived in Hertfordshire), putting up stretches of cork board so that I could put up a 'collage' of posters on my wall (a demand in my bedroom when we lived in Cumbria), and agreeing to what – I am certain in hindsight – was a rather grotesque pink and grey striped carpet (a demand made in my room in Northampton). I think, for me, my bedroom became an important space amidst all of the moving around the country that I did with my family when I was growing up, when we occupied a total of four houses in a period of around eight years. It was the one space in each of our houses that I could replicate in a new home, that I could call my own, while other important aspects of my life such as towns and villages, schools and friends changed around me. I even remember visiting my father in a hotel for a few days when we were in between house moves, and taking ornaments from my bedroom to display for the time I was there. My bedroom always gave me a touch point of familiarity, some sense of permanence in an often impermanent home life. It was also a space over which my sister and I had quite a lot of control; for example, in terms of what our rooms looked like, what colour they would be, the choice of wallpaper and carpets, and so on. I suspect this was a conscious decision on the part of my parents to grant me and my sister this prerogative, perhaps in an effort to compensate for what seemed like constant moving around. My sister's bright purple room in our house in Cumbria was indeed a testament to this.

My bedroom was also a place of 'escapism'. I would spend a lot of time in my room, particularly as a way to escape from problems related to family and school. It was a space within which I would attempt to work out why I was encountering particular problems, why members of my family did particular things or to use the fantasy worlds created by music, books and pop magazines to withdraw myself from the problems and remove myself from a reality that I would rather not face head on. It was a space within which I would try and deal with overwhelming feelings of being completely alienated from my friends and peers, especially in my later teen years, not being one of the 'clever kids' when at sixth-form college, while throughout my teens and early twenties it was a space in which I indulged in the very secret world of an eating disorder. My bedroom was the perfect place in which to indulge my illness because it was my space and I could be on my own in there and partake in my secret 'disorder' rituals.

But despite remembering these difficult memories, I also have very happy memories of other things that I used my bedroom for. For example, it was a space of discovery, exploration and experimentation, and in fact my memories of the aesthetics of my bedrooms are very much led by my ever-changing tastes in music. From a very early age I was the ultimate poster girl. I distinctly remember being around 7 years old and the first poster I ever had was of the band Bucks Fizz and it hung proudly over my bed – the memorable image of the band taken from their Eurovision win in 1981 with the girls in their red and yellow mini-skirts and the boys in their blue and green velour tops teamed with white trousers. My memories of friends' bedrooms too are largely remembered through the posters in their bedrooms: my friend Lucy, whose bedroom walls were covered in posters of the Human League; my friend Kathy's bedroom, covered in posters of Michael Jackson; my friend Paula's room, covered in Britpop memorabilia. And the poster-clad bedroom continued well into my university years when my bedrooms in my student accommodation were plastered with posters of Suede, Pulp, Radiohead and many other indie bands of the day that hung amongst the numerous gig tickets that I had started to accumulate. I would spend hours and hours listening to music in my room, really filling the space so it resonated with the sound, be it through the volume on my stereo system or through the headphones of my Walkman. I liked to listen lying on my bed, in the dark, I liked to dance or use music as a soundtrack when trying out different outfits, make-up and hairstyles and I particularly liked music that I considered to be powerful, emotional and a bit on the dark side that complemented the often subdued states I was in.

I did, however, also have the obligatory 'teeny-bopper' moments, namely in the form of the Norwegian pop band A-ha when I was around 12 years old and Bros (oh the shame!) when I was around 15 years old. My Bros obsession particularly led to my bedroom almost becoming a kind of shrine to the band and it was also one of the very few times, in my teenage years at least, that I spent long periods of time in my room with other people, namely my fellow 'Brosette' Katie. We would listen tirelessly to their album, watch their tour video and talk all things Matt, Luke and Craig. My sister also partook in this activity from time to time.

In all seriousness though, I would state without equivocation that 'my bedroom' has been a crucial space present throughout my life and, as you will see throughout the book, bedrooms play a significant, and sometimes fundamental, role in the lives of many young people today. The experience of a bedroom and 'bedroom culture' can be immensely personal but it is also a space within which the very essence of youth culture can be captured and understood both within and outside the four walls of that space.

Youth culture

Youth, Paul Willis claims, is not just a biological stage in a young person's life that 'enforces its own social condition' but is a stage within which, critically, young people 'form symbolic moulds through which they understand themselves and their possibilities for the rest of their lives' (1990, p. 7). The concept of symbolism that Willis draws on here is by no means unfamiliar in the literature surrounding the emergence of youth cultures and youth subcultures, particularly in the work of the Centre for Contemporary Cultural Studies in Birmingham (CCCS). In fact, symbolism was one of the key notions through which subcultures were made sense of. For example, Hebdige (1979) used the conceptual tool of 'style' to explore the ways in which youth subcultural groups such as the Teddy Boys, Mods and Punks would use visual symbols such as clothing, hairstyles and make-up as well as material adornments such as motorbikes or scooters to symbolise their 'membership' and allegiance to a particular subculture. At the same time, their 'style' visually represented to a mystified public their group solidarity with like-minded individuals together with whom they felt alienated from the wider, dominant hegemonic culture (Hall and Jefferson, 1975). The term 'youth culture', then, has become synonymous with explicating a particular way of life that has specific values and meanings which are unique to those young people experiencing them (Frith, 1984). Youth culture is often understood as an alternative, meaningful route for young people who, when going through their turbulent teenage years, are able to find cultural outlets that help them express how they feel, and give them a sense of meaning and purpose when they cannot necessarily find this in other social structures such as school, the home or family.

The term 'youth culture', then, is necessarily tangible, fluid and dynamic, which, on the one hand, helps us understand some of the common patterns in young people's lives and the ways they make the world around them meaningful, while, on the other, helps us explore the highly individual ways in which youth cultures are navigated and experienced by young people themselves; how they drift and flow as they transit towards their adult years. Not surprisingly, then, it has been argued that youth cultures should be understood within the discourse of identity and there have been a number of studies that examine youth cultures within this context (see, for example, Epstein, 1998; Bennett, 2000; Miles, 2000; Muggleton and Weinzierl, 2003). Into the equation of youth cultures and identity this book will also add the question of space. Specifically it will suggest that youth cultures are also about the search by young people for meaningful 'identity spaces', and the bedroom can take on this function particularly well. Through a study of bedrooms it is possible to see 'in action' the ways in which young people articulate their own personal and private spaces as sites of youth culture; how such spaces represent these articulations both as highly individual and personal experiences and as experiences that are shared with other people. In many ways, the teenage bedroom is a 'prism' through which one can explore youth culture and young people's use of it as well as examine the numerous ways in which this space, and youth cultural pursuits themselves, shift and change accordingly.

Private space

A young person's bedroom is what can be considered a 'private' space, although the level of privacy that a young person is afforded within it can vary greatly and is subject to different rules and regulations, many specific to their household. In the context of young people and youth culture (as in many other contexts in our highly mediated world of exposure) the word 'private' is difficult to define. As I discuss in the chapters of this book, the significance of private space as an important youth cultural site has largely been ignored, even in the traditional youth cultures literature of the CCCS where only McRobbie and Garber's (1975) essay 'Girls and Subcultures' serves as any kind of corrective to this. However, while this account was important in British youth cultural studies and is still cited in recent research on the subject, it presented 'the private' as the reserve of only teenage girls and as a realm that is rather isolated from the world outside of the bedroom door, from public spaces. As will become evident throughout this book, private space has a role to play in the lives of young women *and* young men alike, and as others have argued (Livingstone, 2005; Abbott-Chapman and Robertson, 2009;

Pearson, 2009), the word 'private' in this context is not simply a binary opposite to 'public' space, one being 'inside' and one being 'outside'. It is a space that is integral to the overall life-worlds of young people and is adapted by them accordingly. For example, as Abbott-Chapman and Robertson argue, private spaces such as bedrooms are:

> Places that convey 'peace, quiet, sense of space, relaxation, seclusion' – what we have termed *private spaces of withdrawal* ... we suggest that these reactions may result from the need of young people to escape daily pressures in our time/space compressed world and to re-define for themselves the boundaries of 'private' space in which to reflect and make meaning. (2009, p. 431)

Other scholars who have an interest in private spaces such as bedrooms describe them as important sites in the making of a young person's identity (Steele and Brown, 1995); solitary spaces within which teenagers shift in and out of public and private realms through the media (Larson, 1995); sites of 'resistance' and alternative spaces, particularly for teenage girls placed in passivity in public spaces by their male counterparts (James, 2001); as ever-changing cultural constructions that accommodate a young person's leisure interests inside and outside the home (Abbott-Chapman and Robertson, 2009); or as important sites of meaning making through the media (Baker, 2004; Kearney, 2007). In the context of this book, it is appropriate to consider what the young people who took part in this research project considered 'private' space to be and what such spaces meant to them. Such definitions have informed my understanding of the word for the purpose of the following discussions and for the role and meaning of private space in the lives of young people today. Examples from my participants included:

> It's my room; it's my space to do my stuff. (Sonia, 22 years old)

> It's really important because if I'm with others [all day] then it's nice to come in here and be on my own. (Nina, 20 years old)

> I think it's important because you need your privacy; I think that is the main thing, that you need to be creative, which is difficult if you've got loads of people around. You can invite people in, which is good, because you have got privacy but you can decide; you have got more control over your own space and you can decorate it how you want. (Erin, 18 years old)

In terms of privacy I think this is the best space I've had. (Richard, 18 years old)

Everyone has days when they prefer to chill out and have time on their own. (James, 16 years old)

This small selection of quotes from my participants represents a number of the major themes that run through my discussions in this book. One of the points that was repeatedly emphasised by my participants was the desire to have access to private space as part of their everyday lives, with the bedroom being able to accommodate this need. This space, however, is not isolated from the rules and regulations that govern each household in which the bedroom exists and it is not immune to 'invasions' from parents, siblings, friends and peers from time to time, which can make achieving privacy difficult.

Bedrooms are also important identity spaces, spaces in which young people can 'be themselves' away from the pressures of life in other realms such as school, college or work and engage in different cultural pursuits. Bedrooms can also be decorated according to the current (and past) cultural interests of their young occupants. As Erin states above, young people often have some level of control over what their space looks like, for example in terms of how it is decorated, and this means that young people can use their bedrooms as a 'canvas' to display who they are and what they like.

Young people also associate 'private spaces' such as their bedrooms with having a sense of autonomy and independence, using their rooms to spend time on their own, should they choose, with their friends or as a 'portal' of communication through which they access the virtual worlds of social networking. In this way, in their bedrooms, young people can be alone while together with others at the same time. The bedroom, then, is not just a private space isolated from the public realm, as early studies of bedroom culture inferred (McRobbie and Garber, 1975) (although as noted by Bennett in the foreword to this book this study was undertaken in a pre-digital era and in a time when patriarchal norms held much greater sway in many households), but, perhaps more than ever before, in an age of digital media, bedrooms are integral, interconnected hubs of communication as well as personal, private identity spaces 'marked out' as such through the objects, items and things collected within it. It is this interplay that informs the forthcoming discussions.

I begin in Chapter 1 by revisiting what has been termed 'traditional' youth cultural theory, particularly focusing on the emergence of the study of youth cultures and subcultures in the UK as pioneered by the Centre for Contemporary Cultural Studies. While providing an overview of some of the key debates in this work, for example in reference to the teenage delinquent and the teenage consumer, I establish from the outset where the 'gaps' in the coverage of private space may exist in such discourses. I suggest here that the context of the private or domestic setting for potential youth cultural activities is primarily located within discussions of under-represented groups of young people, namely young women engaging in what McRobbie and Garber term 'bedroom culture', and the efforts to locate young women in youth cultural discourse. As I will demonstrate, the context of the domestic can be explored as a youth cultural space for both young women *and* young men as part of their everyday lives in both the public and the private realm. I will also suggest in this chapter that private and personal spaces might have been explored in traditional subcultures – for example, when reflecting on the highly stylised subculture of Mod one might assume that spaces for getting ready for nights on the town required a domestic setting – but CCCS researchers chose not to occupy themselves with such questions. In this respect, I argue that the role of the private is by no means insignificant in such contexts, yet it is by and large ignored or marginalised in those studies (for instance, in Hebdige, 1979).

While the concept of 'subculture' that informed much of the CCCS' work on youth cultures is still considered to carry much theoretical weight in understanding contemporary youth cultures, since the early 2000s there have been efforts to critique and update the concept through what has been termed 'post-subculturalism' (for example, Muggleton, 1997, 2000; Bennett, 1999; Stahl, 1999; Miles, 2000; Muggleton and Weinzierl, 2003). This approach, which questions the imposition of 'structural' categories such as social class and considers them rigid and largely intangible concepts, sets out to account for the fluid, multi-interpretable nature of contemporary youth cultures. Specifically it aims to capture the significance and meaning of youth cultures to young people themselves who shift and change in accordance with their collective identities as well as individual lifestyles (Miles, 2000). Such an approach, I argue, more readily lends itself to the exploration of young people's private spaces within the context of neoliberal society that is characterised by individualisation and 'risk' and within which personal and private spaces such as bedrooms are becoming ever more important. This is because they represent spaces where youth identities can be articulated, displayed and captured as young people move through youth cultures and transit towards adulthood.

In Chapter 2, I take the reader on the 'methodological' journey of my research, exploring young people, youth cultures and private space using ethnographic methodologies. One of the criticisms of traditional youth cultures studies was that, despite their claims that they had used empirically informed methodologies (namely ethnography in Hall and Jefferson's (1975) *Resistance through Rituals*), the conduct of their research was not necessarily done with the rigour required to represent young people participating in youth cultures and subcultures as accurately as might have been the case. In fact, as Coles (1986) points out, many of the representations of young men, particularly in the subcultures literature, were largely not recognisable to the young people themselves. Since the 1980s, this problem and other relevant criticisms have been addressed, particularly in the sociology of youth, with questions of methodology emerging as a key component in discussions of young people's youth cultures (Bennett, 2002). In this chapter, then, I discuss in depth the research process undertaken to explore young people in the context of private space, and especially their bedrooms.

Dickinson et al. (2001), Pink (2009) and others have argued that there are certain realms, for example the private or the domestic, that do not readily lend themselves to traditional ethnographic practice. I critically reflect on the suitability of these 'orthodox' approaches to the study of youth cultures in private and domestic settings, particularly focusing upon the problems, issues and dilemmas one is faced with when doing research in highly private and personal domains such as a young person's bedroom. In doing this, I discuss the methodologies I employed throughout the research process and which have been informed by the more classic ethnographic tradition of participant observation and interviewing, as well as more contemporary approaches, such as sensory and visual ethnography (Pink, 2004, 2007, 2009). I argue that, while an 'orthodox' ethnography may not be wholly appropriate to contexts such as young people's bedrooms, a combination of methodological approaches that draw on this tradition but also include other elements such as photography can not only produce rich data but also mimic contemporary youth cultural practices that by their very nature are highly visual and sensorial. Crucially, such an approach has enabled me to explore in detail the space of the bedroom itself as an ethnographic text that, as I argue, should not be disassociated from the practices that take place within it.

In Chapter 3, the first of the chapters in which I draw on the research data and 'peer' inside a young person's room, I ask what appear to be two rather simple questions: what is a young person's bedroom used for and what is its significance in contemporary youth culture? In exploring these questions, it becomes apparent that while a young person's bedroom is first and foremost a functional space in which they sleep and perform everyday tasks and routines, it is also a 'work upon' space of identity; a place of escapism; a site of experimentation; a space in which to be alone as well as to socialise with friends or siblings; a site of transitions and a portal of communication. In this sense, then, a young person's bedroom is a complex space of youth cultural activity subjected to a number of different negotiations that emerge from its varying uses. The bedroom, of course, does not exist 'in isolation' and as I argue, these uses are implicitly and explicitly informed by the context of the household and family within which the bedroom exists, as well as by the public sphere.

'Age' has emerged as a key concept through which to understand this use and the extent to which the boundaries between public space and private space become blurred in young people's lives. I draw on a number of examples to explore this blurring, such as the ways in which young girls use their bedrooms to get dressed up to 'look' a particular age so that they can get into nightclubs, how bedrooms are used in conjunction with the availability of leisure facilities in a young person's locality and how bedrooms are transformed from solitary to social spaces when young people have their friends round or are getting ready for a night out. Age is also an important element within the wider context of the home, for example, with parents exercising control over who can and cannot enter their children's room, how the space can or cannot be decorated or siblings sharing a room and having to engage in a series of negotiations about how that space will be used and who has ownership of it. Finally, age is also important in the context of transitions, with a number of my participants accounting for changes in their bedrooms following experiences of transitions such as preparing for exams. In reaching such points in their lives, young people often see this as a time to reflect upon their personal space, their use of it and what is in it. It is often at these times when the content of bedrooms shifts from representing an occupant who is a child to one who is emerging as an adult.

I explore this idea further in Chapter 4 in which I provide an in-depth exploration of the 'materiality' of bedroom spaces, which in many of the existing discussions around bedroom culture is often touched upon, but is not really considered in any detail (see, for example, Larson, 1995; Steele and Brown, 1995; James, 2001; Abbott-Chapman, 2000, 2009; Baker, 2004; Abbott-Chapman and Robertson, 2009). The significance of materiality in bedroom space is notably absent from McRobbie and Garber's canonical study 'Girls and Subcultures' (1975). In this chapter, I argue that young people's bedroom spaces in the family home, as well as in other locations such as university halls of residence, are 'worked upon' and can therefore tell stories about their young occupants and their social and cultural lives. Importantly, in this chapter I explore how bedrooms, through young people's possessions, can be understood as sites of identity construction and management that are, on the one hand, controlled by young people themselves, while, on the other, are managed within a context of what Rose (1999) and Strickland have defined as the 'relentless pressure to consume' (2002, p. 7). Using my research data I illustrate how young people's bedroom spaces are ever-changing (even if they are not used to any great extent) in terms of their content and the significance of this content as part of young people's emerging biographies. Objects, items and things, I argue, are constantly moving in and out of the space, representing who young people are, their interactions in the public realm and what their interests are at any particular moment in time. At the same time, I propose, young people's possessions become important 'anchors' that 'fix' elements of their identity, and are important in today's fast-paced cultural world. Finally, in bringing forth a new dimension to discussions of the interplay of public and private realms in young people's bedrooms, I consider how the materiality of bedrooms is not just articulated by young people through the objects and items they have in it, but also in reference to the shops from which items are bought. I argue that emulating the style of particular shop layouts (in this case, Topshop and Urban Outfitters) represents the ultimate in 'bringing the outside in' and the extent to which the consumer world seeps into the space of the domestic in various ways.

In the penultimate chapter I use the concept of 'zoning' (Lincoln, 2004, 2005) as an approach through which to explore young people's bedrooms that are always 'under construction' as dynamic spaces and within which there is an interplay of physical and 'mediated' spaces. The concept of 'zoning' that takes its theoretical cues from McRobbie's 'coding' allows for an exploration of the teenage bedroom as a dynamic space within which young people are constantly shifting in and out, opening and closing different 'zones' both within private space as well as in public. As I demonstrate in this chapter, young people's bedrooms are spaces within which the blurring between public and private life is often captured, both in terms of the bedroom's uses and its content, and this is particularly pertinent in the context of teenagers who find themselves in various states of 'in-betweenness' as they move from dependence to independence, adolescence to adulthood. In the context of post-subculturalism, I argue that bedrooms are important sites within which young people are what Miles has called 'youth stylists' (Miles, 2000). I explore the various ways in which young people select from different media zones to construct their identities in a context of 'relentless consumption' (Strickland, 2002).

I begin the chapter with an historical overview of the relationship between the teenager and the media, particularly within the context of the 'consuming teen' of the post-1945 era. In this respect, I demonstrate, as indeed others have (see, for example, Frith, 1984; Epstein, 1998; Osgerby, 1998; France, 2007), that there has always been a relationship between the two, and that media markets have been very much influenced by this lucrative group of young consumers. I then consider the role of the media in 'traditional' bedroom culture, namely reconsidering McRobbie's analyses of *Jackie* magazine as a set of codes impressed on the life of the teenage girl before reflecting upon the role of the media in more contemporary discussions and debates (for example, Larson, 1995 and Abbott-Chapman and Robertson, 2009).

In applying the concept of 'zoning' to young people and bedroom culture I explore 'zoning in action' in three ways. First, I consider the ways in which bedroom spaces can be 'transformed' by the activities that take place within it (for example, by playing music or through the room's decoration). I illustrate this by drawing on various examples from my research data, including Nina, 20 years old, who had recently moved into a room in halls of residence. In 'zoning' her bedroom Nina was able to transform a mundane, generic space into a space of zones that represented her and her new life at university whereby she would be studying, socialising, experiencing new aspects of independence, as well as maintaining connections with her family, friends and loved ones back in her home town. I explore the complexities of this sort of zoning that demonstrates the intertwining of public and private and physical and virtual realms and how the space of the bedroom is transformed according to the activities that take place in this space.

Second, different zones can have different significances in young people's bedrooms, and for that reason one can detect both 'foreground' and 'background' zones. I argue that foreground zones tend to be more 'worked upon' spaces, in terms of their physical appearance and of young people's interactions in them. Further, foreground zones can overlap with or seep into background zones. These discussions demonstrate the different levels at which bedroom zones can 'resonate'. Music, for example, is often part of the fabric of young people's rooms and the examples that I draw on from the data in this chapter show how music zones are constructed.

Finally, I continue to use music as an example of a bedroom zone. Music has been cited in previous bedroom cultures studies as integral to teenagers' private space (Larson, 1995; Steele and Brown, 1995). Not only does music enable young people spending time in their rooms to explore their own individual musical tastes and identities, and to indulge different moods, feelings and emotions, it also activates the bedroom into a social zone when friends spend time listening to music together. Using the example of James, 16 years old, and his friends using iPods in their bedrooms I demonstrate how music as a main zone in a young person's bedroom is engaged in, both as a solitary activity and a social one. Through the development of new media technologies such as the iPod, music zones (and indeed other media zones) can be 'zoned' further, achieving different levels of intensity on listening as well as facilitating the social interactions taking place in that space. These 'zones within zones' are opened and closed according to the boys' interactions, the technologies on which they listen to the music, the other technologies they engage with in addition to their iPods and the consequences of this listening in terms of their consumption practices beyond the realm of the bedroom. This, I argue, demonstrates the complexity of zoning in bedrooms as well as the integral role of the media used by young people in experiencing bedroom culture.

In the final chapter of this book I consider the ways in which the concept of 'bedroom culture' can be understood outside of its traditional physical and domestic domain and within the context of virtual spaces, within which so many young people now communicate and interact. I draw upon the notion of the spatial metaphor of the 'teenage bedroom' that I first explored with Paul Hodkinson (2008), primarily within the context of the weblog or 'virtual diary' LiveJournal. In this chapter, however, I expand upon these initial ideas through a consideration of the now ubiquitous social networking sites (in this case, MySpace and Facebook). In doing this, I explore how a teenager's private and personal life is not just lived within the physical realm and how in many ways themes such as identity, privacy and control pertinent to the lives of young people in their bedrooms can also be translated into these virtual spaces. However, such a translation is by no means straightforward and building on an emerging body of work that explores some of these themes in the context of young people and social networking sites (for example, boyd, 2006, 2007, 2008a; Mallan,

2009, Pearson, 2009; Robards, 2010), I explore some of the complexities and 'multiplicities' of this public and private dynamic.

In exploring these complexities, I draw on a number of themes already addressed throughout this book. For example, I explore the ways in which the 'virtual bedroom' can be understood as a site of identity (or identities), akin to a bedroom, on which one's personality can be stamped, constructed and displayed; how the use of social networking sites can be understood as representative of transitions (for example, going to university and 'graduating' to Facebook from MySpace); how such sites show up complex negotiations in relation to control and ownership; and how the physical bedroom itself can be understood as a portal of communication from which these virtual bedrooms are accessed. One of the central discussions in this chapter is in relation to the concept of 'authenticity' (Mallan 2009; Sessions, 2009) and the consideration of a 'real' identity by young people themselves in a social world dominated by self-exposure (Orlet, 2007; Mallan, 2009). As I demonstrate, in reflecting upon their use of social networking sites, my participants began to reconsider the importance of the space of their physical bedroom as the place within which their 'true' identities could be displayed and explored. This finding demonstrates strongly the continuing importance of the bedroom in the lives of young people.

1
Exploring the Private in Traditional Youth Cultural Theory and Beyond

> Rather than being marked off by a set of objective and
> unchanging distinguishing features, the concept of
> 'youth' is a social construct. As such, its boundaries
> and characteristic qualities have varied between dif-
> ferent societies and across different historical periods.
> (Osgerby, 1998, p. 17)

At the start of the second decade of the third millennium the task of
making sense of young people and their cultural lives in an increasingly
globalised world is becoming ever more complex and difficult. This is
not least because as Miles (2000) and others have argued, notions of a
globalised world bring with them new ways of thinking about young
people and their youth cultures, and indeed the very concept of youth
itself is no longer seen as the reserve of the young but rather a lifestyle
choice of those well beyond younger years. These new ways of thinking
encompass a variety of approaches, for example post-modernism, 'risk',
globalisation and what has been termed 'individualisation' (Beck 1992;
Miles 2000) whereby notions of 'boundaries' and 'characteristic qualities' as identified in traditional youth cultures are no longer so easily
recognisable or definable in a contemporary youth cultural context.
In a relatively short period of time the concept of youth culture has
shifted from one that is understood and observed primarily as collective
action, to action that is increasingly individualised, arguably more self-
motivated and fragmented and consequently much more complex.

As I explore throughout this book, the *spaces* of youth cultures have
also become more ambiguous within the context of globalisation and
the 'risk society' (Beck 1992), which suggests a shift from the dominance
of place-based youth cultural activities to those that can be described

as more 'space-based' and 'private', i.e. those that take place within the context of the home or within virtual and mediated environments (Steele and Brown, 1995; Miles, 2000).

Just in the last two decades for example (1990s and 2000s), we have seen significant changes in how the media and their corresponding technologies have become embedded inextricably into many young people's daily lives (Tutt, 2005; Walsh and White, 2006; Hulme, 2009). Indeed, it has been argued that young people form a particularly lucrative media technologies market segment, a market that affords them connections and communications that go far beyond their physical locality. In addition to this, the technologies themselves have become multi-functional, highly portable, affordable and consequently ubiquitous, changing significantly the ways in which young people live out their everyday lives, especially in the realms of leisure, education and work, and seemingly making their connections to multiple spaces of culture easier than ever before.

For young people, in particular, the ownership and use of such technologies have multiple meanings in relation to consumption, communication, relationships, cultural interests and social life, and in many ways have changed the meaning of traditional structures of friendships and family life and our interactions within them (boyd, 2007, 2008a). Moreover, technologies such as mobile phones (now multimedia technologies in themselves) and social networking sites are not simply used to facilitate these interactions but have become *embedded* in them and in many ways have become the very essence of a young person living out his or her daily life (Hulme, 2009; Livingstone, 2009). As a result, the media and the technologies associated with them have opened up a number of 'other' social and cultural worlds and spaces through which a young person may constantly shift in and out of and connect to. More than ever before, young people have their life-worlds literally at their fingertips, experiencing a connectedness in and interchange of multiple spaces that span many aspects of their social and cultural lives (Muggleton, 1997, 2000; Stahl, 1999; Bennett and Kahn-Harris, 2004; Hulme, 2009).

The discourse of 'connectedness', a theme that runs through this book in relation to young people's uses of private spaces such as bedrooms (for example, connections to home, family, friends, peers, personal identity), is a familiar presence in the history of youth cultures and subcultures. In that history, however, connectedness tends to be a theme that begins on the premise of young people's position of 'alienation' (Epstein, 1998) or dislocation, especially in relation to dominant (middle-class) hegemonic structures and 'parent' cultures (Hall and

Jefferson, 1975). In the classic British youth cultures literature of the 1970s, for instance, as I shall explore later in this chapter, the emergence of youth cultures and, particularly, of subcultures has arguably been contextualised within a discourse of 'connectedness' inasmuch as young people who feel in some way isolated from society at large (for example in the realms of education or employment) are seeking alternative ways of life and connections through which they are able, with like-minded people, to make sense of the world around them, sharing values and concerns that make sense to them and create a more meaningful reality for themselves.

The traditional accounts of youth culture written by the Centre for Contemporary Cultural Studies, Birmingham in the 1970s, for example, were largely about young people connecting with others who had common experiences relating to their social and economic background through place-based activities, which goes some way to explain why subcultures in these accounts tended to be highly 'visible' (for example, being lived out in the street) with cultural values articulated through subcultural 'style' (Hebdige, 1979) which, as Brake suggests, 'allow[ed] an expression of identity through a deliberate projection of self-image, which claim[ed] an identity "magically" freed from class and occupation' (1985, p. 15).

As a consequence of their perceived alienation from the social world young people would seek out alternative spaces of leisure practices and lifestyles, 'reclaiming' and giving new meaning to those spaces that existed in their locality and frequently used as part of their everyday lives, for example, street corners, bars, clubs and shops where they could come together and 'freely associate', as Hebdige (1979) argued. At the same time they would share the same institutional position and the same social problems as their parents albeit approaching them with a distinct 'problem solving function' (Frith, 1984) that came in the form of youth cultures and subcultures.

Such a discourse of connectedness can also be seen in the CCCS literature through the use of the concept of 'membership' (Hall and Jefferson, 1975; Clarke and Jefferson, 1976; Hebdige, 1979; Brake, 1985), which, according to Cohen (1972) and Hall and Jefferson (1975), made youth subcultures resemble 'exclusive' clubs. This exclusivity clearly marked out its 'members' as different from the general, ordinary public through highly stylised clothing (for example, the Edwardian suit of the Teddy Boy) and fashion, and demanded a commitment from its members to the subculture in order to maintain their role and status within it. Such rigidity in terms of who could and could not be part of a particular group suggests that in fact subcultures could be very insular, the domain of the privileged few, rather than open to any young person feeling a sense of isolation. This issue has since emerged as one of the key criticisms of traditional youth cultural research (Shildrick and MacDonald, 2006). Coles (1986), for example, argues that such a rigid category-defined approach somewhat excluded 'ordinary kids' who did not necessarily fit into the 'rough/ respectable dichotomy' (1986, p. 79, see also Miles, 2000), while a number of studies that were published in the 1980s (Jenkins, 1983; Brown, 1986; Wallace, 1986 [cited in Coles, 1986]) began to challenge the rigidity of social structures such as social class imposed on subcultural activity. Subcultures, Brake argued, could exist amongst ordinary young people, given that the majority develop a complex framework of motives as they struggle to find their footing in an adult world (1985, p. 79). This suggests, then, that ordinary young people may 'drift' in and out of many different aspects of different subcultures as they progress on the road to adulthood (although arguably their participation doesn't strictly end there). They may not necessarily show a firm commitment to one particular subculture as a common practice, but connect to a variety of different ones, a notion that has been suggested and explored more recently in the post-subcultures literature (Miles, 2000; Bennett and Kahn-Harris, 2004), as I discuss later on in this chapter.

The discourse of connectedness in much youth subcultures work was also articulated through other key concepts such as resistance, rebellion and delinquency (see, for example, Cohen, 1972; Hall and Jefferson, 1975; Willis, 1977; Hebdige, 1979). The use of such concepts by the CCCS primarily grew out of an American sociological tradition, which Hall and Jefferson (1975) cite as one of their key influences in writing about subcultures in the 1970s and 1980s. In the Chicago School tradition, for instance, rebellion and delinquency were primarily made sense of through what was termed 'labelling' theory (Becker, 1963; Matza, 1964) discussed in more detail below. The implication of this theory was that young people seen to conform to the dominant ideologies of wider society were likely to 'label' those who didn't conform as 'deviant' (as opposed to the label emerging as a response to deviant, rebellious or resistant behaviour 'in action', which was a reality on the streets). Not surprisingly, the term 'subculture' became synonymous with delinquent or rebellious behaviour that did not conform to the 'norms' of a moral, upstanding society.

However, as I discuss in Chapter 3 of this book, there was a notable shift particularly in the study of British youth cultures in the post-Second

World War period. This was signalled by the rise of 'teenager' as a social category and the emergence of what appeared to be a rather distinct youth 'consumer' group in British society as noted in Abrams' study in 1959 entitled *The Teenage Consumer* (cited in Frith, 1984). In this piece of work, which was largely constructed on the basis of data collected by empirically driven market research, Abrams argued that by the late 1950s a new consumer group had emerged in the UK, one that was accompanied by an equally distinct consumer market (France, 2007). Importantly, Abrams noted that the behaviour of young people was no longer to be understood primarily within the discourses of 'rebellion' and 'deviance', as was previously the case in studies of youth culture (for example, see Whyte, 1943; Mays, 1954; Miller, 1958), but within the discourse of consumption as, for Abrams, young people's consumer choices indicated a new form of demarcation for them:

> As a consumer group, young people were distinguished from other age groups not by their 'bad' behaviour, but simply in terms of their market choices and it was these choices that revealed a new 'teenage market'. (quoted in Frith 1984, p. 8)

In many ways, the interpellation of young people as a 'discrete consumer group' (Osgerby 2002, p. 16) seemed more positive than earlier approaches. However, given the Marxist roots of British subcultural studies there was cynicism with regards to the positioning of the teenager within a market (created for them rather than led by them), especially as the primary market for the production of youth culture related goods was a working-class one. While working-class youth were displaying their consumer power through the consumption of mass produced 'popular' goods and, as Osgerby (2002) notes of the US context (similarly embracing the emergence of the teenager and associated niche markets particularly in the post-war period), while teenagers were exercising a never-before-seen spending power, they were arguably still subordinate in terms of their 'fixity' within their class structures. This suggested limited possibilities in terms of class mobility, particularly in the realms of education and employment. Additionally, this consumption of popular goods could be interpreted as working-class youth 'buying into' a mass consumer culture, which, instead of providing them with a social status of any kind, defined them first and foremost as hedonistic leisure consumers (Miles, 2000; Osgerby, 2002). Arguably, then, this perpetuated their fate as a distinct social group that was 'different' from dominant 'adult' society and therefore in positions of subordination. Consequently, it has been argued, subcultures arose as a rebellious response to the domination of mass culture and the positioning of the teenager within it (Hall and Jefferson, 1975; Epstein, 1998), for example through targeted marketing techniques and niche marketing (Osgerby, 2002).

However, more recent accounts of youth culture that tend to focus on the more everyday practices of young people explore how forms of 'rebellion' are embedded not just in class resistance but in wider identity formations too, through which a young person is gaining independence while realising that their parents are not necessarily always right. For example, Larson argues:

> Adolescents in our culture place increasing importance on who they are and what they will be in the future. They partially shed the secure and unquestioned sense of self acquired from their families and begin to look for a more personally determined sense of identity. (1995, p. 536)

This proposition is very much in the spirit of Erikson (1968) who identified adolescence as the period in a young person's life when one ceases to be a child and has to make decisions about the future, a time when young people's emerging adult identities begin to be formed. Epstein argues that it is in this period in particular when young people may engage in youth cultures and subcultures as part of an identity forming process (1998, p. 4) and, drawing on Erikson, argues that subcultures provide 'simply a mechanism of identity protection', particularly for young people who fall out of the education system or who are perceived as 'downwardly mobile' in the job market (p. 4).

One of the criticisms of the CCCS studies of youth culture, besides the often cited arguments that they tended to be class-biased, male-biased and ethnicity-biased, is that very little attempt was made to understand the relationship between youth and family in the discourse of the formation of youth cultures (McRobbie, 2000, p. 26) or the ways in which forms of resistance or rebellion may manifest themselves, not just in class politics, but in relation to the family structure or within the domestic or private spaces within which family life is organised. Such discussions in a contemporary context have become particularly important because, as Miles (2000) notes, young people are becoming more and more economically dependent on their parents and for longer periods of time, which changes the nature of their transitions from childhood to adulthood (Molgat, 2007) while also affecting significantly the structure of the family itself.

In addition, one could argue that the absence of the youth and family discourse in traditional CCCS accounts was the result of another bias, one related to the *spaces* within which youth cultures and subcultures could be lived out. Specifically, by and large, in the CCCS accounts we see the dominance of public street-based spaces over other potential spheres such as the private or the domestic, which, as I outline later on, were marginalised, secondary and predominantly understood as exclusively 'female' spheres (Marshall and Borrill, 1984; McRobbie, 1991).

Over the years many reasons have been cited as to why the focus in these discussions should be on public spaces. For example, McRobbie (1991) suggested that private and domestic spheres were almost impenetrable to the male researcher (with the majority of CCCS researchers being male at this time). As a result, a significant proportion of young people, and especially young women, were absent from these accounts because, as she argues with Jenny Garber (1975), girls occupy different youth cultural spaces, ones associated with the domestic sphere. As she puts it:

> When girls do appear, it is either in ways that uncritically reinforce the stereotypical image with which we are now so familiar ... for example, Fyvel's reference, in his study of teddy boys, to 'dumb, passive teenage girls, crudely painted' ... or else they are fleetingly and marginally presented. (McRobbie, 1991, p. 1)

This bias, McRobbie argued, clearly suggests that only one half of the youth cultures story was really being told and it was that half of the story that came to be representative of young people as a whole. Of course, public spaces are significant, not least, as I explore later on in the chapter, because conceptual tools such as 'subcultural style', analysed through the application of empirical methods, were about exploring the highly visual representations of different groups or subgroups of young people who would thus make a statement about their place in society, through clothing, hairstyles and make-up (Brake, 1985). More simply perhaps, Miles (2000) points out that because the streets were largely free of motor vehicles (as opposed to the busy streets of today), they made ideal and relatively safe spaces in which young people could spend their leisure time and be within their communities. Moreover, in the decades between the 1940s and 1970s there was arguably a much stronger sense of community life in British culture with the presence of family and extended family in the neighbourhoods, even in the same streets, being the norm and the relative absence of the discourses of fear that dominate how young people use public spaces in more recent decades (as I outline in Chapter 3). Mays (1954) suggested that because of family size (an average of five children per household) the notion of taking part in leisure pursuits within the home was unfamiliar to white, working-class males, a view that persists throughout the 1950s, 1960s and 1970s. For example, of one of his participants Mays said: 'He [Arthur] spent nearly all his non-working hours with his friends and "never thought of staying at home"' (1954, p. 80).

During the 1950s when Mays' study was conducted indoor-based leisure activities were often restricted to middle-class adolescents whose families could afford to buy toys and games that could be played with in the home. The number of children was likely to have been smaller and a larger house would have allowed plenty of 'space to play'. This is particularly significant in terms of the relationship between young, white, working-class men and street-based activities that included petty crime, as the street offered these teenage boys a place to be away from parental controls and siblings. It also meant that the boys were likely to be part of or seen as part of a local or neighbourhood peer-group. And because the rate of crime was relatively high in the area in which Mays' study was conducted the boys were exposed to criminal activities on a frequent basis, which suggests that they were more likely to become part of a criminal or delinquent subculture (see also Miller, 1958).

Such a spatial bias in traditional youth cultural accounts seems surprising on reflection when considering the mass availability and affordability of pop cultural goods made specifically for the teen consumer market, the rise of which marked a key turning point in the recognition of 'teenagers' as a distinct social and marketable group. For example, magazines such as *Seventeen* were made to be read by teenage girls in their early teens and with specific domestic responsibilities, and who were too young to be hanging around the dangerous streets. Such goods were made to be enjoyed with an ease of use both inside and outside of the home. As Osgerby (2002, p. 16) notes:

> this financial power [of teenagers] seemed all the more impressive for the way in which it was unencumbered by domestic responsibilities or restraints – teenage leisure being concentrated into the realm of leisure, style and hedonistic pleasure.

While the public/private debate is a well-rehearsed one in contemporary youth cultural research, particularly within the context of the mass media and the rise of virtual cultures, youth consumerism from the mid-1940s onwards can be identified as a major turning point in those discussions. As Osgerby notes above, the financial power of the teenager from the post-war period onwards purchasing within the domain of leisure enabled such boundaries to be blurred through the consumption of mass-produced, affordable goods such as recorded music (on vinyl) and teen magazines both inside and outside of the home. However, this interplay is not readily seen in the subcultures literature.

This meant too that engagement in youth cultural practices was not just the privilege of the teenage boy, as the CCCS studies present, but could also be undertaken by the teenage girl. This point is identified by McRobbie and Garber (1975) as one of the main absences in these studies. As argued in their essay, given the context of the teenage consumer the questions of why young women were largely missing from those traditional youth cultural accounts and why they should be dismissed as subordinate to their male counterparts in terms of their part in youth culture certainly need to be asked. Equally importantly, there were no accounts of young men engaging in home-based youth cultural activities.

What I explore in the rest of this chapter, then, is the proposition that there has been disproportionate attention paid to private spaces in the study of youth cultures, particularly those within the domestic sphere, such as young people's bedrooms, and with the focus being on subcultures rather than the cultural pursuits of ordinary, everyday young people. While there is a well-established and highly influential tradition of exploring young people and place (Skelton and Valentine, 1998; Valentine, 2004; Shildrick, Blackman and MacDonald 2009; Hopkins, 2010), and while an ever-growing body of work has emerged in youth cultural studies that considers 'other' realms, such as virtual spaces (boyd, 2007, 2008a; Hodkinson, 2007; Hodkinson and Lincoln, 2008) within which youth cultural practices exist, the study of youth cultures within private spaces has remained under-researched comparatively. This is especially surprising, given the relatively well-established tradition of what Kearney (2007) refers to as 'room culture scholarship'[1] (see, for example: Larson, 1995; Steele and Brown, 1995; Abbott-Chapman, 2000; James, 2001; Baker, 2004; Lincoln, 2004, 2005, 2006; Abbott-Chapman and Robertson, 2009; Glevarec, 2009), and the recognition – as far back as the 1980s – in youth cultures research of a need to explore both the public and private realms in the lives of ordinary young boys and girls (Wallace, 1986 cited in Coles, 1986; Reimer, 1995).

In attempting to address this gap, in this book I argue that an understanding of spaces that can be considered 'personal' and 'private' and exist in the domestic realm, such as a young person's bedroom, is crucial in making sense of the role, significance and changing nature of contemporary youth culture in the lives of young people. What is more, I argue in later chapters that 'private' spaces such as bedrooms are currently more significant than ever before. Through an intimate study of them, one is able to discern a conceptual shift from youth cultures as 'intensive communication' (for example, through subcultural style and membership in relation to subcultures whereby a dedicated participation is required [Mitterauer, 1992, cited in Miles 2000, p. 68]) to youth cultures that are 'intensive communication' *of young people's choosing*; more fragmented in their nature and arguably affording a young person more control over their cultural identities. What I will demonstrate in this book, then, is how in many ways the space of a young person's room acts as a site of 'legitimation' (Miles, 2000, p. 79) of these identities for young people. This is because it provides a space within which they are able to unite with other young people (for example in their uses of the mass media [Reimer, 1995]), while at the same time asserting their individual identities, as those are articulated, for example, through the objects, items and things, the 'consumer artefacts' (Miller, 1987, cited in Miles, 2000, p. 29) found in their bedrooms as well as through their cultural practices.

Before considering this further, however, I continue my exploration of some of the key approaches to the study of youth culture, highlighting throughout where the discourse of 'private space' is perhaps missing. In this way I would like to establish why it is an important area of study in the context of youth culture.

Private space and traditional subcultural theory

The work of American sociologist Howard Becker (1963) is cited in the introduction of the CCCS' seminal text *Resistance through Rituals* (Hall and Jefferson, 1975) as one of the key influences in their work. Becker's 'labelling theory' was considered by Hall and Jefferson as a 'break in mainstream sociology' (1975, p. 5) which recognised that through the power of some to 'label' others, a socially constructed subculture of deviancy could emerge, perpetuating the diatribe of youth as a problem, something we 'ought to do something about' (p. 9). Epstein (1998) suggests that some groups of young people were more susceptible to this 'labelling' than others, and as is borne out in a number of the CCCS' studies, labelling was very much articulated within the axis of 'class', with working-class kids being regarded as 'troublesome' compared to their better-behaved middle-class counterparts. What is clear from the outset of the American sociological tradition, and particularly in the work of the Chicago School, is the domination of accounts of 'sub-groups' (later to be termed 'subcultures' by the CCCS) occupying public spaces. Most notable perhaps is the work of William Foote Whyte, particularly his study *Street Corner Society* (1943). Whyte's study of the social life-worlds of street gangs offers a traditional description of youth as deviant through a discussion of the 'corner boys' who live in an Italian slum in an American suburb. He refers to the corner boys as

> a group of men who center their social activities upon particular street corners...They constitute the lower level of society within their age group and at the same time they make up the majority of the young men of Cornerville. (Whyte 1943, p. xviii)

Although the boys were growing up amongst other predominantly working-class families, Whyte suggests that there was still a feeling of class subordination that contributed to the emergence of tight-knit, gang-like groups of young men in public spaces and on the street corners, for example those truanting from school. Whyte typically highlights education as a middle-class privilege, which has allowed what he refers to as the 'college boys' to gain a social status that is regarded as consistently 'above' that of the 'corner boys'. He also suggests that being part of a subordinate (working) class means that the 'corner boys' have little hope of developing within the dominant political and social culture in which their group is operating because the opportunities offered outside of their local culture do not account for or benefit the lower classes. We see similar accounts later on in British sociology, for example Willis' study of the 'lads' and the 'ear 'oles' in his monograph *Learning to Labour: How Working-Class Kids Get Working-Class Jobs* (1977) where young working-class males appear to be placed in a structural opposition to their middle-class counterparts whereby they have little choice but to perpetuate their own fates of a life of manual, low-skilled work like their fathers. In relation to the corner boys, Whyte argues, this establishes barriers within a specific physical neighbourhood or public social space that, arguably, aggravate and encourage 'rebellious' behaviour, particularly by gang-like groups of young men who feel they have to prove themselves through an alternative route to social status. Whyte stresses throughout his study that the social organisation of the street-corner gangs consisted of non-delinquent activities as well as those activities considered by adult society as delinquent, even though such pursuits were considered to be the norm for the street-corner gangs who had grown up in a high-crime area.

The youth cultural groups of the street corner explored by Whyte are also studied in relation to the dominant authorities operating within the same social spaces and specifically to the 'racketeers and politicians' (Whyte, 1943, p. xix). Whyte explores the relationship between the 'big shots' and the ways in which the corner boys and college boys operate in relation to them. Although the majority of the boys in Whyte's research are aged 20 years and over, his core thesis is to demonstrate clearly how street cultures develop and how a pattern of social interaction with people considered of a higher 'social standing' emerges. Mays points out how the gangs in Whyte's study of Cornerville are constituted through regular interaction that produces the social order of the group:

> [Whyte] found the social structure of the district well organised and hierarchical. The patterns of the gang were remarkably fixed, the members coming together every day and freely associating with one another for long periods of time. (Mays, 1954, p. 14)

Much like the accounts offered by the CCCS, the focus in Whyte's classic study is on the young working-class male who spends the majority of his leisure time occupying the streets, often as part of one gang or another. While, indeed, Whyte's account is ground-breaking as it explored the complexities of youth activities in relation to authorities and institutions as well as age and age-related hierarchies that reveal the intrinsic workings of subcultural life, there are still 'gaps' in this representation of life in Cornerville. Most notably, these are in relation to the role of the young women as these accounts of youth culture are dominated by young men actively engaged in street-corner society. Mays, for example, in his study of youths growing up in the city of Liverpool, suggested that the teenage girl only socialises on the streets with young men with the intention of finding a potential husband (a criticism later taken up my McRobbie and Garber [1975] in relation to the CCCS studies). There is a social status to be gained through having a boyfriend, and not having one compromises a girl's social status and peer acceptance:

> as far as girls are concerned matrimony and maternity present the only way of life open to them … Girls think of marriage much earlier than boys and competition to secure a regular 'boyfriend' begins as soon as school is left behind. A girl's status is appreciably raised

upon engagement and consolidation by subsequent marriage. A girl without a 'fella' feels ashamed and inferior and if the condition is long continued she becomes the object of contempt and pity. (Mays, 1954, pp. 88–9)

Additionally, as with Whyte's study, we have a limited understanding of what these young people's lives might have been like in the domestic sphere and in relation to the family, other than knowing that they were young men who had grown up in an area of high crime, suggesting that a culture of criminality was indeed generational. This, we can argue, gives us a 'snapshot' (Brake, 1985) of life in a subculture within very specific spaces, rather than one that acknowledges the other spheres within which young people were also living out their everyday lives. Similarly, these criticisms have also been associated with the British youth cultures and subcultures research tradition, particularly as this was presented by the CCCS.

Taking a Marxist standpoint, influenced by the Chicago tradition, and following on from Stanley Cohen's influential work *Folk Devils and Moral Panics* (1972), youth cultural researchers at the CCCS focused on 'class' as a central structure and struggle around which cultures operated and through which 'ways of life' for young people were dictated and restricted. With the primary focus of their research on the young male generation of the working classes, the image of 'youth as trouble' was emphasised by the opposition between the working class and the middle class, with the latter in a position to represent 'itself as *the* culture' that dominated social, economic and political spheres of influence:

It tries to define and contain all other cultures within its inclusive range. Its view of the world, unless challenged, will stand as the most natural, all-embracing, universal culture. Other cultural configurations will not only be subordinate to this dominant order: they will enter into struggle with it, seek to modify, negotiate, resist or even overthrow its reign – its *hegemony*. (Hall and Jefferson, 1975, p. 12)

From a middle-class hegemonic perspective youth cultural groups were seen as threatening to the moral stability of society. This created a sort of panic because, ultimately, young people were (and are still) viewed as the future of society and the visible opposition of specific groups of young people to mainstream cultures was considered potentially unsettling and damaging, with the threat of breaking through dominant structures and ideologies.

Drawing on work by Antonio Gramsci, Hall and Jefferson believed that cultures provide specific 'maps of meaning'; maps through which members of a social group make 'things intelligible' (Hall and Jefferson, 1975, p. 10) in terms of how culture is 'experienced, understood and interpreted' (p. 11) in relation to dominant structures and ideologies. Building on the notion of 'subgroups' offered by the Chicago School, the CCCS set out to examine the relationship between the dominant and parent culture alongside a subgroup or, as they termed it, 'subculture'.

As 'subsets', subcultures have to be distinguishable from other subcultural groups so that they may stand out alone through 'certain activities, values, certain uses of material artefacts, territorial spaces, etc.' (Hall and Jefferson, 1975, p. 14). At the same time, as a peripheral part of a working-class culture, a subculture also shares a number of elements with its parent culture. For example, parent culture and subculture are united in their position in relation to the dominant sphere of the middle classes that so often render them as insignificant and subordinate. Hall and Jefferson identified such 'subcultural' groups emerging in the 1950s, 1960s and 1970s, such as the Teddy Boys, Mods, Rockers and Skinheads who, they suggest:

> May walk, talk, act, look 'different' from their parents and from some of their peers: but they belong to the same families, go to the same schools, work at much the same jobs, live down the same 'mean' streets as their peers and parents. (1975, p. 14)

It is through their image, demeanour and argot that they 'project a cultural response' (1975, p. 15) to the same problems that are faced by other members of the parent culture. Being part of a subculture is a form of reaction that is different from the mainstream, an alternative way of interpreting 'focal concerns' common to both the parent culture and subculture. And while, indeed, the popular media at the time were quick to associate the actions of young people in subcultures with deviance, criminality and resistance (Osgerby, 1998), it was predominantly through the tool of 'subcultural style', rather than behaviour and social patterns, as was the case in the earlier work by the Chicago School. 'Style' was refined as a conceptual tool with which to analyse youth subculture by Dick Hebdige in his work *Subculture: The Meaning of Style* (1979). His focus was the 'spectacular' subcultures that were highly visible and style-driven and followed Cohen's (1972) analysis of the stylistic form of the 'Teddy Boy' as the first subgroup of young people using style as a political and social statement against their position in 1950s society. As Hebdige put it:

> The stylistic innovations were seen – and quite rightly so – as being not just ones for dress, but as heralding a new cultural contour to be taken into account in society's normative map making. (1979, p. 183)

Style is a component in a cultural map of meaning through which a particular group claim their identity through a set of signs. This identity conforms to their subculture rather than to the dominant culture. Subcultural style, then, provides a context for innovative, self-styled, individual identities to be formed. Stahl describes the very essence of stylistic descriptions of subcultures as encapsulating 'the heroic rhetoric of resistance, the valorization of the underdog and outsider, and the re-emergence of a potentially political working-class consciousness' (1999, p. 1). The use of distinctive stylistic forms and their reproduction by the media was one of the ways in which society came to understand these subgroups of young people as 'alien', incomprehensible to 'society at large' (1999, p. 1) and therefore, a threat to moral and social order, much as we see in the earlier accounts offered by the Chicago School.

While the analysis of subcultures through the conceptual tool of 'style' offered an empirical approach to the study of youth cultures whereby a researcher was able to observe 'meaning making' as produced by young people themselves, this approach was not without its criticisms. For instance, the stylistic analyses offered by the CCCS were primarily only an interpretation of a minority of young people, as mentioned earlier in this chapter. First, it has been argued, this was because the majority of ordinary, everyday young people were not involved in subcultural activity (Coles, 1986) but rather just the everyday pursuits associated with a young person growing up. Unfortunately, there was very little written about this 'majority' group at the time, hence 'youth' as a social category was largely represented by the minority of young people involved in subcultures. Second, these accounts were based largely on what was 'observable' on the streets and in public life. There is no mention, for example, of the domestic life of the Mod, but we are offered insights into his nights out on the town or clashes with the Rockers (McRobbie, 1991; Osgerby, 1998).

McRobbie and Garber's essay 'Girls and Subcultures', published in Hall and Jefferson's collection *Resistance through Rituals*, set out to be a 'corrective' to some of those areas they perceived to have been overlooked by much of the work on young people being undertaken at the CCCS. Most notably, their essay aimed to 'add on' the teenage girl to subcultural accounts, on whom, they claimed, very little seemed to have been written. Additionally, however, while trying to account for the missing girl and arguing that alternative spaces of culture and leisure existed for her, McRobbie and Garber conceptualised what they referred to as a 'culture of the bedroom' (1975, p. 213). Kearney (2007) notes that in the post-war period teenage girls were more likely to be focused on a life in the domestic sphere than their brothers, learning how to become wives and mothers, which implied the existence of a home-centred culture as the primary space within which teenage girls were living out their cultural and social lives. This culture, McRobbie and Garber argued, was more fitting with their domestic responsibilities because it was not a culture that demanded the level of membership synonymous with street-based youth cultures; it was a culture which the girls could float in and out of accordingly.

While this essay still remains a key turning point, particularly in discussions of girl culture (Kearney, 2007), it is not without its criticisms. Most pertinent to discussions in this book is the criticism that in many ways McRobbie and Garber did just what their male researcher counterparts did, that is, also concentrated on 'telling one side of the story' in their recounting of girls in their bedrooms. Was the bedroom not the domain of the teenage boy as well, albeit in different ways? If, for example, we were to reflect on the highly stylised nature of subcultures such as the Mod, one would assume that there must have been intensive 'getting ready for a night out' rituals that were very likely to have taken place within the domestic sphere, within their parents' homes and most likely in a bedroom. Interestingly, although a fictional account, such scenarios are illustrated in the film *Quadrophenia* (Franc Roddam, 1979) that depicts Mod culture in the 1960s and the famous Brighton Beach clashes between the Mods and the Rockers.

The highly stylised nature of this subculture is reflected upon in Hebdige's essay 'The Meaning of Mod' (in Hall and Jefferson's *Resistance through Rituals*) where he talks of a *Sunday Times* magazine feature that included an interview with 'Denzil, the seventeen year old mod' (p. 90). In the interview Denzil describes 'the average week in the life of the ideal London Mod':

Monday night meant dancing at the Mecca, the Hammersmith Palais, the Purley Orchard, or the Streatham Locarno

Tuesday meant Soho and the Scene Club
Wednesday was Marquee night
Thursday was reserved for the ritual washing of the hair
Friday meant the Scene again
Saturday afternoon usually meant shopping for clothes and records,
Saturday night spent dancing and rarely finishing before 9.00 or
10.00 Sunday morning.
Sunday evening meant the Flamingo or, perhaps if one showed
signs of weakening, could be spent sleeping. (Hebdige in Hall and
Jefferson, 1975, p. 90)

By his own admission, Hebdige acknowledges that this rather gruelling
social timetable may well have been fabricated for the purpose of the
interview, not least because of the cost involved in maintaining such
a lifestyle that could only have been afforded by the privileged few.
But the leisure foci, characteristic of Mod suggests a great deal of time
getting ready for these numerous nights on the town and a ritualised
pattern of going out to different places on different nights. Given the
highly stylised nature of Mod, a culture in which clothing was everything, it might be assumed that such a hectic weekly social calendar
afforded different outfits; it was unlikely that a Mod would be seen
wearing the very same outfit twice in a row. This by default suggests
that spaces were likely to have existed for both Mod boys and girls
within which these preparations took place and that these spaces were
likely to have been bedrooms within the domestic sphere of the family
home. Interestingly too, in Denzil's timetable above, sleeping, which
would most likely take place in the bedroom and almost definitely back
at the parental home, is identified as a sign of weakness and an activity
reserved only for those who did not have the stamina to keep up with
the relentless going out. In this case, then, the context of the domestic
is placed as a subordinate sphere in comparison to the context of the
club, bar or dance hall.

   Despite these possibilities, virtually nothing appears to have been
documented about these practices as a prequel to the endless nights
on the town. Instead, the focus has been on what happens when they
actually reach town; as McRobbie says 'no-one seemed interested in
what was happening when a mod went home after a weekend on speed'
(1990, p. 67). Mod, then, could have served as a useful example of the
significance of the domestic realm in its construction, its use by Mod
girls and Mod boys and the ways in which the two spheres of the public
and the private intertwine.

Youth culture beyond the CCCS: creating room for the private?

The concept of subculture, as I have discussed above, has provided a useful theoretical framework through which to make sense of young people's cultural activities, although, as I have also pointed out, such an approach has not been without its problems conceptually and, as we shall see in the following chapter, methodologically. However, it has maintained its currency as one way through which to make sense of youth cultures and has in more recent times been reassessed and updated in terms of its potential for understanding contemporary youth cultures and lifestyles (Bennett and Kahn-Harris, 2004). As I explored earlier, while the CCCS approach might not have considered the role of home, family, the domestic or the private sphere (as well as neglecting to a large extent issues of gender and ethnicity) as important in the making of young people's subcultural lives and was arguably (over) reliant on its key concept of class, there are aspects of their approach that continue to be instructive and useful in the study of youth culture and private space (Lincoln, 2004). For example, while CCCS studies of subculture focused solely on the public domain, their understanding of such spaces through concepts such as 'style' and 'membership', were in essence about young people marking out and forming their identities as distinct from dominant, everyday, cultures and environments. Additionally, although the physical context of their activities was important, it was predominantly the body that was used as the Barthesian sign that marked out their subcultural allegiances (for example through clothing, hair and make-up) and whose presence in a particular physical location gave that space an alternative meaning. This in turn meant that subcultural activity was very much the practice of those 'in the know', who were highly stylised and who demanded a dedication to subcultural style that seemed to exclude ordinary young people somewhat from such practices.

The notion of identity marking is as pertinent in the context of private spaces such as bedrooms and, much like the adorned body in subcultural style, provides a canvas on which young people can display who they are and what they are into. However, a spatial analysis alongside an understanding of a young person's ever-changing cultural practices suggests a methodological shift from the semiotic reading of subcultural signs and symbols, as championed by Hebdige (1979) and others, to an analysis of the meaning of a bedroom's contents constructed through young people's own accounts that change alongside their interests.

In the subcultures literature one gets the sense that young people belonged to one subculture only, were fully paid up members for a short period of time, before moving outside the domain of 'youth' into the worlds of work, family and domesticity. A more fluid understanding of identity marking allows for an understanding of the potentially multiple, shifting and changing cultural interests of a young person. It also enables us to capture engagement in youth cultures that may go beyond one's teenage years and importantly, allows us to see how youth cultures are experienced not just by the subcultural few but by ordinary, everyday young people within the context of their own unique lives.

Additionally, discussions of subcultures tended to be focused on the 'spectacular' (Stahl 1999), namely, the highly stylised clothing of, for example, the Teddy Boy, Mod and Rocker rather than (or in addition to) those things associated with their mundane everyday lives. For example, the highly visual, subversive styling of punk was not easily appropriated into the workplace, so was left at home until they returned only to be worn again in appropriate contexts. This arguably skews one's perceptions of what life in a subculture for a young person was really like in relation to other aspects of their lives, for example education or family, associations with other friends or peers and interests beyond their subcultures. In contrast, then, by studying the spaces of young people as well as the practices within them, we are able to explore the intricacies and mundanities of everyday life, the many layers that make up a young person's youth culture within the wider context of their lives, while also examining how and why these cultures shift and how they are consumed.

Miles (1995) reiterates this point in his critique of subcultural theory when he argues that in the subcultures literature there has been a tendency to focus upon the 'symbolic aspects of subcultural consumption at the expense of the actual *meanings* that young consumers have for the goods that they consume' (Miles, 1995, quoted in Bennett, 1999, p. 602). Miles suggests that in their quest to 'impose' rigid theoretical frameworks onto the actions of young people, primarily understood through subcultural style, CCCS researchers did not consider what the actions of young people really meant for them as 'youth stylists' (as opposed to them just being 'members' of a subcultural group). What Miles means is that the items, objects and things that young people would consume as part of their cultural lives are not purely symbolic but have a very specific meaning and styling appropriated to an individual's youth cultural pursuits and the context of their construction. Miles argues that the focus by the CCCS on what styles and activities *appeared* to mean primarily as semiotic texts subsequently produced accounts of subcultures that were largely unrecognisable by their members.

Such discussions can be contextualised in what has been termed 'post-subculturalism', an approach that emerged in youth cultural studies at the turn of the new century that considers the usefulness of subculture as a key conceptual tool in post-modern, contemporary youth contexts. As Bennett (1999) argues, such an approach considers notions of identity as 'constructed' rather than 'given', and 'fluid' rather than 'fixed' (Bennett, 1999, p. 599).

The premise of the post-subcultural approach is that the term 'subculture' carries much theoretical weight but that on closer inspection it is not necessarily the most useful way to make sense of the ever-changing patterns of contemporary youth lifestyle (Bennett, 1999). Thus, it is a term that has been revised in light of a contemporary post-modern youth context. Stahl, for example, called for:

> a thicker description of the multiple forces and vectors that shape them [cultural practices] ...The (retreat to the) spectacularization of subcultures offers ineffective descriptive tools and often obscures the complexity of current cultural practices that constitute and are constituted by, the aleatory effects of a globalized cultural economy. (1999, p. 2)

Stahl suggests that when considering the life-worlds of young people in late modernity, there is a need to employ a flexible conceptual 'framework', one that enables the researcher to explore and understand the complexities of the contemporary cultures of young people and in the malleable state in which they are found. An understanding of cultural practices, particularly in the contemporary, ever more globalised world, he argues, should be free of rigid theoretical structures such as social class 'imposed' on subcultural groups as practised by the CCCS. Rather than imposing a rigid analytical framework on the culture that is being studied, a framework should be developed that is amenable to describing the constant reconfigurations of *spatiality* and their effect on social relations (Stahl, 1999) and thus 'undermin[es] any notion of a single determinant, often cast in essentialist terms (class, ethnicity, age, gender)' (Stahl, 1999, p. 2). This brings the notion of 'space' to the fore in the post-subcultural debate and an understanding of spatiality as instrumental in the construction of youth cultures and definitive of the ways in which young people move in and out of them.

Furthermore, Stahl argues, as does Miles (2000), that youth cultures should be understood as lifestyle formations that unfold in a world dominated by consumerism, the media and globalisation and in some-what adverse conditions. Rose (1999) argues that young people are particularly susceptible to the relentless pressures to consume from an ever-changing variety of products or as he refers to it a 'repertoire of wants' (p. 231). On the one hand, he argues, such desires are promoted and legitimated through the mass media, for example through advertising, while on the other, such desires are experienced in such a way that they appear as personal wants. This, Strickland (2002) argues, makes it very difficult for young people to ever be completely in control of their emerging selves and their individual lives. This pressure, as well as the quest to maintain control over one's life, is one of the reasons Miles (2000) suggests, that explains why in contemporary times we have seen a weakening in the 'power' of subcultures as a 'single unifying group' (p. 68). Subcultures, he argues, have in some respects lost their unifying function for young people. In the face of a supposed freedom of choice young people no longer feel obliged to do what others are doing but are increasingly engaged in 'doing their own thing'. Miles suggests that this is potentially a reason for the increased significance of private spaces such as bedrooms in the cultural lives of young people. Such spaces accommodate the 'do your own thing' ethos of contemporary times, while at the same time acting as a portal from which to communicate with the outside world with an intensity of their choosing.

However, this 'choosing' exists, according to Rose (1999), within a very particular framework. In his book *Governing the Soul: The Shaping of the Private Self*, Rose argues that one of the key identifiers of modern-day lifestyles, particularly in western societies, is that of 'choice', the opportunity to select from a range of goods, products and services that, we believe, will make our lives better. This right to choice has been encouraged and cultivated by the rise of neoliberalism, which, according to Rose, promotes a society of entrepreneurs who can shape 'their lives with the choices they make among the forms of life available to them' (1999, p. 230). This means that 'choice' is permeated by a very specific form of governance whereby we are making decisions about how we live out our individual lifestyles not from an infinite set of options but rather from 'a variety of marketed options' (p. 230). 'Within this new rationality of government,' Rose argues, 'a space has opened within which the precise standards of conduct, routines of life, values and aspirations of a particular family or individual can vary' (p. 230). This space has allowed the regulation of the self to become a highly individualised pursuit (Roberts, 2009), as we are encouraged to account for ourselves rather than allow ourselves to be regulated by traditional mechanisms of control and governance, such as the welfare state, which until recently had been undertaking that function. Importantly, Rose goes on to argue that it is within the sphere of leisure that this notion of self-regulation is most appropriated. He refers to leisure as the 'domain of free choice *par excellence*' (1999, p. 231) and likens modern life more generally to this arena. As he puts it:

> However constrained by external or internal factors, the modern self is institutionally required to construct a life through the exercise of choice from among alternatives. Every aspect of life, like every commodity, is imbued with a self-referential meaning; every choice we make is an emblem of our identity, a mark of our individuality, each is a message to ourselves and to others as to the sort of person that we are, each casts a glow back, illuminating the self of he or she that consumes. (p. 231)

For Rose, consumer choice in a neoliberal context is one that is, in part, defined by what he terms a 'therapeutic culture' or the 'therapeutic imperative' (p. 218), a culture that is very much perpetuated through the mass media. For example, we are exposed on a daily basis to a plethora of information advising us on how to better our lives, how to deal with our innermost problems, how to work through our 'hang-ups' and how to cope with our insecurities. For Rose, discussions that were once exclusive to the consultation room and remained within the sphere of the private, have now, through the mass media, become the 'staple fare' of the public domain (p. 218). Consequently, individuals are embroiled in a continuous hunt for who they are; their identity within a culture of consumerism demands a relentless revision of the self, a self for which we are primarily responsible and with which we are never truly satisfied. As Rose argues:

> Advanced industrial communities are no longer culturally positive. Individualism rules, the links that once bound each person into the chain of all members of the community have been severed, the possibility has emerged of everyone living a truly private life ... in the absence of any belief in positive community, the good life is the negotiation of a private life of personal relations rather than participation in a public life of shared activities. (p. 220)

In the culture of the therapeutic imperative within which the intricacies and mundanities of everyday life are laid bare in a very public manner, it can be argued that the realm of private space is one that offers some kind of refuge from such exposure and is a realm within which individuals can perhaps feel more in control of their identities and their personal relationships. This proposition is addressed throughout this book. However, the concept of control, as we shall see, operates at both the micro and the macro level in young people's bedroom culture. At the macro level it materialises in the realms of media and consumption cultures through which young people shape their youth cultural practices and identities. At a micro level, it operates through the realm of the domestic sphere within which a young person dwells, usually with their parents and other family members. Young people's uses of 'private' locations as cultural spaces, then, much like their 'public' counterparts, are part of often complex 'webs' of both identity and spatial politics. Young people often find themselves suspended in this web (Sibley, 1995; Livingstone, 2005) and have to find ways to work through it. Bedroom culture, it can be argued, is one of the ways in which this 'working through' can be represented not only in terms of the practices that take place within it, but through the space itself.

Conclusions

In this opening chapter I have explored what I consider to be some of the key limitations in the CCCS youth cultures literature when focusing on the marginalised positioning of 'private' spaces that are, by and large, absent from those traditional accounts. In revisiting this literature, I have identified the locations of those theoretical gaps and the increasing significance of the role of private space in relation to contemporary youth cultures. In such a context, private spaces such as young people's bedrooms are arguably important 'touch points' of the legitimation of youth identities, as Miles (2000) argues, of stability and authenticity in an unstable, globalised world within which consumer choice is bounded in a variety of ways. In this respect, while a well-established body of literature on young people's engagement in culture is located within the context of individualisation, globalisation and post-modernism the focus has remained largely on the public, with spaces considered to be 'private' such as bedrooms still receiving comparatively less attention.

But before elaborating on these themes, in the following chapter I recount the research process through which this study has been produced. In doing this, I consider another major critique made of the CCCS subcultures tradition, namely their choice of methodological approach in the study of young people in subcultures, which has been criticised for being predominantly based on the imposition of rigid theoretical concepts such as 'class' rather than on fieldwork. As Bennett (2002) argues, while some allusions to empirical fieldwork were made in the CCCS accounts (for example, through their observations of sub-cultural activity on the streets and through the concept of subcultural 'style' based on semiotic analysis), empirical work of an in-depth nature whereby the experiences of those young people could be told by them and not *for them* was not deemed particularly enlightening. It was commonly thought amongst CCCS researchers that empirically informed approaches were simply a form of validation of what they already knew based on their theoretical analyses. However, as I explore in the following chapter, much contemporary youth cultures research is empirically grounded and the research presented in this book is no exception.

The question that underlies the following discussions is how we go about doing research in youth spaces that are not public but private. With this in mind, in the following chapter, I take you on my 'research journey' exploring the private spaces (namely bedrooms) and cultures of young people.

2
Researching Young People's 'Private' Space

They seem to think that teenagers aren't very bright.
But I haven't found that to be the case. I listen to kids.
I respect them. I don't discount anything they have
to say just because they're only 16 years old. (John
Hughes, filmmaker [1985] *Chicago Herald Tribune*)[1]

All of us reading this book will have been a teenager at some time or
may even still be experiencing those years. While there are underly-
ing 'biological' and 'psychological' effects of this experience that may
indeed be similar across the generations, there is also a plethora of
cultural and social differences that in many ways make the experience of being a young person a very individual and unique one. These
experiences change from decade to decade, year to year, even month to
month in a rapidly changing global world (Miles, 2000; Muggleton and
Weinzierl, 2003; Nilan and Feixa, 2006) and in what has been termed a
'risk' society (Beck, 1992; Mythen and Walklate, 2006) in which young
people have to negotiate the many twists, turns and contradictions
that make up their biographies and which infiltrate their everyday lives
(Furlong and Cartmel, 2006; Roberts, 2009; Woodman, 2009). Each of
us grows up in quite different circumstances all of which have an effect
on how our teenage, and thus adult, lives 'shape up', which, consequently, makes understanding young people's lives as a sociological
phenomenon a difficult and complex task.

This book is one such attempt to undertake this task of exploring
young people's lives and identities today as lived out within the context
of what can be understood as 'private' or 'personal' space. Specifically,
I focus on the teenage bedroom as an example of such space, a space
in which youth subjectivities are understood as fragmented, multiple,

fleeting, impermanent and often bewildering (Bennett, 1999; Stahl, 1999, Muggleton, 2000) as well as collective, holistic and affirming. It is an attempt to make sense of the ways in which young people use their proximate spaces or their 'immediate life spaces', as Willis (1990, p. 2) refers to them; spaces that are situated in the home and are part of their social and cultural lives as they embark on their journeys towards their 'emerging adulthoods' (Arnett, 2004). It is also an attempt to understand how such sites potentially afford some sense of permanency, stability and identification for a young person in a post-modern, risky world.

Earlier on in the introduction to this book, I outlined the different ways in which the concept of private space is understood by young people themselves in the context of their individual lives. In summary, private space has been described by the participants in this study as a solitary space, a space of autonomy, of escapism, one that is removed from the public sphere, a space of ownership and control, hierarchical and multiple, 'controllable' and controlled. Private space also acts as an identity space, a space of production, consumption, conformism, resistance and rebellion, among many other things. Often these experiences are intermittent and interchangeable, with the meaning, significance and relevance of bedroom culture changing frequently. Private space and bedroom culture, then, are integral to the everyday lives and experiences of young people, at whatever level they participate in it, yet dependent on many different factors, including, among others: age, gender, geographic location and family formation.

Given the complexities in understanding the different conceptualisations of bedroom culture and the different interpretations of private space by young people in the context of their social and cultural lives, it is important to consider how one might go about doing research in this context in order to capture and bring to life what goes on in such a culture and a space. By taking you on my research journey in this chapter I explore matters of research practice with a number of focal points, including: assessing the methodologies I utilised; discussing the issues, problems and dilemmas I encountered along the way with particular reference to the methodological tools I used; exploring the role of the young people themselves in the research process; and assessing the 'authenticity' of the research findings given the context of private space and my position as a researcher spending time in both young males' and young females' bedrooms.

My exploration of young people and bedroom culture drew on an ethnographic approach. Ultimately in this chapter I ask the question of how one goes about doing this type of research into young people's cultures and in a private and potentially sensitive setting.

Ethnography and the study of young people's private space

> In its most characteristic form [ethnography] involves the ethnographer participating, overtly or covertly, in people's daily lives for an extended period of time, watching what happens, listening to what is said, asking questions – in fact, collecting whatever data are available to throw light on the issues that are the focus of the research. (Hammersley and Atkinson, 1995, p. 1)

There exists a well-established body of literature that examines ethnography as a research methodology and debates how it can be practised and critiqued in a variety of social and cultural contexts (Burgess, 1982, 1991; Delamont, 1992; Gilbert 1993; Coffey and Atkinson, 1996; Atkinson et al., 2001; Machin, 2002; Hammersley and Atkinson, 2007; Fetterman, 2010). As a methodology, ethnography has had a long history with its main roots stemming from anthropology. As the quote above suggests, ethnography, in its traditional sense, requires the researcher to 'go native', to become immersed as far as possible into the culture that he or she is exploring, observing the actions and routines of people in everyday life. For the ethnographer, it is the ordinary that is extraordinary (Willis, 1990; Baker, 2004), and this extraordinariness comes to the fore through careful and extensive observation and engagement in the field.

However, as a methodology ethnography has not been without its criticisms. These have centred, among other issues, on the partiality of the ethnographic account, its supposed dependence on subjective views (given that many ethnographies are conducted by one researcher or a small research team) and the role of the researcher and the management of the reflexive self (Barnard, 1990; Coffey, 1999). As Clifford Geertz put it in his seminal text *The Interpretation of Cultures*:

> this fact – that what we call our data are really our own constructions of other people's constructions of what they and their compatriots are up to – is obscured because most of what we need to comprehend, a particular event, ritual, custom, idea or whatever is insinuated as background information before the thing itself is directly explored. (Geertz, 1973, p. 9)

Gilbert Ryle's notion of 'thick description', which was discussed specifically in two lectures published in 1971 and was adopted by Geertz,[2] provides an anthropological account that recommends ways in which research should be conducted when attempting, as the ethnographer does, to put together as complete a 'picture' as possible of the lives of their participants, of a specific set of people existing in the particular culture or society under study. Geertz argues that the descriptions the researcher provides through their analysis of the data collected should be comprehensive to a level whereby those descriptions can be recognised by the subjects as themselves and their activities make ample sense to them. This has not been always the case in ethnographic studies of youth subcultures, and the partiality of some accounts by CCCS researchers where a qualitative tradition was claimed has been well documented (Clarke, 1981; Waters, 1981; Bennett, 2010).[3]

Geertz warns us, then, that we must be aware of the fact that our analyses are by and large our own constructions of other people's constructions. McRobbie makes a similar point when she acknowledges that research is constantly influenced by the historical moment in which it is set and that different historical circumstances can influence research in a variety of ways. As she put it:

> No research is carried out in a vacuum. The very questions we ask are always informed by the historical moment we inhabit – not necessarily directly or unambiguously, but in more subtle ways. (1991, p. 64)

Since the beginning of the 1990s, scholars such as Barnard have argued that social scientists have become increasingly disillusioned with the term 'ethnography' and the ways in which ethnographic methods can be applied. Barnard went as far as to argue that there has been an ethnographic 'crisis' centring around the notion that ethnographers have found themselves in a methodological and interpretative 'cul-de-sac' in terms of the 'politics of interpretation and representation', articulated clearly in the question: 'what is the position of the researcher in relation to the objects of research?' (Barnard, 1990, p. 71).

Barnard's discussion traces the beginnings of an ethnographic research approach rooted in the anthropological tradition (established largely by Malinowski in the 1920s) whereby the researcher followed a given 'set of rules' that mapped out the ways in which the research should be conducted. These 'rules' included: the selection of 'a closed community – tribe, caste, village, community, or urban ghetto – in one of the colonial or neo-colonial territories for in-depth study'; 'resid[ing]' there 'amongst the chosen people' for a specific period of time; and, finally, upon return, the production of a 'series of ethnographies which capture this life as a whole' (Barnard, 1990, p. 59). Increasingly, this method became criticised predominantly by those who were the subjects of the 'anthropologist's gaze' (p. 59). In light of a wave of decolonisation, these groups argued that the ethnographic tradition constituted part of the larger colonial tradition and that its activities were both 'intellectual as well as political' leading the subjects to increasingly question the methods being utilised on them (p. 59).

Similarly, in the 1970s, feminism critiqued anthropological ethnography on the basis that it excluded or marginalised women. For example Morgan describes the 'brave' male researcher returning from the field: 'the lower depths, the mean streets, areas traditionally "off limits" to women investigators' (1981, quoted in Burgess 1991, p. 91). This representation very much defines CCCS youth cultural studies that were dominated by male researchers. Further, their findings rendered the female research subject invisible and insignificant, dismissed as being 'passive' or 'giggly' and harder to reach than their male counterparts, and therefore seemingly not having the same subcultural 'role' as the boys. McRobbie and Garber's work on the bedroom culture of girls was born specifically out of this critique. As a methodology, ethnography continues to be critiqued from feminist perspectives. For example, the power relations between the researcher and the researched have been questioned as well as the inherent inequalities associated with the author 'speaking' on behalf of the participants through their analyses (Skeggs, 1994; Van Zoonen, 1994; Harris, 2004a).

Despite the numerous criticisms, however, ethnography re-emerged as an important research tool in youth cultural studies in the 1980s particularly in light of the CCCS' questionable ethnographic approach to the study of British subcultures (Barnard, 1990, p. 69), which appeared partial and incomplete (for example, in relation to young women, ethnic minorities and middle-class youth that seemed to be excluded). However, Clifford (1986) argues that ethnographies are by their very nature 'constructed narratives' and therefore can only 'tell part of the story … [are] inherently *partial* – committed and incomplete' (quoted in Pink, 2007, p. 10, original italics). This suggests that while the ethnographer can go some way to enlighten us about a particular culture or aspect of it, they will nonetheless not be able to ever construct a 'complete picture'. By its very nature, then, ethnography is destined to remain open-ended and 'incomplete'.

The methodological problems associated with ethnographies of youth culture have been also highlighted in more recent times. An example of such a critique is Bennett's (2002) work which questions more recent qualitative studies on youth (for example, Redhead, 1997 and Richard and Krüger, 1998, cited in Bennett, 2002), particularly in relation to popular music. While these studies have made an effort to critique the CCCS' methodologies, and despite a substantial level of thoroughness in terms of methodological choices, Bennett argues that they still failed to critically engage with the research methods they used to produce their research findings. It is the lack of critical engagement with the sources that provide this type of 'insider information' that, for Bennett, creates compromised ethnographic accounts, irrespective of the degree of influence that some of these studies achieved in the field of youth studies.[4]

Discussing 'the craft' of scholarship more generally in academia Back draws a quote from John Berger's *And Our Faces, My Heart, Brief as Photos* (1984), which is particularly telling of the relationship between researcher and subject:

> What separates us from the characters about whom we write is not knowledge, either objective or subjective, but their experience of time in the story we are telling. This separation allows us, the story-tellers, the power of knowing the whole. Yet, equally, this separation renders us powerless; we cannot control our characters, after the narration has begun. We are obliged to follow them, and this following is through and across time, which they are living and which we over see.
>
> The time and therefore the story, belongs to them. Yet the meaning of the story, what makes it worthy of being told, is what we can see and what inspires us because we are beyond its time. (Berger, 1984, pp. 30–1 in Back, 2007, p. 171)

When reflecting on ethnographic practice this passage underlines the problems in the relationship between the researcher and the researched and the extent to which, in the context of ethnography, we are placed in a position whereby we are retelling the 'story' of our informants. However immersed in a culture we get, we are still in many ways separated from the people we study, cannot have access to them in their entirety and are always 'positioned' to some degree as 'the researcher'. The subjects' experiences are inevitably different and temporally shaped and determined – so while we might be able to relate to them we should not forget that these are experiences that are very specific to a certain place in time (as McRobbie [1991] also suggests and as Bennett [2002] finds problematic in some recent studies of young people and music).

This is particularly pertinent when we are trying to 'get inside' the world of a young person. We try, through spending time with them, observing them, participating with them, to make sense of their worlds, but when doing this research we are aware that we are trying to make sense of worlds that are constantly shifting and changing at an accelerated pace, and that we, the researchers, will no doubt have trouble keeping up. We are observing these young people going through a complex series of experiences and transitions – sometimes collective, sometimes individual – and we aim to provide as complete a picture as possible under these conditions.

Ethnographic methodologies do, however, afford a greater understanding of young people in ordinary everyday life, not just as part of 'spectacular' groups (for example the Teddy Boys, Mods, Rockers and Skins) as early CCCS research favoured. Ethnography entails the placing of participants 'centre stage' in organically evolving analyses rather than 'pushing' them to a marginal position when a theoretical framework is imposed on them – as was the case with the subcultures approach in the 1970s and 1980s (Bennett, 2002), thus creating a narrative around their activities that might not necessarily be recognisable to the participants themselves (Waters, 1981). In this respect, there have been criticisms of many ethnographies of youth subcultures conducted in the UK during these two decades, criticisms that raise the lack of interaction on the part of the researcher with the actual 'social actors' themselves (Hammersley and Atkinson, 2007). Bennett (2002) has argued that those approaches tended to be grounded in preconceived theoretical notions, which are, then, inevitably imposed on the subjects rather than shaped by them. Bennett gives the example of Stanley Cohen who in his book *Folk Devils and Moral Panics* (1972) provides criticisms of his own research methods and approaches. He also reflects on those accounts of other CCCS researchers, who barely touch the surface of what could be considered as ethnography today. As Bennett writes:

> The structuralist narratives produced by the CCCS served to render fieldwork redundant in social settings deemed to be underpinned by irremovable socio-economic determinants which, it was argued, fundamentally shaped the consciousness of social actors. (Bennett, 2002, p. 453)

Taking their theoretical direction from subcultural theory, it is not surprising that the CCCS approaches were deeply grounded in questions of political hegemony. Such grounding is something that contemporary researchers try to avoid and criticise, especially in light of what has been termed a post-subcultural approach (Bennett, 1999; Stahl, 1999; Muggleton, 2000; Muggleton and Weinzierl, 2003; Bennett and Kahn-Harris, 2004), which proposes that the cultural activities of young people can no longer be understood simply as being 'fixed' in place by subcultural theory. Rather, as Bennett puts it, young people's activities should be considered as 'prime examples of the instability and shifting nature of post-modern society' (1999, p. 603). Bennett argues that there is a need for alternative ways in which to understand the actions of young people in culture, ways that are flexible enough to encompass the complexities and ever-changing shape of youth culture, its 'fluid boundaries and floating memberships' (Bennett, 1999, p. 600; see also Stahl, 1999).

In more contemporary ethnographies, then, the researcher utilises his or her skills to place the subjects themselves in a position in which they can 'tell their story' (Hammersley and Atkinson, 2007).[5] Rather than simply being 'mapped onto' existing theoretical frameworks, as was the case for the CCCS studies, the subjects have a significant role to play in shaping the resulting data and their analyses. Importantly, the power dynamic between the researcher and the researched should at the very least be more balanced, if not in favour of the subject. This then allows for a series of 'micro' ethnographic studies, which enable the ethnographer to piece together the relationship of, for example, 'local' and 'social' processes in the lives of the young people who are the focus of the research, to engage with the complexities of those processes (Bennett, 2002, p. 455) and to understand associations between the micro and the macro, between structure and practice (Skeggs, 1994, p. 74). Crucially, the ethnographer does not aim to achieve a body of research that is 'bounded' by particular theories or concepts, as according to Hammersley and Atkinson, 'the boundaries around ethnography are necessarily unclear' (1995, p. 2).

Additionally, in critiquing the work of Paul Atkinson, Sarah Delamont and William Housley, Sarah Pink argues that in contemporary settings, which are defined by fragmented lifestyles and cultures, there is no longer necessarily a 'standard way of doing ethnography that is universally practised' (2009, p. 8). Pink argues that while 'classic' ethnography is defined by participant observation and ethnographic interviewing as well as other techniques that promote participation that adhere to a form of 'holistic' practice, more fragmented approaches to ethnographic research need not necessarily be frowned upon. Further, it can be argued that a more fragmented approach to ethnography indeed complements the contemporary youth lifestyle that is often defined as fleeting and momentary rather than stable and fixed. Ethnographic practice that diverts from traditional methodological approaches, Pink argues, is still 'a reflexive and experimental process through which understanding, knowing and (academic) knowledge are produced' (p. 8) and need not privilege a particular methodological approach. In her presentation of sensory ethnography as a critical methodology Pink suggests that such an approach demands a diversity in methodological perspective and style that can be shaped by the experiences of the ethnographer in the field, particularly given that the use of the senses to experience culture is 'of the moment' (for example, selecting music to listen to as the mood takes us). Pink draws on the work of O'Reilly who, in reviewing varying ethnographic approaches, has suggested that ethnography necessarily draws on a 'family of methods' (O'Reilly, 2005, p. 3 in Pink, 2009, p. 9) selected according to the contexts that define the everyday lives of the participants, an approach I adopted in producing this study. This alternative approach contests the more traditional definitions offered for example by Delamont (2004) and others who suggest that ethnography is more strictly living and dwelling in the research field and necessarily utilises participant observation as a key ethnographic research tool (Delamont, 2004, cited in Pink 2009, p. 9).

'Keep out!!!' The problem with ethnography in young people's private spaces

While ethnography in the anthropological sense (of being on site and being or becoming an insider) is a highly effective and appropriate methodology in the study of youth cultures (see, for example, Thornton, 1995; Bennett, 2000; Hodkinson, 2002) I would argue, as indeed others such as Pink (2009) and Dickinson et al. (2001) have done before me, that there are some domains and cultures that do not readily lend themselves to this type of intensive participation, not least because of the ethical implications of doing ethnography in this way. A young person's bedroom is an example of this. This is not to say that gaining access to and dwelling in youth cultures in the public domain is by any means easy and indeed, as Cohen (1991), Thornton (1995), Hodkinson (2002) and others testify, the process of becoming an 'insider' is complex and requires careful and critical reflection in relation to the ethnography produced. But the very fact that these cultures exist primarily in public spaces does present potential for ease of access and an opportunity for 'dwelling' that is not readily found in the private domain. For example, access to a club (the research site of Thornton's study) as a customer is fairly standardised across clubs (and bars) in the UK in that it requires one to be over 18 years old,[6] to behave appropriately (for example, not to [appear to be] drunk or on drugs or to be suitably dressed). Adhering to such regulations is likely to get you access and, in addition, instils an initial level of trust on behalf of the staff regulating 'the door' that is sufficient to get you 'in' at least.[7] Access to the private domain, on the other hand, is different. While age, behaviour and dress (or 'impression management' as Hammersley and Atkinson [1995] refer to it) are indeed important,[8] there are also other factors, as Dickinson et al. note:

> Studying the social dynamics of domestic interiors is notoriously difficult in Westernized societies, where the home is a geographical site for several types of activity and to which others can legitimately be denied entrance. Regarding the home as a type of sanctuary is bolstered by highly valued notions of privacy and claims to certain types of freedom and rights. It is one of the social settings that is particularly impervious to sociological or social anthropological observation. (2001, p. 242)

The home, then, by its very nature, according to Dickinson et al., is a domain whereby one has the right to maintain one's privacy and a domain over which its owners have the right to regulate who enters and who does not. And while indeed this type of regulation can be in operation in the public domain (and within virtual spaces also), the privacy that is afforded within the context of the home in western societies is increasingly protected in a world of self-broadcast and exposure (Orlet, 2007; Burgess and Green, 2009; Mallan, 2009), which makes domestic spaces difficult to gain access to, let alone dwell in.

In her discussions about the space of the bedroom more specifically Baker reiterates Dickinson's observations, while also reflecting upon the reasons why there is still a relative paucity of research on young people's private spaces. She remarks:

> Of course, part of the problem is that bedrooms are difficult research fields to gain access to. This is because the home is deemed a private space, a space free from the prying eyes of outsiders (the researcher). To conduct fieldwork in someone's home as a stranger – observing, questioning, taking notes – breaches the traditional boundaries between the public and the private. (2004 p. 76)

Adopting an 'orthodox' ethnographic approach (Atkinson, Delamont and Housley, 2007 and others) for my study was difficult for a number of reasons. First, given the ethical issues of doing research of this nature (which I discuss in detail below) and the age range of my participants, with a significant number of them being under the age of 18 years, an orthodox approach would have demanded that I spent a sustained period of time within the actual space of a teenager's bedroom. The highly private, and potentially sensitive, nature of the space, as well as the domestic sphere more generally, as noted above, meant that this was not viable. Indeed, while parents were happy to allow me to spend short periods of time with their children in their bedrooms, 'living' with them in those spaces was not a possibility. This was further problematic because my research was also conducted with teenage boys. It was therefore crucial to select methods whereby I could 'get inside' and to some degree participate in the private spaces of both young males and females without being able to 'dwell' in those spaces in the traditional anthropological sense.

Second, there was the issue of household dynamics that Dickinson et al. discuss in relation their study of household organisation and consumption. The family homes in my research sample were not just inhabited by teenagers but were also inhabited by a number of other family members, each living out their own routines. In this respect, while, as I document below, other family members were very happy to welcome me into their homes on the occasions of my research visits, actually living in that space was not practical, especially given that the study in total has amounted to working with over fifty young people.[9] In addition to this, and as I note in Chapter 3, a number of the teenagers in my research sample had more than one bedroom, for example, if their parents were divorced and were living separately. This further added to the complexities of dwelling for an extended period of time in these spaces, the dynamics of which could be captured through the use of other ethnographic tools, and also potentially meant engaging in complex and difficult family relations, again compromising my ethical position.

Finally, there was the problem of my presence interfering in the everyday lives of other household members who would no doubt feel that they have to 'accommodate' me in various ways. This meant that my presence would have been an interruption to their everyday routines and thus I might not necessarily have been able to gauge an 'authentic' household experience within which a teenager's bedroom is located. I was interested primarily in how a teenager articulates the use of his or her bedroom in reference to the dynamics of their individual households, thus demonstrating the plurality of bedroom cultures as well as the different, and similar, experiences of such a culture by young people.

My approach

In order to explore this and in attempting to overcome some of the problems and issues outlined above, I drew on three strands of ethnography. Firstly, I drew on the more traditional anthropological strand whereby I conducted in-depth ethnographic interviews and observations with participants, in their bedrooms. Secondly, I drew on what has been termed '(multi)sensory' ethnography (Pink 2004, 2009), a strand of ethnography that, according to Dicks et al. (2011), 'mean[s] anything from research using video recorders, observation of bodily movements or analysis of material objects and environment' (p. 228). Thirdly, I incorporated elements of visual ethnography (Banks, 2001; Pink, 2004), namely photography (Collier, 1995 [1975]). Given that the majority of the research was conducted within the space of the bedroom either in small friendship groups (Griffiths, 1995; Hey, 1997) or on a one-on-one basis (Spradley, 1979),[10] I felt that it was important not only to be able to articulate the range of social and cultural practices that go on in the space but also to be able to explore in detail the role of the bedroom itself in the lives of my young participants. This is not least because, as one of the first spaces a young person can call their own, they are quintessentially spaces of emotions and these emotions are not just expressed through speech, but also (sometimes even more so) through visual and aural elements.

However, while I state that I drew on these traditions, it is important to acknowledge that the three strands do not exist in isolation and that in many ways the ethnographic interview, the starting point of my data collection, is by its very nature context-dependent (Pink, 2009, p. 83). This means that it draws on a range of senses and therefore relies to some extent on the implementation of visual and aural techniques to work effectively. The awareness of context in a study of this nature in which I was actually spending time in bedrooms with my participants was crucial. As I note above, being privileged to obtain access to such personal and private spaces and to overcome many of the reservations other room culture scholars have faced in terms of actually entering into these spaces as sites of fieldwork meant that I had to conduct the research in very specific ways. I had to be sensitive to the context of the private and the domestic and operate with some degree of reflexivity with regards to my own feelings, emotions and experiences (Rubin and

Rubin, 2005), especially as I used to be a teenager who spent a lot of time in my bedroom. This sensitivity manifested, not only in what questions were asked, how, with what intonation and with what forms of bodily expression, but also in some of the minute details of the interviews: for instance, when first entering the bedrooms I would always ensure that I asked the participant where they would like me to sit. I did not just assume it would be fine to sit on the bed, the obvious place to sit on entering this space. The bed is probably one of the most personal things in a bedroom (an example of the private within the private), as it is a place to sleep, masturbate, have sex or to read, listen to music, check Facebook and so on. It may have been considered an invasion of personal space and may even have had sexual connotations and thus serious ethical implications, particularly in a boy's bedroom, had I just assumed it was OK to sit on it. This was especially so given that I was an adult and a relative stranger rather than a parent, friend or sibling. If my interviews took place on a one-to-one basis, then I was normally invited to sit on the bed. If I was working with a small group of friends, we usually sat on the floor together making it easier to talk to and see each other.

In considering this need for sensitivity, my approach complemented contemporary feminist perspectives on qualitative research (Skeggs, 1994; Van Zoonen, 1994; Harris, 2004a; Rubin and Rubin, 2005). For example, the positioning of my participant within their own personal space empowered them, particularly when reflecting upon their positioning in relation to myself as the researcher. As I state below, the participants were interviewed in *their* home, in *their* bedroom and with *their* friends, which means that they were not only able to 'talk back' (hooks, 1989, cited in Pink, 2009, p. 83) but also to talk, chat and converse amongst themselves, the anecdotal nature of their discussions providing rich and informative data way beyond the questions I had prepared in advance. Additionally, because my research was conducted with both young males and young females I was able to give a voice to participants (in this case male ones) who had not been considered to any great extent in earlier discussions of bedroom culture (and excluded completely from McRobbie and Garber's [1975] canonical piece). Further, in critiquing McRobbie and Garber's work I was able to gauge through talking in depth with my participants the extent to which the space of the bedroom is connected to the public world rather than being isolated from it, and the ways in which it can act as a 'portal of communication', from which they facilitate many aspects of their social and cultural lives as has been documented by scholars such as boyd (2008a) and as I explore in detail in Chapters 5 and 6.

A space of the emotions: bedrooms and (multi) sensory ethnography

Admittedly, this study started out with many points of contact to a traditional ethnography, and in critiquing McRobbie and Garber's original study on girls and their bedrooms, I was keen to ensure that the research took place within the space of the bedroom itself, rather than within a more public context, as was the case for McRobbie and Garber's interviews with teenage girls (which I discuss further below). But as the research progressed, my findings revealed that the sensorial elements of bedroom spaces experienced by my participants were a key part of their engagement in bedroom cultures. For example, the bedroom was evidently a highly visual space, and indeed each bedroom that I visited was decorated differently and in many different ways represented the interests and identity of its occupant as was revealed during my interviews. In addition to this, the visual elements of the space were further enhanced through the use of media technologies, such as televisions, game consoles, laptops and so on (the significance of which in young people's bedrooms has been well documented by scholars such as Steele and Brown [1995] and Larson [1995]) and, as I explore in Chapter 5, this opened up a range of other visual 'zones' through which bedroom culture could be experienced beyond the physicalities of space. Furthermore, young people immersed themselves in bedroom cultures at different levels of intensity through sound (Bull, 2005), for example by using media technologies such as the sound system or iPod to indulge or deny particular moods, to escape from the trials and tribulations of everyday life or to avoid thinking about or doing particular things (such as homework). On occasions too, the bedroom was a space within which smell played a significant role to its young occupants in creating a particular kind of ambience or was indeed used in more rebellious ways, for example to cover up illicit acts, such as smoking cigarettes or drugs or drinking alcohol.

As a researcher entering into the intrepid domain of the teenage bedroom, all three of these sensual elements experienced by the participants were also experienced by me. For example, I was always struck by the different ways in which a young person's bedroom was decorated and the extent to which the space itself could be read as an ethnographic text, one that changes and evolves all the time giving clues about the emerging identity of its occupant as well as the history of young lives, especially if they have occupied the same room for most of their lives. The visual elements of the space drew out both the mundane and routine aspects of a young person's life as well as those things more unique to them. Sound was also important in my experiences of doing this research, not only in terms of how music contributed to the biographies and identities of my participants but also in how sound contributed to my experiences as a researcher entering into different bedroom spaces. For example, I have very vivid memories of one research interview with a group of four girls aged between 12 and 14 years, who lived in the north Manchester suburb of Gorton.

It was a summer's evening and I had got off the bus a few streets away, so I had to walk a little distance to get to the participant's house. As I entered their street, I could hear voices and chatting and I could see a small group of teenagers gathered outside a house, talking to the girls above who were hanging out of one of the girls' bedroom window. In addition to this, I could hear the 'thudding' of garage music coming from the same bedroom, music that was turned up loud. Its volume in this instance was significant for two reasons. One reason, given by the girls when asked about the music, was so that both they and their friends outside could hear it and no doubt this was an aural statement of the girls being 'in the know' about the latest tunes. It was the type of music they were all into, so they had turned it up loud in order for everyone in the neighbourhood to hear it. This also meant the girls had to shout out of the window to the group gathered below, thus creating more noise outside. The second reason, from the point of view of the researcher, was that the music had probably been turned up for my benefit as well as for the benefit of friends hanging about in the street below. The girls were anticipating my arrival and had no doubt been looking out for me as well as chatting to their friends outside. The music too seemed a symbolic marker of territorialism; they clearly had ownership at that particular moment, of that particular part of the street, and the girls appeared to be held in some esteem by the group on the street who were happy to hover outside (rather than being invited in) while the girls stayed inside (although again my visit may have influenced this). Additionally, there was some feeling of trepidation on my part, not just because of the volume of the music that gradually became louder as I got closer and as I began to think 'I really hope that's not the house I'm going to!', but also the style of music which in itself was rather intimidating. This for me signalled that I had entered into the space of the girls and that I was a stranger there among a group who were clearly very familiar with each other. The use of the loud music had achieved this 'me and them' separation even before I had spoken to the girls.

Finally, smell was significant to my experiences as a researcher, although, perhaps surprisingly given the context, it was the least talked about sense for my participants. According to Largey and Watson (1973), spaces can be defined through smell (for example, a kitchen) and we are often able, through smell, to identify the activities that take place within them or, as Largey and Watson call them, the 'modes of involvement' within a particular space (p. 1027). In entering the domain of a young person's bedroom, smell was an indicator of the 'type' of bedroom I was in. For example, I could identify whether I was in a male's bedroom or a female's bedroom, whether I was in a clean room (and whether the room had been freshly cleaned by a mother for the purpose of my interview) or a dirty room and whether I was in a room that was used often or one seldom used outside of its functional role as a place in which to get dressed or to sleep. When my participants did talk about smell, it tended to be within the context of 'recreating' other spaces so, for example, in Chapter 4 I discuss the ways in which 18-year-old Erin took comfort in smells such as perfumes and washing powder as reminders of home when she first moved into halls of residence at university.

To complement this, then, my methodological approach evolved to adopt a more multisensory ethnographic approach that, alongside the more traditional observation and ethnographic interviews, incorporated a close analysis of the materiality of bedroom spaces, paying particular attention to bedrooms as visual, aural and to a lesser extent, olfactory spaces.

The sensorial experiences of young people in their bedrooms were captured in a variety of ways. The visual aspects, for example, were captured using what Brown and Steele have described in their work on young people's bedrooms as 'room tours' (1995, p. 553), that is, the participants took the researchers on a tour around their bedrooms talking about the objects, items and things found in their rooms and how they were significant to them. Brown and Steele asked their participants to hold a tape recorder while they did this, capturing the data aurally and presumably giving the participants freedom to wander around their rooms selecting the objects they wished to talk about. As an important part of the research process in my own work, 'room tours' were incorporated into the in-depth interviews with my participants and involved them showing me around their rooms and talking about the objects, items and things that were contained within their bedrooms, much like Brown and Steele's participants.[11] The commentary during the 'tours' was digitally recorded and, in addition, I photographed the 'things' the young people talked about ensuring that I captured both an aural and visual record of those things as well as of the space of the bedroom more generally within which those things belonged. I discuss the use of photography in more detail below. During the room tours, the participants spoke about the objects on display in their rooms as well as objects that were not (for example, memory boxes under the bed,[12] beauty products tossed into a drawer or cigarettes hidden away). They also talked about objects that they considered to be significant to both their past and current personal biographies as well as the things that seemed to just 'appear' in their rooms. On a number of occasions participants would say that they had forgotten why a particular object was in their room in the first place or that in fact those objects were remnants from past occupants. In using this approach my participants were able to select the objects that they wanted to talk about; they could tell stories associated with them and the meanings attached to them, locating them within the context of their personal space as well as individual biographies.

The study of 'things' as part of material culture is hardly new and indeed there is a well-established tradition, particularly within the social anthropology of the study of things as ethnographic texts (see, for example, Miller, 2001, 2008; Turkle, 2007). However, traditional youth cultural studies in the UK (such as the semiotic analyses of the CCCS) did little to unveil the ways in which individuals created meaning around objects outside of their subcultural affiliations. As Miles (2000) has argued, those objects remained at the level of representation of subcultural membership, which left wide open the question of what subcultural artefacts meant to members not only as part of their subcultural identities but their everyday identities too; more generally, how did the 'spectacular' elements of subculture fit into aspects of a member's everyday life?

The role of sound, and especially music, in the creation of a bedroom culture was mainly captured through the more traditional method of the research interview in which each of the participants spoke in depth about many aspects of their social and cultural life both in and outside of the home. Of course, the significance of music in the lives of my participants was also clearly documented within the space of the bedroom though posters, postcards, gig tickets, vinyl and CD collections captured in room tours and photographs. Discussions about music formed a significant part of the interviews with participants talking, in many cases extensively, about their engagement in music in their rooms. Themes included how music created a form of 'soundtrack' to the participants' lives and their evolving biographies (DeNora, 2000; Bull, 2005; Lincoln, 2005); how the seemingly mundane space of the bedroom can be transformed into a dynamic cultural and social space (Baker, 2004; Lincoln,

2005); the motivations of musical choice and how music facilitates interactions among young people in both public and private space and across multiple media. On several occasions, music was actually playing in the bedrooms during my research visits allowing me to experience some aspects of their bedroom culture, as I note, for example, in one of my research diary entries after a meeting with the four girls from Gorton, north Manchester, I talked about above:

> They had some music on in the bedroom, which they told me was UK garage music. They told me that this was the sort of music they listened to most of the time. I thought it might be better if the music was left on because the girls liked to have a bit of background noise and it allowed them to have a level of control over the music in their own familiar space. One of the sisters had said to me beforehand they she always had music on in her bedroom and that often it was on really loud.

Other room scholars such as Baker (2004) have used alternative research techniques in order to capture how young people use music as an integral part of their bedroom culture. For example, in asking her participants to record anything they liked from their daily lives using tape recorders, some participants had created 'pretend' radio shows, recorded in the familiar and safe space of their rooms.[13] Notably, though, Baker did not conduct research into her participants' bedroom by entering this domain herself. Instead, Baker incorporated observations with the use of cameras and small portable tape recorders by her young female participants. In doing so, Baker argues, she was given insights into the girls' world beyond the school setting within which the interviews took place. As she notes:

> The cameras and tape recorders could be taken by the girls into spaces that, as an adult researcher, I may not have been able to readily access – the bedroom being one such space. (Baker, 2004, p. 79)

For Baker, the use of audio and visual technologies by her participants allowed her to break away from more traditional ethnographic methods, such as participant observation, that she suggests (and as I note above) do not readily complement research within the private sphere. In using this technology, the girls were ultimately in control of the data collected, could record what they please, thus producing what Wallman et al. (1980, cited in Baker, 2004, p. 79) called an 'ethnography by proxy'. Baker's work is particularly interesting because she considers how young people (specifically pre-teens in her work) engage in both the consumption and the production of music in this private space.

'My bedroom is me': bedrooms and visual ethnography

While the use of photography in ethnographic studies has received its fair share of criticism (for example, see Collier 1995 [1975]; Prosser, 1998) on the grounds of its 'subjectivity, bias and specificity' (Pink, 2007, p. 9), scholars such as Baker (2004) and Steele and Brown (1995) have demonstrated its use in difficult-to-access spaces such as young people's bedrooms. Steele and Brown, for example, incorporated photography into their study of adolescent room culture and the media. While they claim that initially the idea of using photographs was to enable the researcher team to share data across US states, they subsequently found that 'these photos and the bedroom culture they captured opened up an unexpectedly rich vein of information about adolescent identities and media use' that came to form a greater part of their study than initially anticipated (1995, p. 554). The visual representation of their participants' room gave them another source of rich ethnographic data that enabled them to further understand young people's bedroom cultures.

Having been able to gain this access and seeing for myself the highly visual nature of bedroom spaces, I was keen to incorporate visual data into my study and thus bring bedroom spaces 'to life', visually as well as orally. Knowles and Sweetman (2004) argue that the use of visual material such as photographs in ethnography 'is worthwhile because ... photos can achieve something that methods relying on speech and writing cannot' (quoted in Rose, 2007, p. 238). In the case of a bedroom, a photograph can capture how the space is used by its young occupants as a visual representation of their identities, interests and cultures, an identity that might not be so easily (or creatively) articulated through speech.[14] Visual material, Pink argues, '*become[s]* of interest' (2007, p. 6, original emphasis) through its relationship with other aspects of the research process. In this respect, rather than relying solely on spoken accounts of the uses and meanings of their bedrooms, I also used photographs as a data resource that provided rich representations of the bedroom cultures I was experiencing.[15]

All of the photographs that appear in this book I took myself using a digital camera and were taken during the 'room tours' with participants. The decision to take the photos myself rather than asking the participants to do it (as Baker [2004] did with her participants) was made after attempting to issue a small number of my participants with disposable cameras during the early stages of my data collection. Although I had some success in employing this method during my pilot study, its implementation was not so successful this time. This I surmised, was for three main reasons: first, because I had simply asked the participants to photograph any aspect of their daily life (including life in their bedrooms) rather than giving them a specific brief, they were a little unsure what they should take photos of; second, and mainly because of my failure to give them a specific brief, the participants got a little bored with the task, which suggests the collection of questionable visual data; and third, those who did take photographs (or who claimed that they did) did not return the cameras, despite me giving them a prepaid envelope in which to do this.

The decision to take the photographs myself came with a number of considerations regarding my position as a researcher, what I took photographs of, how the participants would respond to this and the extent to which the power relations would shift between researcher and participant.[16] This point was particularly pertinent given the feminist leanings of my approach whereby I was constantly conscious of the positioning of the participant within the research process and in relation to me, as I discuss above. For instance, while I considered it essential that the research take place within the space of the participants' bedrooms or at the very least in their homes whereby the participants were the ones inviting me into their homes, inviting me into their bedrooms and introducing me to their friends, and while, despite undertaking semi-structured interviews, I was more than happy to observe and listen to the exchange of stories and anecdotes between close friends, taking the photographs myself seemed in the first instance to detract from this consideration of empowerment. However, by taking these pictures during the 'room tours' I was able to shift some of that power back onto the participant. This was because it was them that led me around their rooms and showed me the things they felt were of interest or had a story to tell. I would then photograph these objects and items or the section of the room that the object was in more precisely so as to be able to see the context within which the object appeared. Because the photographs were taken digitally I was able to review the photographs with the participants at the end of the interview and the technology also meant that rather than having to carefully line up the shot, I could 'point and shoot' while talking to the participant quite discreetly and ensuring a continued flow of conversation. In reviewing the photos too, I was able to 'banter' with the participants about my novice techniques, for example looking at very blurred shots that I had taken quickly and they in turn would sometimes talk about taking photos themselves, especially with mobile phones and on nights out when they would often get a series of blurred shots, as I discuss in the final chapter.

Once taken and uploaded onto a laptop, the images could then be analysed, both in their own right and alongside the interview and observational data. Pink claims that there are 'no fixed criteria that determine which photographs are ethnographic' and that the meaning of a photograph is 'arbitrary and subjective' (2007, p. 67) and dependent on who is doing the looking. Indeed, a researcher's reading of a photograph of a room under examination will be different from a reading by a participant who spends large amounts of time in that space. Both are likely to notice different things. Therefore, a discussion with the participant about their rooms alongside the visual images is important. The researcher is then able to construct a narrative that makes sense of the life-worlds of the participants as well as making sense to the participants themselves. The researcher is also able to undertake forms of micro-ethnography, looking in detail at the images, considering the placing of objects and exploring how the space can be understood as a microcosm of a young person's identity. As Dodman (2003, p. 294) argues, a photograph can be 'a more transparent representation of the life experiences of participants'. In this way, the subjective nature of a photograph in a context such as a young person's bedroom can be very useful in determining the different ways in which bedroom cultures can manifest, shift and change over time.

Another issue that I had to consider in using photography to document bedroom spaces was of an ethical nature. Given I was photographing highly personal spaces, it was a stipulation of ethical approval for the project that none of the participants would appear in the photographs or, if they did, their identity was to be made anonymous. This, I felt, somewhat compromised the cultural considerations of the work. In understanding the cultural practices of a young person I have argued above that the spaces within which these practices occur should not be distanced from the practices that take place within them and that in the example of the teenage bedroom, the space itself plays a vital role in the understanding of bedroom cultures. However, the visual representation of bedroom culture that my photographs presented dislocated my participants from the object of study; I had a series of photographs of bedrooms but without the occupants in them I felt I was missing what Becker (2002) refers to as the 'real, flesh and blood life' (quoted in Rose, 2007, p. 238) of the photograph. On the other hand, however, Knowles and Sweetman (2004) suggest that social science researchers should perhaps not be concerned with such considerations because the secondary nature of photographs in ethnographic data collection makes them 'simply means to certain ends' (quoted in Rose, 2007, p. 238). In this respect, Knowles and Sweetman propose that researchers should emphasise 'the analytical and conceptual possibilities of visual methods' (p. 238) on the basis of what photographs can achieve as opposed to what photographs are as a technology of vision. In this case, then, the photos capturing the spaces of my participants offered endless possibilities in terms of their analytical power and are very rich sources of data. The 'real, flesh and blood life' that Becker requires is, I would suggest, evident in the material presence of the participants' space and objects, despite the absence of the participants themselves.

For the remainder of this chapter, I wish to turn my attention briefly to some of the more practical issues that I have encountered in doing research with young people in private spaces. By doing this, I will highlight some of the problems, issues and dilemmas that the researcher faces when doing research in such a context and reflect upon the extent to which my chosen methodologies enabled me to gain a meaningful insight into young people's private spaces. Below I discuss how I 'found' my participants, how I negotiated access, the ethics of doing this type of research in private space and my role as a female, adult researcher in a young person's space.

Finding participants, gaining access to young people's private space

Finding participants to take part in a project of this nature can be difficult, not least because of the ethical implications of an adult researcher entering into and spending time in the personal and private environments of young people as noted above. Being mindful of this fact when undertaking this research, it was my intention at the start of the project to go about recruiting my participants through formal educational settings (schools and colleges, for example), a method popular with youth researchers because it potentially enables access to a large number of participants on one research site (Heath et al., 2009). However, an initial pilot study demonstrated that this was not going to be the most suitable method of access given the type of study that I wanted to undertake. There were a number of reasons for this, including 'research saturation' in my research sites of Manchester and Liverpool, both large university cities in the north of England with a high number of students trying to gain access to schools to do research; the problem of a long and potentially complicated consent process, starting with head teachers and ending with the young participants; and my commitment to remaining as true as possible to the context of the research given my criticisms of early studies of bedroom culture (namely McRobbie and Garber's 'Girls and Subcultures' [1975] in which the research was undertaken in youth clubs rather than in bedrooms).[17]

As an alternative strategy, I decided to draw on my own, less formal 'social networks' of family and friends. Through this route and through making initial contacts this way my sample 'snowballed', often exponentially, as on several occasions I found myself talking with parents, siblings, participants' friends as well as other family members, such as cousins, aunts and uncles, people I would not have spoken to had I pursued access through the more formal education route. This method proved particularly useful with regard to issues of trust that are so central in any kind of ethnographic work. Using informal social networks meant that colleagues and friends could act as 'gatekeepers' to my research sites, introducing me to parents and to the participants. This introduction was particularly important given that I was an adult researcher going into young people's private spaces. More often than not, however, the participant's (and participant's parents') relationship with the gatekeeper was much more established than mine which proved beneficial to the positioning of the participant and the researcher within the research context. Essentially I had been invited into *their* home, by *their* friends or relatives, thus they were in a position of power when it came to the research context.

One of the drawbacks of using a 'social networks' approach came to light during the pilot study, as using these networks produced a predominantly white, middle-class sample. To avoid this in the research that followed, I strategically sought out teenagers living in areas of the city that were more likely to be inhabited by working-class populations and ethnically diverse groups. However, unlike CCCS youth cultural analysis in the 1970s and 1980s, it was not my intention to deal with the issue of class as central to my research project. As McRobbie herself has argued in a more recent study that critiqued her work in the 1970s, class was too big a determinant in these studies, often at the expense of other significant discourses:

> I ... went to great lengths to grapple with both class and gender in my early study of 14-year-old girls in Birmingham. I brought in class whenever I could in this study, often when it was simply not relevant. Maybe I was just operating with an inadequate notion of

class, but there certainly was a disparity between my 'wheeling in' class in my report and its almost complete absence from the girls' talk and discourse ... Being working class meant very little or nothing to these girls – but being a *girl* over-determined their every moment. (1991, p. 64)

The flexibility of a post-subcultural approach that has influenced much of my work as well as an engagement in ethnographic practice whereby I draw on a range of methodological tools, has meant that structural categories such as class and gender were not 'imposed' on the analysis of the data, but rather my discussions of them are led by the articulations of the participants themselves. Furthermore, I found that 'class' as a discourse through which to make sense of youth cultural activities, while indeed significant, was dominated by age, geographic location and gender as more important discourses in young people's articulations of their use of bedrooms. With regards to age, both male and female participants would talk about how the look of their room had changed especially as they moved through their teenage years; for example, I talk about James' room renovation when he turned 16 years old and 14-year-old Natasha's move from her 'girly' peach-coloured bedroom into her brother's old room in Chapter 4 and how each of them banishes teddies and similar childhood objects from their 'new rooms'.

My sample

My research sample was composed of fifty participants, half of them male and half of them female between the ages of 12 years (just entering their teenage years) and 22 years (having not long left their teenage years) living in the north of England either in Manchester or Liverpool. The majority of the research took place in Manchester between 2001 and 2003 as part of my PhD research at Manchester Metropolitan University, with additional research being conducted between 2008 and 2009 in Liverpool. The sample included young people from a variety of different backgrounds and cultures, for example participants came from both working-class and middle-class backgrounds. Furthermore, there was also some variation in ethnic backgrounds (for example, I interviewed young people with Bangladeshi and Jamaican parents although all of the participants had been born and raised in the UK). All of my participants had access to a bedroom with the majority having their own rooms (sometimes in two homes if their parents had divorced), while others shared with siblings or on one occasion with a friend. In terms of the content of the bedrooms, all of the rooms had a bed in them and most had a wardrobe, a desk or a table, a dressing table or surface for products or cosmetics and shelving. All of the bedrooms that I visited contained pieces of technology with variations of televisions, games consoles, stereo systems, PCs and laptops, MP3 players and mobile phones. In the earlier stages of the research very few participants had access to the internet in their bedrooms, but by the later stages of the research in 2008 the majority had access, either via a PC or laptop (sometimes located in their rooms but also commonly in a shared space in the house, such as in the dining room or living room) or in a few instances via the mobile phone although this is now very common.

Bedrooms

Although throughout the book I use the word 'bedroom' rather generically, it is possible to distinguish different 'types' of bedroom in this research. First, there was the bedroom to be found in the parental home, the type of bedroom I visited most commonly, and if the participant's parents were separated or divorced, it was likely that they had a room in both their mother's and their father's home. For the majority of young people who participated in the study the bedroom I visited was the one they had had from a young age and often the only bedroom they had had. Some of the participants shared a room, with male participants sharing with their brothers and female participants with their sisters, although in some instances brothers and sisters had shared at a younger age. I came across examples of shared rooms that were often 'divided' into two, for example using books and clothes piled up to create two bedrooms in one space. Each side was decorated differently with posters, pictures and photographs so as to clearly mark out two individual sides belonging to one or the other. I discuss this type of 'marking out' of space further in Chapter 4.

The second 'type' of bedroom I conducted research in was rooms in halls of residence (university student lodgings). 'Bedroom culture' is not just the reserve of the family home as has previously been explored in the literature, so I was keen to at least make some first tentative steps in young people's bedroom cultures outside of the family context. Halls of residence, largely taken up by first-year university students, are interesting spaces to explore because for many of their residents, this is the first time they have lived away from home and the 'bedroom' they are allocated in halls not only becomes multi-functional (the place where they sleep, wash, eat, work and so on) but is an important site of identity display for their new 'hall mates'. Additionally, young students are experiencing a major transition from dependence to independence and having to fend for themselves in a variety of different aspects of their lives (Kenyon, 1999; Heath and Kenyon, 2001; Kenyon and Heath, 2001). Their rooms in halls are visual markers of those changes as well as spaces in which to remember 'home'.

In addition to this, there has been a marked change over recent years in young people's transitions. As Molgat argues, the 'transitions to adulthood are becoming increasingly de-standardized, reflecting more reversible, fragmented and uncertain "yo-yo transitions" between youth and adulthood' (2007, p. 2). In other words, while many young people may leave the parental home to pursue further education or job training, they may return to the family home after this period, perhaps in order to save money to pay off accumulated debts or to save for their own home, rather than following the 'traditional sequence' of finishing school, leaving home, gaining employment, getting married and having children (Molgat, 2007).

The third 'type' of bedroom that I refer to particularly in Chapter 6, is what Hodkinson and Lincoln (2008) have termed the 'virtual bedroom'. In exploring how, for contemporary teenagers embracing the world of social networking and virtual media, the concept of a bedroom culture exists beyond the 'traditional' confines of the physical space I consider what analogies might be drawn between their use of their physical bedroom and their online profiles, such as those on Facebook. Hodkinson and Lincoln (2008), who explore the bedroom analogy in the context of online journals, suggest that many of the ways that young people use their bedrooms to establish and exhibit personal identity and to engage in social as well as personal interactions translate into personal spaces online. In the final chapter I explore the ways in which young people engage in multiple bedroom cultures both on and offline, the interplay of which has interesting implications in relation to their youth cultural identities.

'How did you get into young people's bedrooms?' The ethics of research in young people's private spaces

A research project of this nature is fraught with ethical implications and indeed the ethics of doing research in private spaces is something that I am often asked about by students and by colleagues alike who are intrigued to find out about my experiences and the issues that I had to overcome. While it would be impossible to discuss all of them in a small section, I have selected some of the most interesting ones to discuss here. As I mention earlier, I believe that the use of 'social networks' in the production of the research sample alongside the role of the 'gatekeeper' were vital in gaining initial access to participants and their bedroom spaces. As noted above, having a person who is known mutually by both the researcher and the participant is beneficial because it instils an adequate level of trust from the outset. This is important not only for participants who are letting a relative stranger into their private space and for their parents or carers who are granting access to their home but also for the researcher, perhaps even more so the female researcher, entering into both male and female teenage spaces. There are, however, a number of observations that can be made with regard to the ethics of research in private and personal spaces such as bedrooms belonging to young people.

The first observation is concerning my presence in the participants' bedrooms. Cohen (1991) notes in her ethnography of the Liverpool music scene that her presence in (male-dominated) spaces, for example backstage at gigs or rehearsal spaces where wives and girlfriends were explicitly barred, may 'have made some people uneasy' (p. 205) and that in her quest to gather in-depth, extensive ethnographic data and to become an 'insider' she had in fact become the opposite, an 'outsider' at least with regards to her position as a woman in a male dominated environment:

> my activities obviously conflicted with those normally expected of a woman. I attended gigs alone, expressed interest in the technicalities of music making and in the attitudes and concerns of those making it, and contradicted in other respects most women many of the band members were familiar with. (Cohen, 1991, pp. 205–6)

Similarly, in my study my presence in young people's bedrooms spaces was essentially conflicting with 'normal' behaviour within that space and from the outside could be perceived as rather unusual. A young person's bedroom does by and large tend to be inhabited by teenagers, adolescents, children or young adults, whereas 'grown ups' do not usually hang out there. While indeed parents do go into their children's bedrooms (either with or without permission) to tidy up, to pick up washing, to retrieve cups, plates, to tell them that their dinner is ready and so on, parents and their children do not ordinarily spend time together in this room and more likely they will spend time together in a more communal area of the house, such as the living room or the kitchen. Moreover, many young people are adamant that their parents are not welcome in their bedrooms and the use of 'do not enter!' signs is testament to this kind of regulation.

Second, while on the one hand I had to contend with the issue of being a researcher entering into personal and private space, I had the additional problem of being an *adult* researcher. Proweller (1998) and Moore (2003) argue that age is a significant factor in being able to conduct research of this nature effectively, and while I do think that being in my mid-twenties and, additionally, female (would I have been granted access had I been a male in my fifties?) did have its benefits (for example, in terms of knowing what contemporary bands the participants spoke of or which stores they shopped at or in terms of what I wore and how I carried myself [see note 8]), ultimately I was an adult and a stranger in a young person's personal and private space. This will undoubtedly have impacted on the responses I received from participants. For example, there are likely to be things that the participants did not want to tell me, things that they would only discuss with their friends. Nevertheless, I do feel that my participants spoke honestly to me and engaged with interest in the project, and despite my initial worries I did not find myself at the end of the stereotypical 'teenage' grunt of 'yes' or 'no' in reply to my questions.

Third, and in a similar vein to the issue above, while I tried to mimic closely the interactions in bedroom space (for example, by conducting interviews one-on-one or in small friendship groups like those that might gather in a bedroom), my presence undoubtedly interrupted normal *patterns* of behaviour. And although, as I suggest earlier, I did attend interviews with a series of questions to guide discussion, I was very happy to let the stories and anecdotes between friends flow and often this resulted in the best data. However, realistically this 'flow' would not have been the same had it just been friends gathered together. Their discussions would more likely be more mundane: about their day, relationships, plans for the night, weekend and so on rather than the more meaningful responses to questions or recalling stories for the benefit of a researcher. The use of friendship groups, however, was undoubtedly a successful method that placed my participants in an empowered position: they knew each other well and were clearly comfortable in each other's presence and in familiar surroundings.

Finally, and in addition to the ethics of an adult entering into a young person's personal and private space, I was a female adult going often into a young male's space. This was ethically sensitive for a number of reasons. For example, for younger teenagers particularly, having girls in the bedroom might not be permitted by parents, although this rule may indeed be violated regularly. In this case, then, there are implications for a female researcher entering into a personal and private male space.

Again the role of the gatekeeper becomes significant here, particularly in gaining permission from parents to enter these spaces. Through the use of the gatekeeper, a friend known to the participant and often their parents, I was accepted as a trusted, professional adult. As mentioned above, I was particularly careful in my male participants' bedrooms to ensure that I asked where I should sit, rather than assuming that the bed was fine, and as with all the interviews the bedroom door was left ajar, with a third person in the vicinity. In comparison to my female participants, there was undoubtedly at times a display of sexual bravado in some of the boys' interviews. For example, some in their mid-teens who were just becoming interested in sexual relationships and some of whom were already engaging in them, were happy to draw my attention to posters on the wall of, for example, half-naked women. One in particular belongs to James, who was 16 years old, and depicts a women bending over to pick up a bottle of beer from the bottom of a fridge with the caption 'why guys always keep their beer on the bottom shelf'. While such imagery did make me feel slightly uncomfortable, I was able to take it for what it was: essentially a visual representation of James' sexuality/activeness.

In addition to the observations above, I also encountered other ethical issues and dilemmas that had to do with consent, anonymity and confidentiality. However, these issues are commonly encountered in much qualitative research with young people and are discussed in detail elsewhere in the literature (see, for example, France, 2004; Heath et al., 2009).

Conclusions

In this chapter I have taken you on my journey of conducting research with young people in and about personal and private spaces, especially their bedrooms. In doing this, I have explored the use of ethnographic methodologies in studying young people, questioned their suitability in the context of private spaces and cultures and outlined the various methodological strands that I drew on in order to conduct this study. I have presented an approach that encompasses both more traditional anthropological strands as well as more contemporary sensory and visual approaches that are arguably more readily adaptable to research contexts such as mine and I have suggested, as indeed others, such as Pink (2009), have, that an ethnography that breaks away from traditional methods can still produce vivid and insightful representations of the culture under study. Finally, I have reflected critically upon some of the major ethical implications of doing research in young people's personal and private spaces and considered my role as an adult female researcher entering into those spaces.

In the chapters that follow, I open the doors to a young person's bedroom exploring in depth its uses, meanings, practices and culture. In the next chapter, then, I begin with what are seemingly two very simple questions: What is a young person's bedroom for? And what is its role in contemporary youth culture?

3
The Role of Private Space in Contemporary Youth Culture

In the previous chapter, I examined in depth the research process undertaken to explore private and personal spaces such as bedrooms in a young person's life-world. I considered the various issues and dilemmas in taking an ethnographic approach to research in this context, explaining how my methods were selected, how I created my research sample, and the ethical dilemmas I faced. One of the concerns I raised, as others such as Dickinson et al. (2001), Baker (2004) and Pink (2009) have done before me, was in relation to the suitability of 'traditional' and 'holistic' ethnographic approaches that are led by participant observation and interviewing and that strive for immersion and intensive participation on behalf of the researcher. In exploring contexts such as the personal and private domestic spaces of young people, such techniques are not necessarily the most suitable ones and, moreover, given the fragmented and fleeting cultural lifestyles of many young people, not always complementary to these. In this respect, I have argued that it is more insightful in such contexts to draw on a range of ethnographic methods, which in this study are drawn from traditional ethnography as well as from more contemporary sensory and visual approaches.

As I will go on to demonstrate, drawing on a range of ethnographic approaches still allows the researcher to explore in depth the ordinary world of a young person's private space, in this case their bedrooms; to explore its intricacies and complexities as social, cultural and identity spaces. In the four chapters that follow, then, I consider the significance of such spaces in relation to the social and cultural practices that take place within them, explore in depth the space itself, which, I argue, can be understood as a visual representation of a young person's evolving identity, and examine the many ways in which bedroom culture can be understood as a 'mediated' culture. In doing this, I explore the significance of 'bedroom culture' to young people.

Private and 'personal' spaces, such as young people's bedrooms, are not just simple functional spaces. Bedrooms are worked upon, albeit at varying levels, and even when the space seems to change very little visually, the mere presence of a young person within it, living out their social and cultural lives, means that it is a space that is never static. Moreover, for many young people, these are 'worked upon' spaces of identity and biographical display, capturing both through cultural practices and the materiality of the space itself those often turbulent transitional years of growing up (Griffin, 1993; Roberts, 2008). Young people's bedrooms are also quite complex spaces to understand. For example, they can have a dual role as both spaces within which to stabilise and authenticate one's identity, as well as to play and experiment with it (Baker, 2004). They are spaces that can offer refuge at difficult times, but also spaces within which those difficult times can be experienced. They can be spaces to escape to, from the control and regulation of parents, but also spaces subjected to this type of regulation too (Heath, 1999, 2004). They are spaces whose use is influenced by geographic location, familial formations, gender, social class and age, all of which are complexly intertwined. In addition to this, the significance of bedrooms to young people is rarely stable, fading in and out throughout their teenage years and even beyond. The experience of a bedroom culture then, is, arguably, unique to each and every young person.

In attempting to explore a number of these complexities and in stepping inside the world of a young person's room, I begin with this chapter in which I ask what on the surface appear to be two simple questions. First, I ask what a young person's bedroom is used for and second, what is its role in contemporary youth culture?

What is a young person's bedroom for?

Young people's bedrooms are full of activity and while in this book I am interested in how these rooms are used by young people as 'identity spaces', it is important to consider how the activities that take place within bedrooms are regulated by the wider context of the domestic and family rules, regulations and responsibilities as well as by the realm of 'the public'. As Hollows (2008) argues in relation to the home more generally:

> The ability to experience the home as a site to 'be yourself' – or create 'the self' – is constrained by power relations within the home and by

wider expectations about the performance of 'appropriate' identities. (p. 79)

As I have explored in Chapter 1, early conceptualisations of 'bedroom culture' such as those offered by McRobbie and Garber (1975) were very much driven by the domestic role of the teenage girl who was considered to have certain responsibilities within the home that her male counterpart, engaging in youth cultural activities in public spaces, did not have. In this case, McRobbie and Garber conceptualised bedroom culture as the privilege of the teenage girl and the ease of access to such a culture meant that she could dip in and out of it in accordance with her domestic responsibilities (1991, p. 12). In this respect, she could maintain her identity as a teenager listening to music, experimenting with clothes, hair and make-up and hanging out with her friends as well as her domestic role in the family home. Although this is perhaps a rather anachronistic scenario for teenage girls today (although many do still have a significant role in the household, especially in terms of caring for younger siblings as I discuss below or undertaking specific household chores), both young males' and young females' experiences of bedroom culture do differ in accordance with the politics of the household as well as their identities in public spaces and thus the ways in which bedrooms are used and the levels of privacy afforded can vary. However, before considering some of these dynamics, I discuss more generally the question of what a young person's bedroom is for.

When a child misbehaves, the bedroom is often the place to which he or she is sent as a punishment. Many of us will be familiar with (either we have heard or used ourselves) the phrase 'go to your room!' shouted when disgruntled parents want their child out of their sight. However, as that child gets older, the desire for some privacy and some space of their own becomes more acute and their bedrooms take on a new significance and meaning (Larson, 1995); they want to spend time in it, be alone and in a reversal of fortune, their parents wonder why they are spending so much time in there, wonder why their beloved children no longer want to spend time with other members of the family. So what goes on in a young person's bedroom and what is it being used for?

First and foremost, a young person's bedroom is a functional space. The majority of the bedrooms that I visited did 'look' similar in terms of their 'functionality'. For example, all contained a bed and the majority a wardrobe, a desk or a table, a dressing table or surface for products or cosmetics and shelving as I mention in the previous chapter. In terms of its functions, the bedroom is a place to sleep, it is a place to get dressed and do other forms of 'self-maintenance' such as doing one's hair or make-up. It is the space that most young people start and end their day in (Lincoln, 2004); whether in their own rooms or in somebody else's, alone or with siblings, friends or partners. The bedroom can take on other functional aspects too. A number of my participants regularly ate in their bedrooms, some claiming only to leave their bedrooms to get food and consequently cups and plates from the kitchen would become a familiar part of the space (Lincoln, 2004). Commonly, it is also a space in which to do homework or to prepare for important exams such as SATs, GCSEs and 'A' levels (more about which I discuss below), so it takes on an important role in the 'transitional' phases, such as those related to education, that play a key role in a young person's life (Miles, 2000). As we shall see in Chapter 4, bedrooms are commonly moved around and re-arranged in order to accommodate (or indeed provide escape from) exam preparation and school or college work.

A young person's bedroom is also a space of 'escapism'. In their room, young people can relax, 'chill out', spend time on their 'own' (although interactions with others take place constantly through mobile phone and social networking sites), get away from the stresses of the day and unwind. They may immerse further in this escape by reading magazines, listening to music, playing computer games, watching television, listening to the radio, watching films or on-demand TV on laptops and smart phones, texting and talking on the phone or checking social network sites such as Facebook or Twitter, and often young people do a number of these things at the same time.

The bedroom is a space of experimentation, exploration and 'rites of passage' for young people too. While it was difficult to talk about sexual activity with my participants given the age group and the context of the research in bedrooms, as well as the many other ethical implications related to the research context of 'the private', as documented in the previous chapter, it would be remiss not to at least acknowledge that the teenage bedroom is one of the most common spaces where young people will explore their bodies and engage in sexual activity (responsible or irresponsible),[1] be it masturbation (alone, with pornography, or with someone else) or intercourse. And of course, the fact that the bedroom is in the parental home can add to the excitement of these teenage rites of passage; the fear of getting caught, 'doing it' in your parents' house, trying to do it quietly so that no one else in the house hears (even though the lingering smell of sweat and other bodily fluids gives you away), hiding and disposing of condoms or tissues afterwards. The bedroom is without doubt an important space in this context. Other rites of passage include smoking and drinking, both of which a number of my participants did in their rooms, for example in preparation for a night out or on returning (Lincoln, 2004), when hanging out at the weekends with a small group of friends, when having a house party or other social gathering or just because sometimes there's 'nothing else to do'. Smoking would also be used as a distraction from doing things like homework.

Experimentation and exploration in young people's bedrooms can demonstrate the integral relationship between public and private space and how one informs the other. For example, a number of the younger female participants who took part in this study would spend a number of hours in their bedrooms in front of the mirror, experimenting with clothes, hair styles and make-up (à la McRobbie's findings [1991]) in their quest to 'look just that little bit older' so that they would be able to gain access to pubs or clubs with their peers and their older friends or siblings, thus transferring and legitimising their teen identities from the private space of their bedrooms to the public realm, from childhood to teenage. For example, Sara, aged 12, described to me the outfit that she wore last time she went to a 'teen night' held in a club in Manchester's city centre:

> Last time I went I wore this [she shows me her outfit – a tight fitting dress] with my knee-high boots. The first time I went I wore ... what did I wear the first time? The purple top I think [she points to a purple halter neck top] ... oh no, the purple skirt [she shows me a mini skirt] and knee-high boots, everyone just gets dressed up though ...

Clearly, Sara has selected an outfit that far from being 'girly' (i.e. 'pretty' and 'childish') is one that is quite overtly sexual and revealing (the décolleté halter-neck top that also reveals the back and midriff, the short skirt not quite meeting the knee-high boots). Despite her being old enough to get into the teen night, there is still a deliberate attempt on Sara's part to look older than she is through her choice of clothing. And while she claims that at the club 'it's just dancing and all that', there is no doubt an awareness that there will be boys there as well as her peers in front of whom she wants to be able to demonstrate a 'maturity' beyond her 12 years and to demonstrate a transformation from the 'adolescent' school uniform of her everyday life to the 'grown up' outfits of her nights out. Much time is spent by the girls deciding what they will wear in anticipation of the next teen night (held monthly at the same club) and selecting their outfits was regularly discussed when the girls were spending time together in one of their bedrooms. Additionally, the girls would try on outfits in the presence of each other, getting advice on that final selection.

'Getting dressed up' is essential if you are going to be granted access to the teen night if you are underage, as Sara's sister, Natasha, was. When telling me about the night, Natasha said 'it's like a big club with just music in … It's under 18s. You've got to be 13 to go but I can pretend I'm 13 …' Along with her sister Sara, with whom she shares a room, Natasha experiments with different outfits (something she has to do every time she goes because 'it's one of those places where you don't wear the same thing twice, d'you know what I mean?') ensuring that she selects the one that will make her look at least 13. Sometimes she borrows clothes from her sister because they are the same size, from her friends, or she will buy something new for the occasion. The quest to look 13 is continued through the application of make-up and 'doing your hair' like Sara's friend Angela, already 13, who would 'iron' her hair in order to straighten it, a popular trend that may make you look a little older but also demonstrates an awareness of the latest fashions, styles and trends.

Bedrooms, of course, are not just entered into by their occupants. They can be 'invaded' by other family members (and this is particularly true if bedrooms are shared as discussed below). If this is the case, then young people's bedrooms can take on different meanings, depending on who is and who is not occupying them. Further, their meaning can change, for example, when they are at school, college or work, at a friend's house or even just occupying another room in the house. Siblings, for example, may go 'snooping' into their brothers' or sisters' bedrooms; rifling through their 'stuff', retrieving things that belong to them, borrowing clothes or CDs, going in to get the shared games console that has otherwise been monopolised (McNamee, 1998). Sara and Natasha's 8-year-old sister regularly entered into their shared room much to the annoyance of the girls. Natasha says, 'my little brat of a sister [comes in] … "I want to change my clothes, I want to put my dress on" … it does my head in when she puts stuff in the bedroom that just doesn't go.' For Natasha, the invasion of her little sister into an already shared space interrupts not only what they are doing (as she tends to go into their bedroom uninvited), but also what the room looks like. Sara and Natasha had taken great pride in redecorating their room with a blue and silver colour scheme, but would regularly find things in their room that belonged to their youngest sister, for example a pink desk. This was frustrating for the sisters not only because this is an invasion of their space through their sister's physical presence, but also an invasion of its 'aesthetic' by the insertion of 'girly' pink items that they primarily associate with 'childhood' into their 'grown up', tidy and organised blue and silver themed bedroom.

Parents go into their children's bedrooms too. The frequency of entry and the reasons for it varied in my sample but generally in two-parent homes, it would be mothers who would go in and clean the room, pick up laundry or retrieve crockery as well as have input on how the room is decorated and fathers who tended to have more of a say in how the space is regulated, for example in terms of who was and who was not granted access, especially for teenage girls. However, there were anomalies to this, particularly in single parent homes and I discuss these below.

Bedrooms can be 'invaded' by parents for reasons other than practical ones, for example, if they are curious about what their illusive son or daughter is up to. A number of my participants were aware of this sort of 'snooping' happening when they were not at home and so they would hide things like bottles of alcohol, cigarettes, condoms or pornographic magazines and films inside cupboards, in the back of the wardrobe, in drawers or in among box files for college in the hope that they wouldn't be easily found. One participant, Jonathan, 16, would put an ashtray outside on his window sill so that it was out of view of his parents (and so that there wouldn't be a lingering smell of stale smoke), while another, Ben, 15, hid an ashtray under his bed and while he claimed that his parents knew that he drank alcohol in his room on occasions with friends, they were not aware (as far as he knew) that he smoked. Although not discussed with parents over the course of my research, bedrooms could be 'invaded' for other, more serious reasons too. For example if parents have concerns about their child's welfare (they suspect he or she is drinking alcohol excessively, is smoking or taking illegal drugs, has an eating disorder, might be pregnant or is being bullied) they might resort to entering their children's bedrooms to find clues.

Family dynamics, 'age' and bedroom use

Julie, 13, Sara, 12, Natasha, 14 and Jackie 13, introduced in the previous chapter, live in Gorton, north Manchester. Like all of my participants, the girls spoke about their families and the formations within which they lived out their everyday lives. As a result of my discussions with participants about their families, the theme of 'age' (or what Griffin [1993] has conceptualised as 'age grades', that is the ways in which young people categorise their age group in relation to other family members or peers and how they identify with this specific age group) emerged as a key element in their understanding of their position in the family, their use of the household and specifically the use of their bedrooms. Primarily age grades were experienced through their relationships with siblings (male, female, younger and older), peers (male and female) and parents (including step-parents and guardians) and through articulations of dependence and independence, for example in reference to identity 'markers' ranging from sexual interest to music tastes. Key transitional periods such as doing exams (a number of my participants were doing SATs, GCSEs or 'A' levels) regularly challenged my young participants' relationships with other family members, and were integral to the ways in which age grades and teenage lifestyles both inside and outside the home are structured.

Jones and Wallace (1992) argue that in a post-industrial society family relationships are inherently bound up by inequalities, especially those linked to age and generation, and that these inequalities are constantly changing and shifting from one family member to another as family formations evolve and change. Their argument highlights some of the complexities of the family that need to be unpacked when thinking about the role of young people in the home and specifically the ways in which they are able to live out their social lives within their own private spaces. As I suggest above, I want to consider how age, as a constantly shifting and changing entity, influences household dynamics, with a particular focus on the relationships with siblings and with parents and on how such dynamics impact on private spaces within the home. I give examples of each below.

Sara and Natasha, 12 and 14 years old, were sisters and shared a bedroom. They were two of five siblings living with their mother in a single parent household. Sara and Natasha got on well because they were relatively close in age with only a year separating them. However, in discussions with them, they talked about their more difficult relationships, particularly with their eldest sister and, to a lesser extent, with their young sister who was 8 years old. Their discussions demonstrate the ways in which young people categorise their age in relation to siblings and how their perceptions of household members can conflict and cause friction. For example, as mentioned previously, the two girls shared a bedroom but at the time of the interview the eldest sister who was 18 years old was using their bedroom too as hers was being redecorated. I asked the girls about their relationship with her:

Sara: The oldest one does our heads in, but the next one down [aged 17], she's all right.
SL: Do you argue a lot?

Sara: We both argue with the other one, the eldest one
SL: Why's that?
Sara: Because she thinks she's our mam.

In many ways, being the eldest of five siblings in a single parent family would mean that Sara and Natasha's sister did have significant responsibilities in the family home, not ordinarily undertaken by the 'average' 18-year-old; for example, taking on some of the domestic chores, cooking for her siblings and looking after them while her mother was at work, and indeed the other teenage siblings were likely to have their own roles in the home too. However, Natasha and Sara were not particularly sensitive to her plight and rather saw their sister as somebody 'pretending' to be someone who she is not: their mother. Their rejection of their sister 'pretending' to be older (assuming a mothering role) is somewhat hypocritical given the scenario I describe above when the girls actively 'pretend' to be older on nights out. A projection of appearing older is acceptable to them in the public sphere, but is rejected in the private sphere. In the public realm, this quest to look older is a form of unification for Sara and Natasha as well as an initiation for Natasha into the 'public' teenage world. In their private teenage world, however, friction is created through the 'older' projection of their eldest sister. Natasha and Sara do not see her as worthy of her assumed adult status; instead, they prefer to see her as their sister, still within teen age and with little authority, and thus they reject her assumed 'mothering' status. This 'rejection' was emphasised further by the girls on two other occasions; when the girls talked about how their eldest sister used their bedroom during the time that her room was being redecorated and her relationship with her boyfriend, Lee.

The girls' bedroom, already 'invaded' by their 8-year-old sister and the placement of her 'girly' pink toys in their room, was now 'doubly' invaded by their eldest sister. As explained above, Sara and Natasha's room had just been redecorated with a blue and silver colour scheme with accessories and furniture matching this scheme. They endeavoured to keep it tidy (perhaps a novelty given its newness) and had storage space in which to keep all of their bits and pieces. Their eldest sister however would 'just throw all her college work all over the bed ... she has her homework and everything all over the bed ... and shoes ...' and, as Sara adds, 'I think that bed makes our bedroom look a mess'. So in addition to the girls being 'mothered' by their eldest sister, their space was also being 'invaded' and disrespected by her, causing further tension and animosity. This was further exacerbated by the role of 'the boyfriend', Lee, the relationship with whom, Sara and Natasha felt, added to their sister's adopted 'mothering' role.

Sara:	She's got a boyfriend called Lee and she's like 'oh, I can't go, I'm going out with Lee'
Natasha:	We call her Mrs Lee, us!
SL:	Does she bring him up to your room?
Natasha:	No, not in our room ... oh, this is another thing. Say that we're downstairs watching telly or something before we're going to bed, if Lee comes in we've got to go upstairs.

On the one hand, the role of 'the boyfriend' is viewed by Sara and Natasha as just another way for their sister to establish her 'adult' status. Lee is also used by her as a way to 'control' them and their use of the house. Like children, they are often 'banished' to their room so that their sister can be alone with her boyfriend, especially important for her given that temporarily she doesn't have her own room. The tension is caused by the fact that although all three of the girls are teenagers, the eldest sister assumes a role in the home and an iden-tity outside of it (through her relationship to Lee) that places her in a higher 'age grade' than her siblings; one that alludes to adult rather than teen status. Because of this, the responsibilities she has assumed separate her from her younger siblings, which is a cause of friction within the family.

Oliver, 16 years old, from Sale in Cheshire, revealed how his use of the home was determined by generational differences and how his use of particular rooms was determined by who was or who was not occupy-ing them and what activities he was undertaking in them. For instance, when talking about using the 'landline' telephone, shared with other members of the household, Oliver explained that if his parents were in the living room where one of the phones was he would use the other phone upstairs. This, he explained, was because his parents 'asked ques-tions' and would 'listen' to his conversations:

They're listening and they tell you that they're not listening, but they turn the TV down and they're asking questions about what I've been saying ... you don't want your mum and dad listening.

Oliver's words demonstrate that keeping his social life 'private' from his parents was important to him and that the unavoidable generation 'gap' between them was articulated through his desire to detach his social life from the dynamics of the home and maintain his privacy as much as possible. For example, he said 'normally if the phone rings and mum says it's for me I usually go "male or female" and if she says male, I'll say I'm not in!' At 16, Oliver is obviously interested in girls and he emphasises this shift from hanging out and 'playing' with his male friends to having pubescent, sexual interests. In this respect, his demand for and selectivity of privacy within the home space increases as he transits into his later teenage years:

> Oliver: I have an extension so I can take the phone up ...
> SL: Do you tend to do that?
> Oliver: It depends who I'm talking to.

Oliver's relationships outside of the home clearly determine how he uses domestic space and how he manipulates his uses of shared items such as telephones to achieve his desired level of privacy. A shift in age grade is evident in this example, namely in Oliver's preference to talk to girls rather than boys that is verbalised to his mother. The shift from preferring to talk to platonic male friends to females with a sexual interest is symbolic of Oliver's growing up.

What the above examples demonstrate is that teenage life, age and identities, both inside and outside of the home, exist within a very specific context of household and family dynamics. In Chapter 1, I highlighted that one of the major critiques made of the CCCS accounts of youth subcultures was with reference to the absence of any meaningful reflection on the relationship between youth culture and the family and how the home, like the streets, might also be a site of rebellion and resistance. Further, such discussions were somewhat limited by their cultural Marxist approach whereby 'class' was utilised as the key structural category through which to make sense of subcultures as sites of collectivity and hegemonic resistance. In reassessing the usefulness of 'subculture' as a theoretical tool notions of individual choice and reflexivity (Miles, 2000; Chaney, 2004) are brought to the fore to account for the more fleeting and partial ways in which young people engage in subcultures, not just in public spaces but in private and virtual spaces too. The concept of post-subculturalism that 'centres on the individual as the pivotal node in a network of contacts' (Robards and Bennett, 2011, p. 306) complements the context of domestic private space, particularly bedrooms, as I argue in more detail in Chapters 5 and 6.

However, in a context in which young people are still dependent on adults, the concept of the individual as a 'pivotal node' is somewhat compromised by what might be considered as a more enforced sense of collective identity, one that is provided by the family. In their discussions of consumption in the household, Reimer and Leslie (2004) argue for a cautious approach to the use of individualised notions of consumption practices in the household, which have been understood in contemporary theories of identity and consumption as part of a 'reflexive project of the self' (Giddens, 1991). Instead, Reimer and Leslie argue that consumption practices in the home have to be negotiated as part of a 'collective household identity' (2004, p. 194; see also Boden, 2006) and the example of the girls in Gorton certainly seems to support this view.

In the context of young people's bedrooms, then, a young person's social and cultural life does not exist in isolation from the rest of the family, but is inherently informed by it. I now go on to explore this in more depth as I consider the role of parental control in young people's uses of their bedroom spaces.

Parental control

The activities of young people, whether in public or private space, are subject to a number of adult interventions, some of which may persist beyond the traditional teen age if a young person remains in the family home for an extended period of time. The 'level' of intervention can vary but an examination of how young people use spaces such as their bedrooms needs to be understood within the context of such controls. Very few young people have 'complete' free rein over what their bedrooms looked like or, in some cases, who can enter into them as mentioned above. Indeed, many of my participants engaged in a process of negotiations with their mothers or fathers, ranging from the colour of the room to the furniture in it. For example, James, 16, said: 'she [mum] made a blank canvas and I added ... she chose the carpet but I really like it'. For some of the young people who took part in this research it tended to be one parent or the other who applied forms of regulation within the household. For example, Evie, who was 16 years old, repeatedly mentioned how her father's control manifested in many aspects of her social and cultural life, including the use of her bedroom. Her father would implement curfews when she went on nights out with her friends, which, if ever they were going 'into town' (going into the city centre of Liverpool), was problematic for Evie. As she explained:

I mean, a lot of my friends go into town and stuff, but I've still got the whole ... my mum would be OK with it, I think, but my dad is really ... as long as I knew, as long as my mum knew where I was and stuff ...

And later, in the same interview:

yeah, but my curfew is always quite early when it's somewhere unknown, or somewhere ... you know, it'll be like half past twelve if I came home from town, but everyone goes out that time ... and my parents don't understand that so ... !

This in turn meant that Evie favoured nights spent at other friends' houses because by doing this she did not have to encounter the problems associated with being out in town: 'I would really rather go round to someone's house than go out to town, really 'cos, like, I like the more relaxed atmosphere, I don't really have to think about ... getting home.' This control was further evidenced in Evie's use of her bedroom as this was especially represented by Evie's bedroom door. At one time, Evie had a sign that hung on her bedroom door that read: 'Evie's Room – Keep Out!' However, after her father had decorated the hallway and landing, she was no longer allowed to put the sign up and thus her bedroom door became like any other door in the house rather than signifying Evie's 'own space'.

A series of negotiations about what a bedroom looks like often take place between teenagers and parents because it is the parents who usually pay for many of the items found there. This sometimes includes basic decoration such as choice of wall paint, curtains and other furnishings. Natasha, 13 years old, explains:

My Mum chose the wallpaper but we said 'right, we'll get silver beds and we'll get green sheets and blue things.' So I got the bubble chair for a Christmas present and ... we got silver beds and these colours [points them out]. It's not finished yet as them drawers are getting sprayed silver.

As Natasha demonstrates, some negotiation had taken place here. In this scenario we see her mother making decisions about things in the room that could be regarded as more 'fixed', for example the wallpaper that is likely to be on the walls for some time, while Natasha and her sister are able to make decisions about more movable items such as bedding and the colour of their drawers for storage. As I discussed earlier, Natasha and Sara don't just simply have to negotiate with their

Figure 3.1   The Manhattan skyline in James' room

mother, but they are also involved in ongoing discussions with both their youngest and eldest sisters who are constantly 'invading' their space.

James, 16 years old, had recently undertaken a major 'transformation' of his bedroom which now featured graffiti of the Manhattan skyline as depicted in Figure 3.1. The graffiti mural covered a whole wall down the right hand side of his bedroom and was completed by a neighbour's boyfriend who was a painter. As James states above, his mum had made his room what he described as a 'blank canvas' when she had insisted upon a 'renovation' of his room, choosing only the carpet and letting him decide on how he wanted to decorate the room. James claimed that 'mum would give the go ahead but I'd change things even if she didn't say yes', demonstrating how he recognises some engagement in a compromise with his mother but also how he had significant input in decorating and organising the space in a particular way. In doing the graffiti mural, James had insisted on getting someone to do it that was 'top notch', and on this basis his mother was happy for the mural to be painted. For James it makes the room look 'unique'.

Parental control is, however, not the only form of negotiation that may occur in bedroom spaces. If the bedroom is to be understood as one of the first spaces owned by a young person and one of the first spaces over which they have any control, sharing a bedroom presents a number of complexities in relation to a young person's emerging biography and identity. It also changes the nature of 'private' itself. As I explore in some of the examples below, this can make marking out one's space even more important.

Sharing a bedroom

Identities exist within a paradoxical space in which there can be no fixed centres or margins. In a world where identities cannot be attached to singular uncomplicated subject positions … identity becomes all about multiple locations and performativity within those locations. Under such conditions the main issue associated with such spatial uncertainty is identification. It is through identifications with others, identifications that can be multiple, overlapping or fractured, that identity – that sense of self-recognition and belonging with others – is achieved. (Hetherington, 1998 pp. 23–4)

Hetherington suggests above that 'identities become all about multiple locations', however, locations such as the home can, in turn, be a site of multiple identities for a young person. In the home a teenager may find themselves in a constant series of negotiations about what their bedrooms are for with parents, siblings, family and friends, which in their teenage years often signifies times of tension. It is during these years, then, when the need to be able to find some privacy is of great importance. The quest for privacy, however, becomes complicated when siblings are required to share a bedroom.

A number of my participants shared with their brothers and sisters. For example, Natasha, aged 14 years, shared a bedroom with Sara, aged 12; Bethan, aged 13 years, shared with her 7-year-old sister; Chloe, aged 12 years, shared with her 9-year-old sister; and David shared with his 13-year-old brother. The reasons for sharing had largely to do with the availability of space in the family home, particularly for those who were part of a large family and in some cases of a lower social class (although David was the exception here). Abbott-Chapman and Robertson found in their study on Tasmanian adolescents and their favourite places that: 'younger students, especially from less affluent families in rural and regional areas may not have their own bedroom and have to share with siblings. Usually in homes where space is at a premium, it is the older children who gain a space of their own' (2009, p. 425).

For Bethan and Chloe, whose age differences with their siblings were fairly substantial, making their 'sides' of the bedroom distinct from their younger siblings' was incredibly important. In doing this, they were ensuring a distinction both physically and culturally between their interests and their sisters' interests, between their side and their sisters' side. The girls explained how they would create physical barriers between the two sides of the bedroom to separate them, enabling them to physically claim their own 'space'. Chloe explained that if her sister were to cross the 'barrier' that she had made across the centre of the room with furniture or piles of books then she gets very angry and considers this an invasion of her space and privacy. The infiltration of 'one side' into another or the 'overlapping of identities', as Hetherington calls it, was a signifier of this 'invasion'. This often resulted in Chloe's sister deliberately 'messing up' her side of the bedroom in retaliation and seeing the 'border-crossing' as some kind of entertaining challenge for her. For Chloe, claiming back her space and exerting her position as the 'older sister' could be done through playing music. For example, she was often the first one to put a CD on the shared stereo system and considered herself 'in charge' of the music collection stored on the iPod. Music, in this way, becomes a dominant aural signifier of who ultimately has control and who dominates their shared space.

The search for 'privacy' becomes complicated in such scenarios, as there are no guarantees that when alone in the bedroom, the space won't be invaded. In some cases, then, this may mean some negotiations between siblings in terms of the times when each of them can use the space alone, although this does not easily accommodate the ever-changing moods and feelings of a young person. Bethan was about to move into a new house with her mum and two younger siblings. In their new home, she would be moving into her own room which to her signified a critical moment in her life as she moved towards independence. I asked Bethan what it was like currently sharing a bedroom with her sister. She said:

Bethan: It's Bad!
SL: Why do you think it's difficult?
Bethan: She messes the room up and blames it on me. It's my bedroom and she's always all over it. One day I woke up and her foot was in my face!
SL: So do you have your own space in your bedroom?

Bethan: Yeah, I've put a barrier up. I tell her she'll have to fight me if she crosses the line!

Despite the fact that they share a bedroom, Bethan determines the space as her own and sees her sister's presence as an invasion of her space, much like Chloe does above. This invasion comes in the form of her sister's things in her side of the room, a 'mess' that she supposedly gets in trouble for on her sister's behalf and a physical presence of her sister in her side of the room. For Bethan, the invasion of her space by her sister is age-related and, as with Chloe, she believes that she is at a very different life stage to her sister. This becomes even more clear as Bethan describes what the two halves of her bedroom looked like, making clear distinctions between her younger sister's 'childish tastes' and her more sophisticated 'teen tastes'. For example, Bethan says in her sister's half of the bedroom there are posters on the wall of the 'Tweenies'[2] and Pokémon, whereas on her side she had 'just a little picture of Sisquo'.[3]

For Evie, aged 16 years (introduced above), getting her own bedroom after a period of sharing with her sister had great significance for her in terms of being able to have her own space:

I did used to share it [her bedroom] with my sister when we first moved in ... that was a long time ago ... it was just, dunno ... so much better, just the best thing that ever happened when I managed to get my own room to myself and I think it's incredibly important to have it to yourself, because, you know, sometimes the family is overwhelming especially because we have a very large family and we get invaded ...

Evie got her own bedroom at a point in her life when she 'needed' her own space. As articulated within the discourses of her family life Evie talks about the need to withdraw from the hustle and bustle of every-day family life and the importance to her of having a space of her own within which to do this. Having her own bedroom means being able to spend time alone should she choose to and being able to retire to her 'safe haven' (James, 2001) should her family life become overwhelming. It is an essential part of who she is.

Chloe, who shared a bedroom with her younger sister, said that one of the downsides about sharing was that her younger sister often left her toys and dolls and also piles of clothes all over the floor; she said there would be 'Barbie dolls all over the floor that I fall over'. Such actions raise two important issues. The first one is that as a whole space, the bedroom is being cluttered up with objects and 'things' such as toys but also clothes, all of which have specific storage areas within the bedroom for when they are not being used (for example a toy box or wardrobe). Second, there is the issue of objects from her younger sister's 'side' of the bedroom infiltrating her 'side'. Childhood objects such as a Barbie doll might be found in Chloe's half of the bedroom. This is an object that she did not consider to be 'cool' and that she did not want her own interests to be associated with. Instead, she considered her interests (such as playing CDs) to be more 'grown up' than her sister's.

Sharing a bedroom, then, does highlight some of the issues that can be taken for granted when a teenager has their own space. Sharing bedrooms, particularly with younger siblings, can be frustrating and difficult and often there is an increased desire to demarcate 'sides' in the room in an attempt to visually 'mark out' one's territory. Through the use of materials such as books, clothes as well as furniture, a sense of space and ownership is achieved. And despite the fact that the bedroom is a shared space, the 'two sides' become immensely important and the crossing from one side to another is at one's 'own risk'. This marking out, I would argue, is particularly important for a teenager who is working through their 'emerging identity' and unfolding biography and who wishes to be seen as a young adult and not a child. Sharing a bedroom with a younger sibling brings with it the possibility of 'being seen as a child', identified through all the child-like possessions a younger sibling may have and which may make their way across the 'border'. In this case, then, the presence of items and objects as 'emblems' of teen culture are of utmost importance and must be on display.

The quest for privacy also becomes more difficult because the use of the bedroom as a space in which to be alone can involve a series of negotiations and arguments with siblings and there is always the possibility that a sibling will come in. This can be problematic for a teenager, especially when the need for privacy is important.

Multiple bedrooms

Wallace and Kovatcheva argue that the rise in divorce rates is one of the major factors contributing to a family structure that is becoming ever more 'unpredictable and diverse' (1998, p. 125). This means that for many young people having more than one home is the 'norm' and within those homes they may have very different experiences of a 'bedroom culture', as these are determined by the family formation of which they are now part. For Lisa, 18 years old, a first-year student living in university halls of residence, her room was a crucially important space and has been consistently so throughout her life so far. This was largely tied in with a number of complex family issues that she experienced while she was growing up, including: the divorce of her parents when she was 6, her mother's moving in to live with another partner and her subsequent move abroad when Lisa was 14 years, and her father meeting a new partner. Lisa's parents now live in different towns in the UK, with her mother living with Lisa's stepfather and stepbrother, and her father living with her stepmother and stepsister. Lisa has periods of time living in each of these arrangements. She explained what her bedrooms were like in each of these domestic settings and how they differed:

> Well, I've got my own room at my mum's house in Carlisle but it's more of a guest room, but at my dad's, he still makes jokes that it looks like I never moved out, and there is just as much stuff everywhere there ...

Parental control very much pervades the living experiences that she has in her mother's house, an experience that is quite different to the one in her father's house. For Lisa, this constitutes the difference between having what she considered her 'own room' in her father's *home* or sleeping in the 'guest room' when she goes to her mother's *house*. Historically, Lisa's mother has exerted control over what she can and cannot have in her room and that has resulted in many 'spatial battles' between the two over the years. For example, her mother 'banned Marilyn Manson from her house and [she] hates a *Clockwork Orange*' so she would not let Lisa have related items such as posters in her room. Her dad, on the other hand,

> didn't care – he's just painted my room and I decided to paint squares on one wall and stick things in the middle of the squares and he didn't care, he was just like 'if that's how you want it, that's how you can have it' kind of thing, he just let's me have it my way.

For Lisa, this *is* the difference between having her own space and not having her own space. To be able to make her bedroom look and feel how she wants it to is what makes that space one that she feels at 'home' in. Having this freedom also means that Lisa is able to represent different parts of her life in her bedroom and, as she says of her room in the university halls, her life 'here' (at university) and her life 'there' (at home) with her dad. For example, one of the main artefacts that Lisa had in her room was her collection of photographs that captured both her family life and her time currently at university.

Through discussions with Lisa, it was not difficult to see that her life had been profoundly affected by the divorce of her parents, which had brought with it 'unpredictability' in her family life and 'diversity' in her family formation, especially when her parents met new partners. For Lisa, then, the need to have her own space was paramount, but it had to be a space in which she had relative autonomy, particularly in the ways in which the bedroom looked. Clearly, her experiences of feeling at home and having her own space were felt more at her father's house than her mother's where she was sleeping in the 'guest room' when she went to stay. In her father's house, her room has essentially stayed the same since she moved out to go to university. This stability of space is crucial for Lisa as she is able to return to her bedroom the way she left it in her family home. As we shall see in the following chapter, Lisa uses her bedroom as a 'reference' point in terms of where she is at in her life, with her room in halls of residence being filled with objects and items related to her first year in Liverpool intertwined with numerous memories of home through photos and other keepsakes. This is a space where there is no parental control exerted and she can make it look how she pleases.

Teenage bedrooms as 'sites of transition'

One of the major debates in youth studies has been in relation to the concept of 'youth' itself and what 'youth' actually constitutes in the contemporary world (Wyn and White, 1997; Leccardi and Ruspini, 2006; Nilan and Feixa, 2006). This debate was linked to related discussions around what have been termed 'extended transitions' and, additionally, 'yo-yo transitions' (Molgat, 2007), making the path to adulthood an increasingly individualised pursuit. Within this context, the role of private and 'personal' spaces such as teenage bedrooms has been to act as important 'touch-points' in those often uncertain times, with young people using their bedrooms while staying at home as work spaces or when moving back into the parental home after a period of time spent at university. Additionally, Livingstone suggests that:

> Following an earlier shift away from children having a productive role in the household, and the wider economy (Cunningham, 1995, 2006) in recent decades industrial western societies have seen the extension of formal education from early to late teens and a commensurate rise in the average age of leaving home, this pushing back the start of employment and delaying the traditional markers of adulthood. (2009, p. 5)

In drawing comparisons with McRobbie and Garber's study of teen-age girls, there are clearly stark differences in the context within which a bedroom culture emerges. No longer are bedrooms under-stood as rather temporary spaces of feminine (in this case) explora-tions but instead, they have become integral identity spaces for boys and girls alike in an ever-fragmented, neoliberal environment. They are not just spaces of passive consumerism used momentarily or fleetingly but are 'transitional' in themselves and this is where the concept of 'age' becomes important as a tool through which one can make sense of youth transitions in the context of their private space. Bedrooms can be considered a crucial part of a young person's transi-tions because such spaces are important sites of articulation when a young person is going through 'life-changing' moments, for example when taking important exams. This is illustrated in some depth in the example of Scarlett, aged 13, moving into her brother's bedroom, in Chapter 4.

As a young person moves through their teens towards adulthood, this desire to have one's space becomes ever more pertinent and a marker of one's shift towards independence. Larson shares this view in his own study of young people using the media in their bedrooms when he writes:

> On the one hand, adolescents in our culture place increasing impor-tance on who they are and what they will be in the future. They par-tially shed the secure and unquestioned sense of self acquired from their families and begin to look for a more personally determined sense of identity. (1995, p. 536)

Sonia, aged 22, also talked about how the arrangement of the space of her bedroom changed while she was studying for her GCSEs and how, at a similar time, the decoration of her room changed to accommodate her new interests and tastes as well as creating a space within which to do her revision and studying:

> When it [her bedroom] was pink I took down the pictures of Leonardo DiCaprio and stuff like that, and then I had … I don't really know … I got this furniture built when I was doing my … that and that [pointing to furniture], my mum's friend built them for me when I was doing my GCSEs so I had somewhere to revise. I kind of like things, I like to know where things are, if I'm going to start work, I have to have things tidy …

In a similar vein to Scarlett, as discussed in Chapter 4, when Sonia was faced with doing important exams, her bedroom space changed accordingly. The posters of famous film stars were taken down, signifying perhaps an end to childlike fantasies and crushes and a move towards 'serious' decision-making and hard work, signified through the furniture made to go into the room for Sonia to work on. Undergoing this major transition meant that Sonia changed her space to be more orderly and tidy, a transformation from a relaxing leisure space into a space in which she was able to work efficiently.

For Sonia, her bedroom has taken on a new meaning since she has left university and moved back into the family home. This shift back home represents clearly Molgat's (2007) 'yo-yo transition', as rather than following the traditional pattern of 'home–education–work–own home', Sonia has moved back into the family home after education. This is increasingly becoming a familiar pattern as a number of young people either stay at home longer (even after they secure employment) or move back into the family home after a period of living away. For an increasing number of young people, such as those who have been away to study at university, moving back into the family home is a necessity rather than an option, mainly because students are leaving higher education with increasingly large amounts of debt and are often unable to find graduate work. Once an absolute 'no-no', moving back to the parental home is now often considered the only option available for university graduates. Not surprisingly, this brings with it new articulations of private and personal space to make sense of. No longer is the space of the bedroom a 'work space' in the sense of doing work for school, college or university but it can become (and does become) a base from which one can work. Sonia's experiences are a good example of this.

Similarly, Brigitte, 23 years old, talks of her bedroom in Liverpool where she resides as she studies for a doctoral degree. She lives in a house with three other girls, aged 23 and 24 years old. They have lived there for four years and every year they do a 'straw poll' for the bedrooms in the house – that way there is the possibility that they will be in either a bigger or smaller bedroom than the previous year. This year Brigitte got the small 'box' bedroom:

> It's not very practical at all – if it was just an office it would work, if it was just a bedroom it would work but as it's both it's just a mess ... Well, size, is the thing that's the biggest issue I'd say, but even when I was in a double room it was still a pain, because whenever I'm

working, I'm a paper person, I have everything on paper and I'd just have these notes everywhere around me, and whenever I needed to go somewhere I had to move them around so that I could get out. So I need space to spread out when I'm working but I don't want that around me when I'm doing something else because you can't relax if you have work around you.

As we will also see in the example of Evie in Chapter 4, there is a preference for the 'zone' of work to be folded up when other pursuits are going on in the bedroom. What this means for Brigitte is that there is a deliberate maintenance of her bedroom as a space of relaxation, despite the size of the room and the extent to which it is filled with papers and other work. Similarly, in the following chapter Evie talks about the placing of her books on her desk that are positioned in such a way that they are not at eye level when she walks into the room. For Evie, the alternative answer to this is to create a 'working zone' in another room in the house, namely the dining room, at least for the duration of her 'A' level exams. As both Brigitte and Evie demonstrate, the visibility of work is not something that makes for a space in which one wants to be able to 'chill out' and relax. In Lincoln (2004) I discuss the 'doing college work' zone which shows some of the ways in which the 'zones' of work and leisure can cross over and spill into one another. As the example of Kate demonstrated in that essay, although there is a 'designated area' in her bedroom, and specifically her desk, which has been allocated for 'doing college work', there are always other items on the desk such as an ashtray or the club flyers above her desk that signify the distractions of other activities and the difficulties in separating these 'zones' when the bedroom is often used to accommodate both (2004, pp. 103–4).

So far, I have considered the question of what young people use their bedrooms for. In asking this question I have explored the complexities of household dynamics and the series of negotiations that young people find themselves experiencing in their uses of their bedrooms and their engagement in bedroom culture. In the second part of this chapter I consider the significance of bedroom culture within the wider context of contemporary youth culture. Specifically I consider young people's uses of and access to youth cultural spaces outside the home and how use and access determined by 'risk' can influence the extent to which a young person's bedroom becomes a key youth cultural site in their social and cultural worlds.

Bedrooms and contemporary youth cultures: public versus private spaces

In their major study *Young People, New Media* conducted in 1999 in the UK, Livingstone and Bovill framed the existence of a 'bedroom culture' in the lives of young people within the context of a large array of leisure preferences and media use, and as an alternative to young people's engagement in public spaces. One of Livingstone and Bovill's findings, drawn from qualitative interviews with young people aged between 6 and 16 years old, was that often young people expressed a preference for leisure time spent outside of the family home. Leisure time inside the home was often considered 'boring' by their young participants, yet they found that much of their leisure time was actually being spent within the domestic sphere. In their explanation of this, Livingstone and Bovill surmised that the widespread availability of various forms of media technology in the home, bought by parents worried about the risks for their offspring playing out on the streets, meant easy accessibility, which young people do find appealing. On the other hand, easy access to media technologies made activities such as watching television seem rather boring, something that adults did, thus making them less attractive as chosen pastimes. In her later work, Livingstone notes that a 'personalised media environment' is taken for granted by many young people for whom this is now commonplace (2007, p. 2). Despite this, however, technologies such as the television have made their way from shared spaces such as a living room or kitchen into the private space of the teenage bedroom (Livingstone, 2007, p. 2) with a number of young people in Livingstone and Bovill's 1999 study stating that they had their own television in their bedroom (63 per cent of their sample). However, as my own research also demonstrated, having a television set in a young person's room did not necessarily mean mindless hours spent in front of the TV. In fact, television has often been considered 'peripheral' to other activities, both inside and outside the home. As Julie, aged 13, said: 'If there's something good on I'll watch it, but I usually have it on and do other things like texting as well.'

While in some ways Livingstone and Bovill's findings 'put paid to any ideas that children are natural couch potatoes' (1999, p. 101), with notable mention of young people participating in activities outside of the home such as going to the cinema, seeing friends and playing sport (p. 101), Livingstone and Bovill also reported a number of 'fears' around the uses of public spaces expressed by both parents and by their offspring (see also Valentine, 1997; Valentine and McKendrick, 1997; Watt and Stenson, 1998) that appeared to be pushing much leisure time back into the sphere of the home. Those fears tended to be articulated through discourses of race and ethnicity, social class and gender. For instance, a working-class Asian mother spoke of facilities such as the YMCA, a leisure centre and a new water park available in her area for her children to attend but which they did not because they felt 'kind of outcast[s] ... because there's not many Asian children around here' (Livingstone and Bovill, 1999, p. 102). The same mother also demonstrated her reluctance to take them there because of 'older children on their bikes, hanging round' and low 'standard' in parks, which often meant lots of rubbish making for an unclean environment for children to play in. Other 'fears' noted by parents in Livingstone and Bovill's study included those intensified by the media, particularly in relation to news coverage on television. They also noted that many parents' accounts cited the news as a source of anxiety but also a reference point to their offspring about 'what might happen' if they stray too far from their homes resulting in few children straying beyond their gardens and instilling 'the idea of danger' (p. 103). In relation to more recent fears, James notes:

> In past times, when security issues and terrorist threats were not the dominant issues they are today, children were much freer to 'play outside' and roam the streets or the countryside with relatively little adult interference or supervision. A British study showed 'that the radius within which children roam freely around their homes has shrunk by almost 90% since the 1970s'. (James, 2007, quoted in Abbott-Chapman and Robertson, 2009, p. 421)

While, undoubtedly, parental fears do play a significant role in the types and amounts of usage young people make of public spaces, as Livingstone and Bovill go on to explore in their study, the ways that young people *themselves* identify with public spaces can inform their uses of private spaces. As we see in the examples below from my research data, young people's uses of their bedrooms can be informed by what leisure facilities are available to them in their localities and the conditions of their use. This in turn reveals some interesting perceptions by young people about their class positioning and what leisure activities this affords them.

David, Adam and Mark, aged between 15 and 16 years old, were from Sale, an affluent town in the county of Cheshire in the north of

England. While they use their bedrooms in quite different ways to one another (for example Mark would spend quite a bit of time playing computer games in his room and spent more time in there than the other boys), they were by and large using their bedrooms very little in comparison to a number of my other participants. This was because they, as they articulated, had access (both in terms of locality and finances) to a variety of different sports clubs that they could attend throughout the week and were all members of different sports teams, both locally and at college level, which meant they were out almost every night playing, for example, football, cricket or rugby. A couple of the boys were also helping run sports clubs for younger children during their summer holidays. The boys also spoke of well-resourced youth schemes set up in the area irrespective of the fact that they did not themselves participate in them. For these boys, discussion of their bedroom was primarily in terms of 'necessities', for example sleeping and sometimes eating rather than as a space of leisure which they primarily associate with the public sphere:

> Adam: Well, we know quite a lot of people through our cricket and football and the tennis club that we go to so we know quite a few people from there and from my cricket team from last year and this year ...

For these boys, leisure time is about being with numerous friends from a variety of places and with links to a number of sports-related clubs. Even if they wanted some privacy with their girlfriends, they favoured the cinema over their homes or bedrooms, despite their parents not minding them coming over. The boys talked about their perceptions of the surrounding area, viewing the nearest 'town' Altrincham as full of 'scallies' while Hale, another local town, was deemed 'okay'. Only David, who was 16 years old, had embarked on 'nights out' in Altrincham and Sale, despite them being what he called 'places where you get all the locals'. David was not yet allowed to go out in Manchester as his curfew was 11 p.m., and so it was deemed 'not worth it'. Much of the boys' experiences of drinking alcohol was from house parties (or 'gatherings' as they called them) with friends who had been given the go-ahead by their parents to have a party.[4] These 'gatherings' were largely peer-related as many of their friends were not old enough (or at least did not look old enough) to drink in bars. There was also a financial consideration as the cost of alcohol was much cheaper (and easier) to buy from the supermarket for a party than to drink in a bar.

Although the boys had several common interests in terms of their involvement in sport, their other interests were quite different and the times spent in their bedrooms varied accordingly. David's use was very basic: 'I sleep and keep my clothes in my bedroom, occasionally I use the phone and it smells a bit!' as he tries to 'spend as little time at home as possible' because he 'gets bored'. It should be noted here also that David shared his bedroom with his 13-year-old brother,[5] altering the dynamics of the space as 'his space' somewhat. Adam claims to 'just watch TV', while Mark would spend much of his time in his room playing computer games. At the time of the interview it was also only Mark who had a PC in his bedroom, which meant that he spent additional time in his room. The boys said that Mark had 'the best room' and his was the one they would hang out in to listen to music or play games if they were spending any time at home. Frequently, all three of the boys referred to their rooms as a space in which to 'do homework' and therefore very much associated time in these spaces with what might be considered 'non-leisure' activities. Mark's passion for gaming may also have been a distraction device from doing homework, while ensuring he was technically in his homework 'zone' (Lincoln, 2004).

For these boys, then, the majority of their leisure time is 'accountable' (particularly by parents) as they are spending much of it at leisure and sports clubs. They are able to do this because all come from fairly affluent middle-class families where there is a disposable income available to pay for all these different activities throughout the year. No part of their leisure time was spent just 'hanging around' in the neighbourhood, but it was highly structured through their sporting interests. There may indeed have been vested interests on behalf of their parents who, in paying for these activities, know that their offspring will be relatively safe and with their friends; indeed, while this example was by no means typical of my research sample, parental fears of public spaces may well emerge as a result of the inability to finance a structured leisure time for their offspring, unlike the case for David and his friends.

Julie, 13, Sara, 12, Natasha, 14 and Jackie, 13, all from Gorton, north Manchester, a much less affluent suburb in the north of England, have had very different experiences of public spaces compared to the boys from Sale. The girls spent much less time together, had less to do with local clubs and institutions and had an apparent absence of 'structured' leisure activities compared to the three boys I discuss above. As a consequence they spend much of their 'unstructured' leisure time in the space of their bedrooms. The following discussion demonstrates some of these issues:

SL:	So do you spend a lot of your free time together?
All:	Yeah
Julie:	Friday and Saturdays nights mainly
SL:	OK, so what sort of things do you get up to?
Angela:	In the street ... talking
SL:	So have you got places where you like to hang about?
Sara:	In the streets
Natasha:	In the park
Angela:	Everyone walks around the street
Julie:	We could have something, but we haven't got owt, have we ...
Sara:	Yeah, we could have a youth club or something, but there's nothing like that, there's only like that over there [a patrolled park over the other side of the road] but you get barred if you're ... you get barred if you cough in there!
Jackie:	I know, and then when you're there ... when you're on the streets because you've got no youth club to go to you get into trouble with the police, don't ya, because you're not allowed on the streets
Sara:	Julie can tell you about the police.
Julie:	I can tell you about the police!
Natasha:	[looking sideways at Julie] Fighting ...
Julie:	All the time, me.
Natasha:	She a bit of a rougher.
Sara:	Everyone around here thinks they rule the world you see, so they're all like ...
Angela:	They just all come 'I am Miss Gorgeous, I love myself, so everyone else has got to love me'.
Sara:	That's what it's like.

While the girls talked at other times about their hobbies such as going swimming or going to 'Sea Cadets' once in the week and shopping at the weekend, the time that they mostly spend hanging around together is on a Friday and a Saturday night. Having grown up in the area and having lived in the same community for all of their lives, the girls were *au fait* with the rules of the streets and its inhabitants (as Angela, 13 years old, said: 'I can tell you about this fizz 'ed [abbreviation of 'head'] that lives up the top of this road ... they got robbed because they kept the door open, it's dead dangerous here'). The girls were known in the area to other local teenagers,[6] some of whom are members of gangs (or *'crews'* as the girls called them) and they were known to the police. Julie, in particular, was known for her bad behaviour and for getting into trouble, mainly for 'fighting' with other teenagers in the neighbourhood. While by and large the girls do not cause any serious trouble, they did identify themselves as potential troublemakers in the eyes of the police, with the act of 'hanging around' being construed as being 'trouble by default'. They associated this and Julie's occasional fights with not having anything to do in their locality, especially at the weekends when they have more time. So, for instance, they say that they do not have a youth club; a space that they could hang out under some adult supervision but without the surveillance of the police. Sara did talk of a 'patrolled park' that existed just over the road from Julie and Natasha's house. They tended not to use it, however, because they perceived it to be 'over-patrolled' ('you get barred if you cough in there!', as Lisa says) and therefore not as a suitable leisure space in which they could just hang out and talk.

These girls, then, spent a lot of their free time in each other's bedrooms and it is easy to see why bedroom spaces are an attractive option for the girls whose leisure time is in stark contrast to the Sale boys. In their bedrooms they can 'hang out' and 'talk' as they wish without the inconvenience of being 'moved on' by the police and without the threat of getting into trouble. It is a space that is warm and comfortable in comparison to the streets with easy access to food and drink, music and entertainment, all things that a youth club could also offer if one were available to them or if there was one they felt comfortable accessing. All of the girls used their bedrooms and would spend time in each other's rooms for much of their free time. From discussions with the girls it appeared that the spaces were primarily regulated by them (for example they talked about having quite lot of say over what their rooms looked like [colour, layout], with little parental interference). They were spaces within which they could entertain themselves, namely through listening to music, trying on clothes, getting ready for parties or other 'nights out', such as the monthly 'teen nights' hosted in a club in the city in which the girls lived. The space of their bedrooms was by and large 'safer' for them than the streets which, according to the girls, offered them 'nothing to do'. This in many ways required them to 'structure' and be creative with their own leisure time in the home.

From the outset it appears that comparisons can be drawn between this example and McRobbie and Garber's concept of 'bedroom culture' for the teenage girl. In some respects, the story of the Gorton girls fits neatly into discourses around 'gender and sexuality', specifically in reference to the 'safety from the streets' debate. Interestingly, though, the girls' accounts of the streets and their reluctance to use them as leisure spaces are not held within preconceived notions of safety in relation to gender. As a matter of fact, there was no mention of feeling in a position of 'subordination' in relation to their male counterparts, and Julie's 'fighting' is certainly a testament to this. Rather, their reluctance to use 'the streets' is reminiscent of traditional male youth cultures and the perceptions of the authorities (as well as of the general adult public) with regard to the implications of them 'hanging around'. Much like in the traditional subcultural discourses discussed in Chapter 1, young people hanging around with nothing to do are seen as a contribution to the moral degradation of society and the inevitability of getting into trouble. The Sale boys, on the other hand, with their access to numerous sporting facilities and their 'structured' leisure time are more likely to be celebrated in the public eye as engaging in 'positive activities' and contributing to their community through their achievements and their participation in community life.[7]

'Risk' is clearly demarcated through public versus private space by the girls and perceived in the context of their locality rather than with reference to their gender. The Gorton girls are placed in a rather vulnerable position within which they have to manage their own 'risky' lives without necessarily having the leisure facilities available to them to potentially minimise this. For these girls, a move of their leisure activities back into the home is a form of 'risk' limitation. As Livingstone and Bovill sum up:

> Social grade makes a difference, for financial constraints make it more difficult for working-class parents to structure their children's leisure in the same way as their middle-class counterparts. (1999, p. 106)

While this is indeed true of young people using public spaces, it might not necessarily be the case when it comes to accommodating a 'bedroom culture' inside the home. Throughout my research I found very little evidence to suggest a marked difference in the 'things' (particularly technical equipment) that young people had in such spaces in relation to 'social grade', although, interestingly, the sources from which these possessions were acquired might differ. For instance, one parent of a working-class male aged 15 told me that while she was keen to make sure her son's bedroom was well equipped with things to keep him entertained, his TV and stereo were 'hand-me-downs' from other family members because she could not afford to buy everything new. The majority of the participants had technical items such a TV, a stereo, a mobile phone and in later stages of the research a PC or laptop through which they could access the internet. This is in addition to more 'traditional' forms of media such as books and magazines.

On several occasions before an interview commenced, I would speak to parents who, at times, voiced concerns about simple issues such as accommodating all the pieces of technology that a young person wanted in his or her room. The parents' concerns were related to the limited amount of space available, particularly if bedrooms were very small, and practical issues such as not having enough plug sockets to accommodate 'modern' youth technological lifestyles. One parent said that she would much rather deal with these types of issues and have her son bring his friends home to play, instead of being out on the streets – 'at least', she said, 'I know where he is and that he's safe.' Such opinions were not uncommon.

One can argue, then, that while young people may show a preference for spending time outside of the home, there are various constraints dictated by accessibility to facilities and the level of this accessibility that social class affords, which means that such spaces are not always readily or safely accessible.

Bedrooms: from private to social spaces

In traditional studies of bedroom culture the space of the bedroom was not primarily understood as a 'social' space. For McRobbie and Garber (1975) these spaces, which were located within the domestic sphere of the home, were spaces in which a teenage girl could 'dip' in and out of cultural practices and activities as part of her wider domestic duties in the home. As a space primarily functioning in accordance with the discourses of romance and of 'finding a man and keeping him' (McRobbie 1991, p. 101) the space of the bedroom was seen as a place within which the teenage girl would primarily be alone. In her bedroom, the teenage girl could experiment with hair and make-up, try on clothes and test out new styles and effectively 'get ready' for the contexts in which she may find herself face-to-face with the man of her dreams.

Given this interpretation of bedroom culture, McRobbie and Garber pay close attention to the role of teenage girls' magazines of the day, taking *Jackie* as their primary example through which one could understand the 'coding' of teenage girls' culture.[8] More specifically, the problem page (for example 'Cathy and Claire' in *Jackie*) was something that teenage girls invariably read on their own, finding out information and advice and importantly finding out how to act with their male counterparts without actually having to ask their friends, which would of course have been embarrassing. By definition, then, the space of the bedroom was primarily linked to solitary activities or occasionally functioning as a space in which the teenage girl would listen to records with a couple of her close friends. While it is still possible to recognise elements of this traditional use of private space in contemporary bedroom culture (see Lincoln, 2004), one can also argue that this is a space that has, in many ways and for various reasons, become much more of a 'social space'.

As discussed earlier in this chapter, the space of the bedroom for young people in a contemporary setting still maintains its traditional role as a space to be alone and it still functions as a space of escapism, a safe haven (James, 2001) or a sanctum (Steele and Brown, 1995) from what might be going on in relation to family, friends, school or work. As is demonstrated by some of my research participants, such spaces are sacred in this context. For example, Lucie, who was 20 years old at the time of the research, has the following comments:

Lucie: I just see it as somewhere to relax really, somewhere to chill out and get ready, listen to music, sleep.

SL: So will you come up here and spend time on your own?

Lucie: Yeah, I'll do things like ... I'll potter around sometimes, a bit of sewing or make some earrings or something like that, on my bed or on the floor or something.

For Lucie, her bedroom has multiple functions. First, it has a practical function in that it is a space in which she sleeps. She also says that it is a space in which to 'get ready', both for college and for a night out. It is also a space in which she can chill out and relax and 'potter around', and in line with her interests at college where she is studying printmaking, Lucie also uses her room as a creative space in which she makes pieces of jewellery or clothing. In this sense, she enjoys being alone in her bedroom and is likely to busy herself with various activities. However, Lucie goes on to talk about how her bedroom is also a social space in which she spends time with friends. She says:

Probably, because we'll be going out or something and I'm always late!, I'll still be getting ready and we'll chat, so rather than sit in the living room they'll sit in here and chat and listen to music and we're out of the way then too.

In this sense, her lateness in getting ready for a night out means that her bedroom transforms into a 'social zone' within which her friends gather. So we see a cross-over of the practicalities of the bedroom as a space in which to 'get ready' and as a space for her friends to sit and chat while she does this. The music that is playing in her room transcends these two zones as it continuously plays both while Lucie gets ready alone and when her friends arrive later. Such activities contribute to the excitement of the evening ahead and may in many ways replicate it (for example through the choice of music played) (Lincoln 2004, 2005), what Hollands (1995) and Hollands and Chatterton (2001) referred to as part of the going out ritual. There is a further practical issue being addressed here inasmuch as Lucie's friends are not left 'hanging around' the house while she gets ready. The lounge or the kitchen, for example, might be occupied by other family members so her going out related activities are confined to her bedroom and do not infiltrate or interrupt the rest of the house, although indeed the music may be heard.

I asked Lucie whether there were periods in her life when she had used her bedroom in different ways and for more or less time than she currently does. She said:

> Yeah, I probably used to use it a bit more when I was about 14 or 15 because I used to make a lot of bracelets and things and I'd be drawing in sketch books and things, so I kind of did most of that in my room. But maybe because then I had a single bed, so the whole of the room was free, so I think that's changed it – changed how my room's set up and how I use it.

For Lucie, the use of her bedroom is determined by her hobbies and interests in jewellery making. Her mid-teens was a period in her life when she was using her bedroom more as a creative space and, crucially, what she identifies here is that the amount of 'free' space she used to have in her room influenced how and to what extent she used it. A simple shift from having a single bed to a double bed has significantly changed the amount of 'free space' that Lucie now has and this makes it more difficult for her to use her bedroom to make jewellery, which demands space to accommodate the various different materials used. For Lucie, then, this is a time that she particularly remembers using her bedroom a lot. In this sense the bedroom became a creative space in which she could spend time alone making jewellery.

Charlotte, who was 18 years old, also reflected on the use of her bedroom when she was younger. In her younger years, her bedroom was used both as an *anti*-social and as social space; a space that is available 'on demand' should she feel the need to escape to it. In this context, the bedroom was interpreted as a space within which to hide away from others and to make a statement by withdrawing her presence from rooms where other family members were. She said:

It's my space if I want it ... if you're annoyed. Like when I was little and I was annoyed I'd just go up to my room and be hidden away. And it's got all my stuff in it, because you try and make it look like how you want it, I like it in that sense. If I shared a room and I wanted to go to bed and they'd be watching TV and I don't have to wait up in case they're late or something.

The bedroom for Charlotte became a space for reflection, a place to accommodate her occasional bad moods, and in this respect, having her own space meant that she could disappear when she wanted to. Larson noted similar uses in his study claiming that 'far from being a happy context, time alone is associated with frequent feelings of loneliness and negative mood' and that '[p]rivate spaces [are] used for self-reflection, emotional discharge and personal renewal' (1995, p. 540). Charlotte highlights the importance of having her own space by comparing it to what it would be like if she was sharing. In this case, she explains, she wouldn't be able to just do her own thing but would have to consider another person's use.

While what we see here are examples of how bedrooms can be used in the pursuit of solitary activities, they can also be understood as highly social spaces too. I suggest this above in the discussion of Lucie and her friends, but it can also be argued that bedrooms can be transformed into social spaces in which groups of friends hang out, which implies the 'zones' within bedroom culture shift and merge accordingly. There are often quite specific contexts in which this will occur. For example, a group of three 18-year-old males, Dean, Alex and Gary, from Abbey Hey in north Manchester, talked about how they would use each other's bedrooms as spaces in which to meet up especially at the weekends.

For them, the bedroom was the ideal social space, first, because they were all working in full-time jobs with different shifts, and second, because they did not always have a great deal of money. The bedroom for them acted as a 'hub' which they could drift in and out of according to their own time frames. So, for example, if one of them was working a later shift, he could easily join the others once the shift had finished. This would potentially be more difficult had they arranged to meet in a bar or a club. The 'ease of access' means that the three young adults just needed some music, alcohol and cigarettes to transform such spaces into social spaces. In comparison to a night out in town, especially at the weekends, this is also a relatively cheap way to relax and enjoy some free time and hanging out together.

In their study *Inventing Adulthoods*, Henderson et al. explain how leaving school or university and going into the world of work can break down existing friendships. This happens even if those young people in the group still live in close proximity or have put in place 'positive strategies' (2007, p. 157) such as making an effort to talk on the phone, using a mobile phone to text and more contemporarily through social networking sites. For many of their participants, there would be some effort put into trying to keep in touch but, in most cases, this would eventually break down and new friendship groups would emerge. However, in the case of Dean, Alex and Gary, using one of their bedrooms as a meeting place worked as a 'positive strategy' for them in maintaining their friendship and accommodating their different working patterns.

The bedroom, then, is a space that can be used in multiple ways, either as a space to spend time alone, as a safe 'haven' from the business of everyday life, or as a social space to which to invite friends. Those uses are often spontaneous, as is the case, for instance, with Lucy whose lateness in getting ready for a night out sometimes means the transformation of her room into a sociable space for friends. For Dean and his friends, the bedroom is an important 'meeting point' that accommodates the differing lives of his friends as they move into the world of work.

Conclusions

I began in this chapter by posing two seemingly simple questions: What is the teenager's bedroom for and what is its significance in contemporary youth culture? In posing these questions, I aimed to reveal some of the complexities in the uses of bedrooms by young people as social and cultural spaces that exist within the context of the family home and its politics. As I have argued, young people's bedroom usage is subject to a number of rules and regulations governed by different members of their household, namely siblings and parents and articulated through the concept of age and 'age grades' (Griffin, 1993). In addition to the internal dynamics of the household, young people's bedroom usage is also influenced by their uses of public spaces and the leisure provisions available in the areas in which they live. Alongside this, the discourse of risk and perceptions of the 'dangerous streets' still underlie the uses of domestic spaces as important sites of cultural and social practices. This has led to a number of parents 'investing' financially in their children's domestic leisure time, spending money on media technologies and equipment in an attempt to create 'safer' environments for them to spend time in with their friends.

Against this backdrop, in the following chapter, I consider more closely the 'materiality' of the bedroom, the meaning of the objects and items found in young people's bedrooms, and the biographical nature of this space, that can tell us much about the lives of their young occupants. In drawing upon the more sensorial elements of my research data, I aim to explore the ways in which the materiality of the space itself is integral to it use and the emerging bedroom culture, a dimension of bedroom culture that is largely missing from the literature. In doing this, I hope to contribute further to the post-subcultures debate, for example, in applying Miles' concept of the 'youth stylist' to the context of private, personal spaces as well as exploring the concept of a bedroom culture within the context of material culture.

4
Young People, Bedrooms and Materiality

> The position of identity – and the lifestyle issues and identity politics associated with it – is one that is topologically complex. The space of identity is a heterogeneous, folded, paradoxical and crumpled space in which a distinct singular position is not possible. (Hetherington, 1998, p. 23)

> all the stuff I've picked myself, even if I haven't meant it to represent me, it does 'cos I've picked everything that's in it, so it does say something about your character, if you know what I mean? (Charlotte, 18 years old)

As one of the first spaces that many young people can call their own and are able to exert any kind of control over, bedrooms can be important 'representative' spaces for them and are representative in a number of different ways. For example, as I argued in the previous chapter, a young person's use of their bedroom can represent their relationship with other family members within the home and the internal dynamics and politics of the household as well as their relationship with friends, peers and partners. Their bedrooms can represent their perceptions of the public sphere as well as their uses of it and they can also represent other aspects of young people's everyday lives too, for example, their hobbies and interests, their consumption practices and even their production practices (Kearney, 2007).

In Chapter 1, I considered a number of the major critiques made of the CCCS' work on youth cultures and subcultures. One of those critiques made by Miles (2000) was in reference to the CCCS' tendency to focus solely upon the symbolic elements of subcultures and the consumption of related goods, rather than considering in any sub-stantial way what those goods meant to young subcultural members. Miles asks what exactly the consumer goods that represented specific subcultures actually meant to those consuming them as part of their individual biographies as well as their collective subcultural identi-ties. In critiquing this approach, Miles proposes that the concept of the 'youth stylist' provides an alternative way through which to make sense of young people's consumption practices in contemporary youth cultures and as part of reflexive youth lifestyles and identities (Furlong and Cartmel, 2006). In conceptualising this, he asks what the goods that young people choose to consume mean to them, in what context and how they 'styled' into their fluid, interchangeable lifestyles.

In his book *Governing the Soul* (1999), Rose states that young people as prime consumers living out multiple lifestyles are particularly suscepti-ble to an ever-changing, consumer market within which their supposed individual consumer 'choice' is legitimised. However, this legitimisation process is bounded, not only by the context of the home and family, but also, Rose argues, by the media (an aspect that I explore in more detail in Chapter 5) as well as by advertising. Given the neoliberal context of the 'relentless pressure to consume', Strickland (2002, p. 7) argues that this type of bounded choice makes it very difficult for young people to have complete control over many aspects of their lives, including social and cultural ones.

Despite this context of compromised choice and the constant pressure to consume, as I will argue in this chapter, the private space of young people's bedroom enables their occupiers to assume the role of 'young stylists' and at times to 'press the pause button' on this consumption and to 'anchor' or 'cement' at least some elements of their identity that form part of their emerging adult biographies. This cementing, I would like to suggest, is achieved through the materiality of their bedrooms, while ownership of objects and other personal goods often found in the bedrooms enables them to legitimate their individual cultural identi-ties, as well as their more communal ones. In a world of instability and uncertainty, I would argue, their bedrooms can offer them a physical space in which their cultural identities may be considered more stable and permanent, and over which they can in some ways exert more control than in other, public, youth cultural contexts.

This is particularly pertinent within a youth cultural context of social media in which young people find themselves in a continual process of identity 'tracking' in their use of social networking sites such as Facebook, embedded into which is the obligatory 'updating' of their status. Besides this, social networking sites require a Goffmanesque 'presentation of the self' and one that is continuously 'edited' for a wide audience of 'friends'. As a juxtaposition to this, and as articulated by my participants, the materiality of bedrooms, in comparison to social networking sites, can be considered part of a more 'authentic' experience of identity construction and display (boyd and Ellison, 2007; Mallan, 2009; Sveningsson, 2009), with the bedroom itself being what Lefebvre called the ultimate 'container of meaning' (1991) for young people. Beyond simply being 'symbolic', as was the case in the classic CCCS subcultures literature, and to an extent in the contemporary context of social networking, as I explore in the final chapter, the materiality of bedroom space is multilayered, worked upon and meaningful and is related to identities, relationships, transitions and emotions. In this chapter, then, in which I continue to draw on my research data, I explore the materiality of young people's bedrooms and the meaning of things to them.

In studying the materiality of young people's bedrooms, I particularly draw on Henri Lefebvre's work *The Production of Space* (1991, but see also Lefebvre, 1971, 1987). In the chapter entitled 'Social Space' Lefebvre proposes that spaces should be understood as ever-shifting containers of meaning, never empty or 'distinct from their content' (p. 87), an idea pertinent to the context of a young person's bedroom and relevant to the context of neoliberalism within which many contemporary youth cultural debates (that see young people in a position of continuous, conspicuous consumption) take place. One can see Lefebvre's view clearly in action in a young person's bedroom. For example, the bedroom is a space in which material items are constantly changing to keep up with the latest fads and trends. Posters are changed on the bedroom wall, better or latest versions of computer games are bought and the old ones abandoned as they depreciate in terms of cultural status or as a symbol of 'cool' (Danesi, 1994). In discussing the history of space, Lefebvre argues that 'representational space', that is, 'the inventory of things in space', its materiality, must be understood in accordance with 'representations of space', that is, spatial discourses (Lefebvre, 1991, p. 116). As I have argued in Chapter 1, in the context of young people's bedrooms, the space itself must be understood as interconnected to the activities that take place within it in conceptualising young people's bedroom culture. According to Lefebvre, everyday life 'figures in representational space' (p. 116), which means that bedroom spaces contain family life, relationships, hobbies, interests, transitions and many other things, as I will discuss below. Lefebvre refers to this manifestation of materiality as an overlapping of the 'practical and the symbolic' (p. 141) and of the public and the private, and I will discuss these configurations more fully in my examinations of the concept of 'zoning' in the next chapter.

However, before I discuss some of these ideas in more detail, I wish to explore closely and critically the concept of 'bedroom culture' for teenagers in the family home, which, McRobbie and Garber (1975) argued, was used as a 'cultural site' located exclusively within the private sphere of the home for the use of the teenage girl. In doing this, I establish why the materiality of bedrooms is so important to consider when making sense of young people's uses of them as youth cultural spaces.

Materiality in traditional 'bedroom culture'

While it should be acknowledged that McRobbie and Garber's approach is now a rather dated one, and that more contemporary studies of bedroom culture have emerged over the past two decades, I would argue that it warrants some close attention in the space of this book. This is because it was one of the first attempts to make sense of youth cultures, albeit girls' cultures, inside private space and outside the 'classic' frameworks of youth culture in public space that dominated those discourses from the 1940s onwards, as I argue in Chapter 1 (see, for example, Whyte, 1943; Mays, 1954; Becker, 1963; Hall and Jefferson, 1975; and others from the CCCS tradition). As I have explored in Chapter 1, the essay 'Girls and Subcultures', although not without its criticisms, was recognised as being crucial in offering an alternative approach by which to make sense of the ways that the teenage girl, in particular, lived out a different cultural life from her male counterpart. As Kearney argues, this was a ground-breaking piece, the 'first analysis of girls' cultural activities' (2007, p. 127). 'Girls and Subcultures' made a case for cultural spaces that 'fitted in' to the domestic sphere and the domestic life of the teenage girl and gave us some insight into how home-based subcultures operate and how their functioning was based primarily on gender differences. I would suggest, though, that in McRobbie and Garber's discussions, much like in other CCCS subcultural accounts, the *space* of the bedroom *itself* remains treated as largely 'functional', a 'convenience', and a means to an end in the production of a 'bedroom culture', rather than integral to our understanding of it and to the girls' uses of it.

As noted in Chapter 1, traditional accounts of British youth subcultures as documented by the CCCS were primarily associated with class oppression and political hegemony. Such interpretations of 'spectacular' subcultural activity were rigidly held within such ideologies, hence the spaces in which subcultural activities were taking place were not considered to be representational in themselves. As part of these traditional discourses, the placing and construction of a 'culture of the bedroom' (McRobbie and Garber, 1975; Frith, 1984) was predominantly associated with the use of domestic home space by teenage girls. Angela McRobbie and Jenny Garber who first coined the phrase 'bedroom culture' in their response to the work of the CCCS argued that the invisibility of young women in such descriptions could, amongst other things, be accounted for in their choice of 'youth cultural site'. They suggested that the teenage girl was living out her cultural and social life primarily in the private space of the home, a peripheral and marginalised sphere in comparison to the dominant public sphere of the teenage boy. They argued that '... the working-class girl, though actively participating in the world of work, remained more focused on home and marriage than her male counter-part' (1975, p. 5). To this end, they suggested that bedroom spaces offered the ideal setting in which to accommodate this for the teenage girl; to dip in and out of domestic duties when necessary. Furthermore, in an updated version of this essay in *Feminism and Youth Culture*, McRobbie argues that girls use this private space as a site in which to 'invest' their leisure time in the pursuit of romance, 'finding a man and keeping him' (McRobbie, 1991, p. 101).

In her later work, McRobbie further argues that the teenage girl's bedroom could be 'mapped out' according to the specific pursuits of being the domestic wife and mother. Using 'codes' such as 'fashion and beauty', 'personal life', 'pop music' and 'romance' (1991, p. 94) she defines how the quest for that crucial romantic encounter works. To some extent, and in line with the discussions around the significance of 'objects' as 'bricolage' in, for example, Hebdige's account of subculture and style (1979) McRobbie's later work does make reference to the 'materiality' of bedroom culture, although there is no rich description of it or its use. The material items mentioned in this account are limited to a record player, make-up and clothes, posters and magazines and, one could argue, necessarily so because the accessibility of 'bedroom culture' in that case relied on its simplicity and the ease of 'membership', and therefore *not* on highly stylised expression as in the visual, 'spectacular' subcultures that were associated with young adults. McRobbie argues:

> This approach, which hinges on explaining the choice of cultural artefacts – clothes, records, or motorbikes – is of limited usefulness when applied to teenage girls and their magazines. They play little,

if any role in shaping their own pop culture and their choice in consumption is materially narrow. Indeed the forms made available to them make re-appropriation difficult. (1991, p. 86)

Bedroom culture in this account and in the earlier 1975 account is meant to be 'almost totally packaged' feeding into particular discourses that include love, romance and femininity (McRobbie and Garber, 1975, p. 220; McRobbie, 1991, p. 11). McRobbie argues that we are led to assume that the pursuit of romance is every girl's goal and that this goal is achieved largely through 'passive' consumption of the material items listed above and that those items offer little creative outlet for teenage girls in shaping their own identities. For example, McRobbie's interpretation of pop music in the lives of teenage girls was limited to the aesthetics of the 'pin-up' (1991, p. 13), having posters of the 'good-looking' male pop star adorning the bedroom walls at which the teenage girl could gaze and drift off into a fantasy world of the romantic encounter with this star. In this account, the record player worked to enhance this fantasy through an aural contribution; with the girl listening to the songs of the favourite pop star, floating away into a fantasy world, sometimes in the company of a group of friends who may have been invited round to listen to records. Finally, clothing and make-up as material artefacts feature in McRobbie's account but again are described within the framework of 'romance'. We do not really find out about experiences of the teenage girl experimenting with clothing, hair and make-up in the context of her 'under construction' identity; instead, there is an argument for a 'manufactured' approach to fashion and beauty dictated through the pages of *Jackie* (a popular 1970s and 1980s magazine for teenage girls, which is highly significant in McRobbie's work, and which she describes as providing an ideological 'map of meaning' for its readers) with multiple warnings of the potential damage of getting it wrong.

What we see in McRobbie and Garber's account and in McRobbie's later work, then, is an application of coding to the subcultural life of the teenage girl and, to some extent, of bedroom spaces. However, such an application renders the teenage girl rather passive, with links to public spaces made through the pages of a popular magazine or through necessity (having a job). We gain little sense of a teenage girl's active engagement in both spheres as cultural and social spaces or any meaningful sense of how one space infiltrates the other, shaping its meaning and significance to the individual and influencing the arrangement and aesthetics of bedroom space. In both these accounts of bedroom culture, objects are considered as a means to an end, the end being the 'romantic encounter' with a male counterpart. Objects are not considered as having meaning in themselves, in relation to a rich, complex and emerging biography of their owner or as objects of 'attachment' for the bedroom occupant. They are far more 'generic' than that in traditional bedroom culture. There is no sense of the continuing significance of items, such as the record player, as the girls get older or temporal considerations of how objects become sentimental and nostalgic. Bedroom spaces, then, are by no means static and, as we will see, are spaces within which objects are moved, placed, displaced and replaced, capturing the often very rapid changes in tastes, interests and lifestyles of a young person engaging in youth culture.

Materiality, consumption and 'bedroom culture'

In stark contrast to the rather sparse material context of the teenage girl's bedroom in the 1970s as presented by McRobbie and Garber (1975), bedrooms in the 2000s are full of 'stuff'. As I note in Chapter 3, it has been argued by Livingstone and Bovill (1999) that one of the reasons for the existence of 'bedroom culture' in contemporary times has to do with the availability of a vast selection of leisure and media products, made for the home and used in young people's bedrooms, to the point at which Bovill and Livingstone identified in their later work (2001) what they described as media rich and media poor bedrooms. In addition to this, they suggest that increasingly, and given the perceived risks of public spaces, parents are undertaking to provide a range of media and entertainment technology for their children in an attempt to create 'safe' leisure environments within the confines of the home. This was also confirmed by my research findings as parents recalled the types of technology they had bought for their children ensuring – as far as they could – that adequate leisure choice was available within the home. This shift of leisure consumption back into the domestic realm emerges against a backdrop of neoliberalism whereby young people particularly are encouraged to consume an endless array of products, which means that an ever-changing movement of consumer goods becomes associated with many aspects of their social and cultural lives. This suggests that, on the one hand, parents are under constant pressure to 'update' those available leisure choices, not always an option for families with minimal disposable income and, on the other, that young people themselves are engaged in a continual updating process in terms of their material possessions, whether inside or outside of the home.

I recall a quote from Rose (1999) referred to in Chapter 1 in an attempt to make sense of this supposed continual movement of objects, items and things in the context of a young person's bedroom:

> However constrained by external or internal factors, the modern self is institutionally required to construct a life through the exercise of choice from among alternatives. Every aspect of life, like every commodity, is imbued with a self-referential meaning; every choice we make is an emblem of our identity, a mark of our individuality, each is a message to ourselves and to others as to the sort of person that we are, each casts a glow back, illuminating the self of he or she that consumes. (1999, p. 231)

In many ways, a teenager's private and personal space is a useful 'prism' through which to explore the definition of modern life for young people as described by Rose above. Bedrooms are one of the very first spaces over which a young person is able to exert any type of control, call one's own, and thus potentially operationalise some degree of choice and autonomy over that space through youth cultural practices (Osgerby, 1998). It is a space that can accommodate constant reinventions of youth biographies as tastes and interests change through time. Of course, there are internal and external factors (for example, parents, siblings and peers as well as financial or educational pressures) that influence that control, many of which I discuss in the previous chapter. But bedrooms are also important signifiers of a young person's shift towards independence and adulthood and I examine this below when exploring the ways in which young people might change their bedrooms around in line with important transitions, such as taking exams or moving out of the family home for a period of time.

The space of the teenage bedroom is also in many ways 'self-referential', as Rose suggests, of aspects of contemporary life. For example, Adam, aged 15, talked about the childhood toys in his bedroom and the meaning they had for him in his teenage years.

Adam: I had about a hundred teddies on one of my shelves but then I shifted them all out and I just kept the better teddies...

SL: Which ones did you keep?

Adam: The ones that looked the newest. I've got this massive dog thing that's about this big [demonstrates size] ... I kept the first one that I had which is called Ben. His arm's falling off, he's in the roof [the loft] now.

Rather than remove all of his childhood toys completely from his room (as is the case with James below who is a year older), Adam goes through a 'selection process', demonstrating an 'in-between' childhood and adulthood feeling, typical of being a teenager. His collection of toys from his childhood is still part of his bedroom space, but there is no kind of playing or interaction with them. James, 16 years old, claimed when I visited his bedroom: '... if you'd have come six months earlier you would have seen stuff from my childhood'. For James, changing his room and moving around the things in it represent his growing up, and in this sense his bedroom can be seen as a self-referential marker as he is able to talk about what it looked like before what he describes as 'the renovation' took place:

> My previous room looked childish. It had kids' stuff, no posters, ted- dies in it and stuff, a thing coming off the ceiling, it looked like a 12 year old lived in it, not a 16 year old. It was bright yellow and in winter it was dark and gloomy, the room was depressing. Now, when it's dark, it's dark and I just put the lamp on. It's nice like this.

In this example, James has consciously undertaken a process of 'self-regulation' in that he is managing his identity through the aesthetics of his bedroom space and the commodities to be found within it. The process of self-referencing takes place through his demarcation of what he considers to be childish (a similar example of which I discuss later in the chapter in relation to Scarlett), for example stuffed toys and teddies, alongside what he considers more 'adult' things. This is indicative of his shift towards adulthood as his 'grown up' interests are clear to see from the collection of beer bottle tops, the posters of nearly naked women ('it took my mum some time to clock [see] it!'), gig tickets, photos of his high school prom, car number plates, and many other objects signalling a variety of 'rites of passage' that have taken over from the 'teddies' and 'kids' stuff'. It is a statement about who James is at the age of 16. In many ways, then, teenagers' private and personal spaces are a 'message to themselves' as well as to others; a statement that declares the fact that 'this is me and this is what I like'.

These messages can also be understood as forms of resistance or rebel- lion and even as metaphors for protecting the 'private self' (Larson, 1995), as visual signs of independence. Parke and Sawin (1979) argue that as young people 'become more vigilant about privacy' (cited in Larson, 1995, p. 540) one may see the strategic placing of 'DO NOT ENTER' signs on the bedroom door or, as used by Millie (depicted in

Figure 4.1), a doorbell that people are required to 'ring' should they wish to enter her bedroom. Furthermore, in this image, the lips, the lipstick (not shown here) and the colour pink function as signifiers of an entrance to other aspects of self-reference, for example, a biography of femininity, one to be fully explored once the bedroom door opens. However, appearances might be deceptive because, as I discuss in more detail later on, as soon as the bedroom door opens, Millie's love of football, which is displayed through posters, photos, football scarves, duvet covers and rugs with the Liverpool Football Club (LFC) logos, is juxtaposed sharply with the 'emblems' of an identity of femininity and 'girliness' evident on her bedroom door as well as in other objects in her room such as fairy lights. This suggests a literal clash of cultures that is primarily signified through the meeting of the colours of shocking pink (from the door bell, fairy lights, etc.) and red (the colour of LFC).

Millie's collection of football memorabilia brings forward another point that Rose has made, namely, that 'emblems of identity' are also

Figure 4.1   A 'DO NOT ENTER!' variation

considered visual cues of our position in society as consumers. Despite Millie's freedom to create her room according to her own vision (and her parents had been very proactive in encouraging her to make the room her own), the existence of so much memorabilia from LFC is a clear indication of consumption practices at work for a number of years. Not only does Millie use her pocket money to save for different pieces of memorabilia, but she also asks family members to buy her pieces for her as birthday and Christmas presents. In many ways Millie is caught up in what Strickland (2002) describes as a 'relentless pressure to consume' (p. 7) as the football memorabilia market is indeed big business and there are at least three LFC stores in her home city of Liverpool in which Millie is able to purchase items on a regular basis. This is also evident in her collection of Disney toys displayed on top of her LFC-branded duvet cover as seen in Figure 4.2. In other words, Millie's selection of bedroom objects demonstrates how young people 'assemble a way of life within the sphere of consumption' (Rose, 1999, p. 230).

Figure 4.2   Millie's football and Disney memorabilia

The teenage bedroom, as I continue to explore in this chapter, is full of visual 'emblems of identity', articulating individual choice and 'unique biographies' (Roberts, 2009, p. 74) which can be discerned particularly in objects and things such as photographs, posters, books, magazines, pictures, music, DVDs, jewellery and trinkets. However, Roberts argues that:

> The uniqueness lies in the ordering, the sequencing, and the particular combinations of experiences that constitute a life. Individualisation is a matter of degree rather than an either/or absolute state. (2009, p. 75)

In the discussions that follow, then, where I explore inside a young person's bedroom, I consider how young people articulate choice and create 'unique biographies' in the context of their private spaces. In doing this, I explore in more detail the suggestion that I made above, namely, that in a cultural world characterised by relentless consumption, fragmenting identities and individualisation, young people's material possessions are not only a product of their consumption but can represent a 'pause' in its relentless pressure, even if this in itself is momentary, and a cementing of elements of young people's biographies through the materiality of their bedroom space, elements that in other contexts are constantly changing. In addition to this, I explore the interplay of the public and the private in the materiality of space and how its materiality works to create not only individual cultural biographies but also histories beyond the present occupant.

Materiality and bedrooms 1: Investing in the private

As a site of identity, personal development, exploration and experimentation, a bedroom is often a most significant and highly meaningful space in the life of a young person. As a 'visual text' it is complex, contradictory at times, the objects within it constantly changing and evolving in line with the activities that take place there. It is both a predictable and an unpredictable space mirroring the very nature of contemporary youth culture itself. As Lefebvre says of social space:

> Social space contains a great diversity of objects, both natural and social, including the networks and pathways which facilitate the exchange of material things and information. Such 'objects' are thus not only things but also relations. As objects they possess discernible peculiarities, contour and form. Social labour transforms them,

rearranging their positions within socio-temporal configurations without necessarily affecting their materiality, their nature state. (1991, p. 77)

The four walls of a bedroom make it rather generic, just another room in a house or an empty space, but it is what is contained within it and the way it is 'styled' by its young occupants that creates meaning and significance and, importantly, personalises that space for them (Búrikova, 2006). This act of 'making the room one's own' is crucial for any young person in the development and unfolding of their biographies, mainly because the act of a young person having their own space and enjoying a sense of ownership and control over that space (for example regulating who is allowed in and who is not) is a rite that resembles a move towards independence. As one of my participants put it:

> If I didn't want something in my room then I won't have it, unless it's storing something for my mum. I still have the choice even if I'm asked to take something down. I let mum come in to drop off the laundry but I don't like it if she just comes in, when I'm angry people know not to come in. I don't need signs on the door, people knock before coming in, they don't just barge in ... they come in when asked. (James, 16 years old)

Once the bedroom door is opened, a 'container of meaning' is revealed whereby initial judgements can be made about the interests and identity of its occupant, for example by gender or by age. Furthermore, objects and items work to 'historicise' space. Although this may appear a surprising aspect of the teenage bedroom, the display of items from childhood to the present day is a visual indication of growing up and of moving through 'age grades' (Griffin, 1993), of which, as Lefebvre would argue, a residue is left (quoted in Moran, 2004).

Nicola's bedroom is an example of this whereby we see 'layers' of her cultural interests building within the space of her bedroom. Her bookshelf (Figure 4.3) shows how this works. We see a photograph of her and her brother when they were both younger (Nicola is now 16 years old) alongside a Beatrix Potter print that Nicola has had from a young age and had in her previous bedroom. Behind the photo and print and propping them up are a number of books, reflective of Nicola's current interests particularly in music and in politics (taking after her father she explained) and her studies for her 'A' level examinations. These objects from childhood have not been moved to a more discreet place

Figure 4.3   The bookshelf in Nicola's room

or hidden away but rather they take up prominent positioning not only on the shelf but in the room as a whole, although often collected randomly, as Nicola says:

> It seems I just collect stuff and it just gets left around or finds a random home at some point. Only pictures have thought behind them; the other stuff I just put down. I hate rooms that are tidy or with not much going on.

For Nicola, these things are still meaningful but their placing is not necessarily deliberate. She talks about how she hates her bedroom to have bare walls and unfilled spaces and how things tend to 'drift' into that space and become a meaningful part of the 'content' of her bedroom. The photographs, however, have not just drifted in, but are deliberately and thoughtfully placed, thus evoking happy early childhood memories and acting as markers of Nicola's life and her family.

James, on the other hand, removed 'stuff from his childhood' when he redecorated his bedroom. He describes his bedroom as if it is a space that tells stories about his life now, aged 16 years. This is a clear example of how the teenage bedroom is not just functional, a means to an end, but is a highly meaningful space deliberately arranged and a space of identity. He says:

> I've stamped my personality all over it, if you'd have come 6 months earlier you would have seen stuff from my childhood. If you're going to live in your room you have to make it everything you like.

Scarlett, aged 14 years, did something similar when she moved into her older brother's bedroom after he had gone to university. This move represented a way for her to redefine her 'teenage' status leaving behind her 'tweenage' girliness (Russell and Tyler, 2002, p. 619) as she moved into a bedroom that she primarily associated with being 'grown up' because it had previously been occupied by her older brother. This represented her move both physically and emotionally towards taking up her brother's role as the oldest sibling in the household now that he was no longer living at home; she had taken up that 'position' physically through the contents of her 'new' bedroom as compared with her old. The markers in her bedroom that represented her shift up in 'age grade' were primarily related to the ways in which her gender was 'embedded' into her bedroom space and her desire to move away from the 'girly' tag that she inextricably linked with being a child:

> I don't know what colour [it will be] yet, but it's not going to be girly at all ... It's just gonna be ... I don't want any teddies in my room when I move. I just don't want it to be girly.

Scarlett defines 'girly' primarily through the materiality of her bedroom. For example, the soft peach colour of her bedroom wall, the pine furniture and her teddies on display for all to see connote, she believes, her girly childishness. Scarlett demonstrates here an inadvertent reference to a sort of 'transitional hierarchy' explicated through femininity, that is, that a move away from the things that she considered girly in her room necessitated a move from childhood to adulthood. By removing these things and painting the room a different, more 'grown up' colour Scarlett believes she can show through her space that she is older now and making steps in a highly visual manner towards adulthood. Scarlett distinguishes what she considers to be childish – her ornaments and teddy bears – and what in her current bedroom is too feminine and girly. In discussion with her friend Bethan below, it is clear to see that she had very fixed ideas about what her new bedroom was going to look like, how her bedroom space would be transformed and how she was actually going to use this larger space:

Scarlett: I used to collect little teddy ornaments, I think they're dead cute so I've got them all on my shelf. But ... I'm not getting rid of them, I'll keep them, but you know in my new room I'm not having them out ... because my room now is like peach with a big picture up ...
Bethan: ... And pine shelves
Scarlett: Yeah, pine shelves and peach ...
SL: What are your plans then for your new bedroom?'
Scarlett: I don't know what colour yet, but it's not going to be girly at all, it's just gonna be ... I don't want any teddies in my room when I move. I just don't want it girly, I want the room bright but I don't want it girly.
SL: Have you got any posters up?
Scarlett: There won't be in my new room, there is in my old room.
Bethan: Just a little picture of Sisquo!
Scarlett: Oh yeah!

Her new bedroom was to be a space in which she can redefine her identity as a teenager, as someone who is more grown up, more like an adult, which is highlighted, in her opinion, by not having posters on the wall. Posters are, according to Scarlett, associated with childhood innocence, whereas as Bethan reminds her, a small picture of Sisquo is an acceptable marker of her more mature teen age. It can be exhibited as a statement of her cultural interests and as part of her 'upgraded' cultural biography as a young woman rather than a child. Transitions also play a vital role in this type of distinction and it is in relation to this that elements of childhood cultures that are no longer used or played with are 'folded up' to occupy a new space within the home (such as a loft) where they can be stored out of sight, and thus no longer considered a symbol of current cultural biography.

In accordance with the idea that youth lifestyles are not static but are constantly shifting and are part of a young person's emerging identity, changing bedrooms around is a popular activity for both teenage girls and boys and one that often involves the moving around and reordering of, for example, dolls, teddy bears, collections and memorabilia – often things that are primarily linked to childhood. This reordering is often done in one of two ways: either through removing the objects entirely from sight by placing them in a cupboard, another room in the house or the loft, as suggested above, or by moving things to a less prominent place within the room (for example from a bedside table to the top of the wardrobe where they potentially will not be seen by friends or peers but are still visible to the occupant as nostalgic, meaningful items attached to a person, place or specific time). Figures 4.4 and 4.5 offer a good illustration of such reordering observed on a number of occasions during my research.

Figures 4.4 and 4.5 are photographs of 15-year-old Millie's bedroom, a small 'box' room that was built as an extension on the family home. Millie's bed ran alongside her wardrobe on the left hand wall of her bedroom, positioned so that she was able to watch the TV and DVDs while lying on her bed. Watching TV, especially the soaps, was one of her favourite activities in her bedroom, especially when she was not doing work for school or preparing for her exams. She said that she watched TV when she wanted to 'chill out' and relax. Millie was also an avid collector of Disney memorabilia, especially stuffed toys, and had been collecting them for a number of years. She told me how friends and family would bring her back such toys if they were ever to visit the

Figure 4.4   On top of Millie's wardrobe 1

Figure 4.5   On top of Millie's wardrobe 2

United States. Millie's practice of collecting such toys is reminiscent of Dittmar who argues:

> If people are asked *themselves* which possessions are important to them, they typically refer to a range of personally owned objects that are relatively durable, i.e. possessions which surround them for some time after they are first acquired. (1992, pp. 14–15)

Despite having had these items for a number of years, for Millie these objects still have much significance in her bedroom and were an important part of the 'biography' of who she is. The stuffed toys that can be seen in Figures 4.4 and 4.5 used to be on Millie's bed and there are a number of reasons why these have been moved and why they have been moved to this particular space. First, they were moved for practical reasons. Millie had more recently started to use her room to study in and because of the size of her room, space in which to do this was limited. To this end, while some of the toys remained on her bed, the majority were now to be found on top of her wardrobe. Second, Millie was also an avid Liverpool Football Club supporter and had collected a large amount of memorabilia in relation to the club. This memorabilia was, she said, taking up more and more of her limited space, which means that other objects and things in her room were being 'pushed out' and moved elsewhere. Unlike Scarlett above, Millie embraces the things (particularly her stuffed toys) that represent the different stages and 'age grades' in her life rather than moving them out of sight and giving them the 'girly'/childish tag. Additionally, despite her love of LFC, her overt 'girliness' is not suppressed or rejected nor does it dominate as in McRobbie and Garber's account of 'bedroom culture'; rather her femininity is intermeshed with her hobbies and interests as a football fan. This is visually represented in her bedroom, for instance, through trails of clashing colours (pink fairy lights draping over a red LFC clock), teddy bears nestling on her bed amongst LFC cushions or through her LFC scarf draped over her curtain pole, again a backdrop of a purple voile curtain juxtaposed with a light pink bedroom wall as depicted in Figures 4.6 and 4.7.

Her 'biography' within her bedroom visually represents what we might describe as a clash between the 'girly girl' and the 'tomboy', and

Figure 4.6   LFC clock and fairy lights

Figure 4.7   LFC scarf, fairy lights and purple curtain

while the LFC memorabilia clearly dominates her bedroom, we are also acutely aware of the backdrop against which this memorabilia is displayed. It can be argued that this is quite deliberate on Millie's part. Nayak and Kehily suggest that gender is 'not simply a matter of choice, but a negotiation which occurs within a matrix of social and historical forces' (2008, p. 5).

Millie's interest in football stems from a long history of LFC supporters in her family, many of whom still regularly attend matches together today. It is a culture that she has grown up in and a culture she clearly feels very passionate about. At the same time, what we see here in these photographs is a kind of 'diluting' of her love of football, not necessarily in terms of her fandom, but in the ways in which is it represented in her space. So, for example, the choice of the purple wall, the draping of the pink fairy lights, the pink beaded curtain that hangs from the doorframe and the 'lipstick' doorbell on the front of the bedroom door, all work to create this 'container' of her femininity that overlaps with her more 'tomboyish' hobbies – she has carefully articulated her cultural identities into her bedroom space. This is further enhanced by the visibility of her Disney soft toys.

Referring back to Figures 4.4 and 4.5 some interesting observations emerge with reference to the symbolic nature of teen private and personal spaces. Despite the practical issues of space in Millie's room, the 'ordering' of this space, particularly above the wardrobe, is highly significant. In Figure 4.4, to the fore is the TV, DVD player, VCR and FreeView box, while clustered behind are the Disney toys. However, as Figure 4.5 shows, the toys are not simply 'thrown' up there, but are clearly well ordered and positioned and, because of their nostalgic value, are treated with respect – put out of harm's way. This is clearly a mini-display in itself 'showcasing' the array of toys collected (or at least a sample of them). The fact that this display has been 'worked upon' by Millie demonstrates that it is still to be seen, it is still a part or 'layer' of the history of Millie and of her personal space but its positioning makes it much less conspicuous and subtle; you would probably only notice it if you were to spend time in the room or if Millie were to show you the collection. In a rather more abstract way, the collection, which started out being on Millie's bed, has been moved away from the centre of the room (where Millie's bed is) towards the door, next to which the wardrobe is placed. This brings us back to Lefebvre who has suggested that:

> Alternatively [space] may be marked abstractly, by means of discourse, by means of signs. Space thus requires symbolic value. Symbols, on this view, always imply an emotional investment, an affective charge (fear, attraction, etc.) which is so to speak deposited at a particular place and thereafter 'represented' for the benefit of everyone else. (1991, p. 141)

Following Lefebvre, one could argue that Millie's room could be understood as symbolic of how the teenager herself is emerging from her childhood into adulthood and how her space is being used to represent this. The concept of 'zoning' (Lincoln, 2004) is applicable here (explored in depth in the following chapter) as it allows us to see, through objects and items, the ways in which spaces within the bedroom are made more or less meaningful and are made to be more in line with the 'current' identity of its occupant. At the same time, the items retain some significance, albeit with some reordering. In this way, they become virtually inconspicuous but are still part of the fabric, flow and meaning of that space, contributing to the ever growing 'layers' of history within it.

Materiality and bedrooms 2: Investing in the public

> Visible boundaries, such as walls or enclosures in general, give rise for their part to an appearance of separation between spaces where in fact what exists is an ambiguous continuity. The space of a room, bedroom, house or garden may be cut off in a sense from social space by barriers and walls, by all the signs of private property, yet still remain fundamentally part of that space. (Lefebvre, 1991, p. 87)

As discussed earlier, the traditional concept of bedroom culture tends to represent it as existing in isolation from the public sphere. Although McRobbie and Garber (1975) were primarily concerned with teenage girls in domestic spaces, the seeming lack of connection to public spheres tended, they argued, to render the teenage girl passive in relation to her engagement with media and cultural artefacts and texts. Using more contemporary examples of teenage life in bedrooms it is clear that one sphere cannot be considered without reference to the other.

> My room now is more about sleep and less about living ... Now I'm older I relax here and go outside, it's still an important space, it's the room I spend most of my time in. (James, aged 16)

Curiosity about 'life in public space' started at around the age of 12 for the young people in my research sample, be it through music, sport or other leisure activities that begin to take them into the public realm of culture as I explore in the previous chapter. 'Looking older' and gaining access to bars, pubs, clubs, etc. become an attractive and necessary challenge and a 'rite of passage'. The concept of 'age-grading' (Griffin, 1993) as introduced in the previous chapter is a useful way to make sense of teenagers' introduction to the public sphere and how young people's negotiations of public and private spaces might be directed, in the first instance, by age. Unlike the more structural reinforcements of age imposed on a young person's social life that we often see in more traditional youth cultural accounts (for example, Hall and Jefferson, 1975), teenagers in contemporary settings are more likely to be directly involved in the creation of identity in cultural or social space, that is, they are active agents who not only use objects as a way of showing collective affiliation with friends or peers but also as expressions of themselves as individuals.

However, Croft (1997, p. 165) suggests that young people identify with age stratification, that they recognise that their lives are both 'shaped' and 'limited' by their age and that while encountering the physical, emotional and mental turbulence of growing up they make a number of choices about their lives as age-related 'rules' are gradually peeled away (p. 164). This makes the relationship of age and the use of space different depending on whether it is in reference to the public or private sphere as there are different sets of 'rules' operating in each sphere, despite the fact that both are predominantly controlled by adults. How, then, might one context be translated into another? In his discussion of social space, Lefebvre adds a further dimension to this when he suggests that the uses of space are restricted by the space itself. He claims 'space lays down the law because it implies a certain order – and hence a certain disorder' (1991, p. 103).

The 'materiality' of being or looking older in public leisure spaces was mostly done by my female participants and through much discussion before nights out or parties as to what to wear, as discussed in reference to Sara, aged 12, in the previous chapter. Being allowed access to public spaces is in itself a defining rite standing for responsibility and increasing independence granted to an adult. It is here, too, that we start to see shifting patterns and new signification of private, personal bedroom spaces. What we also start to see is an 'overlapping' of the uses of public and private space. Of course, the influence of public life is by no means detached from bedroom space before this point in time as the content of the average teenager's space is increasingly mediated (for example through references to particular bands or musicians, TV shows, films, even artists) and technological (TV, DVD player, PC or laptop with internet connection, iPod, mobile phones, etc.), as explored in the following chapters. But the key difference here is that there is a transition from the *influence* of public spaces and the actual *use* of them by a young person.

Dittmar argues that the construction of identity is achieved through 'possessions' (what she refers to as the '*identity of possessions*' [1992, p. 14]) and that our relationship with the possessions that surround us is influenced by the culture which a specific person is part of (see also Dant, 1999). Young people often adorn their bedroom walls (for example, with club flyers) but until they reach the stage at which they are 'allowed' access to public spaces, they can only really imagine what that actual clubbing experience would be like (and this might be supplemented with compilation CDs often produced by 'commercial' clubs such as Ministry of Sound and dancing in the bedroom with friends). In effect, this 'projection' helps shape the biography of that particular young person's bedroom and their self-created identity in that space. It is at this point that we see an overlapping of the public and the private through the space of the bedroom. No longer is the bedroom a space of wonderment and fantasy but it starts to become one in which engagement in public life becomes a reality: going to the clubs on the flyers on the bedroom wall. Gig tickets are another example of this.

One of my participants, Evie, aged 16, had stuck all the tickets of the gigs she had attended onto the doors of her wardrobe as depicted in Figure 4.8. For Evie this display was in many ways 'identity affirming' in that, as she says, her eclectic music tastes can be seen here by anyone who goes into her bedroom. The flyers ranged from contemporary indie bands such as The Fratellis, Franz Ferdinand and Captain to cover bands such as the Illegal Eagles and classic rock events such as Status Quo. The visual display of the gig tickets not only shows that Evie has been to the gigs (participation in public leisure spaces) with her friends but also displays her music tastes (identity construction and management in private bedroom spaces). In this respect, the gig tickets act as significant markers of 'cultural capital' (Bourdieu, 1989) and represent

Figure 4.8   Evie's wardrobe door and gig tickets

this meshing of participation in both the public and private sphere. They also function as a visual marker of Evie's independence to go to the gigs and are a confident display of this leisure activity and of her varying music tastes.

As a young person moves through their teens towards their twenties the negotiation of both public and private space becomes more and more significant. In many ways space shifts from being an evolving, integral, private and personal identity space to one that bridges the public and the private, and which often oscillates between the two. The visual arrangement of private space can also become more significant in terms of transitions, particularly in relation to young people who are working towards important exams. Taking exams is a crucial 'link' in the transition from school to college, university or work, and ultimately to public life. To this end, preparing for exams can lead to a young person reconsidering the role, purpose and use of private space as these are often turbulent and anxious times. Evie, for example, who was preparing for her mock 'A' level exams, talked in depth about the use of the desk in her bedroom (Figure 4.9).

Figure 4.9 Evie's desk

For Evie, the desk was a place to store her school work and books (Nippert-Eng, 1996) but it was not the desk at which she actually did school work; this she did on the dining room table downstairs that had been set up for her to study at. For Evie, it was crucial that her bedroom remained a space that was largely dissociated with doing work for school. She spoke in detail about the 'height' of the things on her desk, and was adamant that her piles of books did not go above eye level:

> I started getting a lot more work and a lot more text books and things to bring home and I had no room to put them and put them all on top of the desk ... I couldn't deal with it and I like, and when I say I like revising with my piles of subject and things, I couldn't do it; and, you know, it's just so much better having the bigger space and you have less on your desk. And having everything quite low as well, I think that's a big thing because it's below your eye line, isn't it? So when you walk in and you just want to relax, it's not kind of in your eye level, is it? It's all kind o'down there, isn't it?

This was part of her endeavour to maintain her bedroom as a space of escapism and chilling out; a space in which to read, listen to music or to play her keyboard or guitar and a space to relax with friends or her boyfriend. She had made the very conscious decision that her bedroom was to be a haven in which she could get away from her studies. This sense of creating a bedroom as a space of escapism was further enhanced through other objects in Evie's bedroom, such as numerous books, CDs, photographs, postcards, lava lamps, posters and musical instruments.

Millie, whom I talked about earlier, did the exact opposite. For her, her bedroom was one of the quietest spaces in the house, a house also occupied by her mum and dad and three siblings. For Millie, being able to escape to her bedroom was as important as it was for Evie, yet she considered her bedroom to be the place in which to get on with her school work and to prepare for her exams. It was clear to see from her bedroom that this space was also a leisure space and the size of the room meant that because there was limited space for a desk, her bed became the place where she would do work. As I discuss above, Millie liked to watch DVDs in her bedroom and, again in contrast to Evie and because her room was often a work space, she had her TV and DVD player on top of her wardrobe, above eye level. Just as Evie tries to avoid unnecessary infiltration of school work time into the leisure zone of her bedroom, so Millie minimises the distraction of leisure time in her work zone. There is a careful and deliberate working of personal and private space here, in accordance with the main activities that take place within the bedroom and in accordance with whoever else occupies the house and other activities going on. The placing of objects in bedroom space is vital in this, as demonstrated by Millie.

There is, then, as seen in the examples above, a constant interplay of public life in private space and there are multiple scenarios within which private space and its content are negotiated. These negotiations are often unique to the young person themselves and are dependent upon multiple contextual influences, both inside and outside of the home. The examples above demonstrate the active way in which young people themselves give objects meaning and how these meanings are contextualised within the spaces where they are found. Objects become part of the 'tapestry' of a young person's emerging and constantly evolving cultural history; they are intertwined. As Lefebvre so eloquently put it: 'Space is never empty: it always embodies a meaning' (1991, p. 154).

Materiality and bedrooms 3: The intertwining of private and public

> Very often independent dwelling away from the childhood home is seen to be both a physical manifestation of independence and citizenship, as well as the arena in which other adult emotional and social developments are most likely to occur. Leaving home is therefore viewed as one factor associated with the complex movement from childhood to full adulthood. (Kenyon, 1999, p. 84)

The 'embodiment' of space through material objects that I have explored so far is important in the unfolding and telling of the biographies of young people as they experience a number of transitions and as they get older and more comfortable with the public sphere as a site of their emerging adult identity (Arnett, 2004). This is not, however, an experience that is simply limited to teenagers living in the parental home as many of the discourses around bedroom cultures to date would suggest (Larson, 1995; Steele and Brown, 1995; James, 2001; Baker, 2004; Lincoln 2004, 2005, 2006; Abbott-Chapman and Robertson, 2009). Personal and private spaces can shift beyond those perimeters in many different scenarios, for example young people living in children's homes, in care or perhaps living with friends or partners or with young families as a result of a teenage pregnancy (Kehily, 2008). Also, a bedroom culture in the domestic family home is by no means universal and is in many cases unfamiliar (as, indeed, is the case for a large number of countries outside the 'western' world). The experiences of 'home' more generally can change throughout a young person's life as they come into contact with different social and cultural worlds (Kenyon, 1999, p. 84).

However, I wish to explore the ways in which the notion of private space and bedroom culture shifts when a young person makes the decision to leave the parental home, for example if they decide to go to university (Christie, Munro and Rettig, 2002). There are an increasing number of young people who are choosing to live at home while studying due to financial constraints, which brings to the fore potentially new experiences of bedroom culture on which there is research to be done. By the same token, there are also an increasing number of young people who are moving back into the family home after graduation, their transitions alluding to what Biggart and Walther (2006) quoted in Molgat (n.d.) refer to as 'yo-yo transitions'. Rather than following 'the quick and synchronized transitions to adulthood ... [whereby] [w]ithin a few years after high school, most young people had left home and gotten married, had found a job and were starting a family of their own' (Molgat, n.d., p. 125), young people are prolonging those transitions, delaying having a family or, in some cases, going to university at a later date.

Youth transitions have become more complex and less synchronised in recent years with young people making individualised choices about their futures at the expense of what was once considered a 'traditional' life-course (Roberts, 2009). This may mean moving back into the family home which has implications in terms of packing up/unpacking one's belongings and limited stretches of 'permanency' in a 'home' space making the search for the familiar crucial as Sonia, 22, explained:

> When I went to uni ... I took everything with me to make my room homely, so when I came back [for example in the holidays and at weekends] it was sometimes a bit depressing so I'd spend a lot of time at my boyfriend's if I came back at weekends. Then when I came back [after finishing her degree], my dad painted it so it felt better.

Going to university, then, I would suggest, opens up new 'private' spaces of identity for young people, outside many of the constraints of the parental home and within new social, cultural and often geographical parameters. Through a series of interviews with young people who were currently experiencing their first year at university, it became apparent that while there was a re-articulation of their domestic space in a new physical space, there was also a re-articulation of what they considered to be 'private space' and what this meant to them in a new context, a context whereby a young person has to constantly manage both their public and private identities in their halls of residence, which in themselves are both public and private spaces (Lahelma and Gordon, 2003). They are public inasmuch as they are inhabited by scores of other young undergraduates over the years, are communal spaces within which their occupants share the kitchen and sometimes the bathrooms and are spaces that become infiltrated with the noises and movements of many different people. They are private spaces inasmuch as each resident (in the majority of cases) has their own room and they can close the door behind them allowing time for privacy which is often desired.

When considering the desire for privacy and personalisation in halls of residence it is important to remember that in many cases (and in the cases of my interviewees), the rooms in halls are largely generic in terms of layout, design and furniture. Therefore, they require rather a lot of physical and emotional labour for their young occupants to make those spaces 'one's own' for that crucial first year. Lisa demonstrates this below:

> [This room] is very similar to my room at home, like I was saying before, and stuff everywhere; I feel more comfortable having things fall on me! It makes it feel more homely because every room here is exactly the same layout and I didn't like going into someone else's room and it being the same as mine so I have had to make it look different. I think it's the 6th year that these have been halls so there has been 6 other people where this has been their home so because it's my room I wanted it to be different to theirs ... it's mine and not someone else's.

For Lisa, making the room *her* room was of vital importance when she first arrived at her halls, trying to make the space different and unique and in some ways 'decorate over' any past occupants. This was going to be Lisa's space for the forthcoming year and she wanted to feel that way about her room. In order to achieve this she used a number of creative strategies, including hanging numerous photographs and collages on the walls.

The photographs and collages of photographs were highly symbolic in her new room, mainly because they evoked many different kinds of memories for Lisa (Kenyon, 1999; Back, 2005). Photographs could be found all over her room, but were particularly concentrated on the wardrobe, as can be seen in Figure 4.10.

Figure 4.10 Lisa's display of photographs

Many of her older photographs captured family times when her parents were still together, a key period in Lisa's life that she holds onto through a visual representation of a time of what she refers to as 'stability' in her life. For Lisa, the meaning of her bedroom was constantly informed by this reference point of 'when my parents were together', a point that clearly shaped the aesthetics of her bedroom. This, she claimed, often resulted in her being considered a 'hoarder' because Lisa liked to hang on to things, not let go of the past. At every point in Lisa's room there was a story to be told about a particular object or item, from the Elvis cushions that her mother had made for her to the homemade 'Sponge-Bob Square Pants' created by her brother. More often than not, these stories would be told within the context of the time when her parents were together, when she considers her world was rather more stable and were a point of reference when things were perhaps not going so well for her:

Ummm … there is pretty much everything, from when my parents were still together, there's stuff from school and then uni ones obviously, there is just pretty much everything from every part of my life like my first day at school ... I think it's because the people in the pictures, if I needed them they would be there for me and it brings back memories looking at old photos so if I am feeling lonely I can look at them and think well it wasn't always like this so it won't always be like it kind of thing it makes you feel a bit better about it.

The use of these photos was essential in the make-up of Lisa's room to create a space where she feels 'herself' and feels 'at home' in. It was her personal space and also it was (by her own admission) spilling over with objects, items and things, all of these things representing various periods in her life that she considered important and 'transitional' times (Moss and Ritcher, 2010). Moving to university was the next big transition for Lisa and she spoke of her bedroom in halls as one within which, like in other periods in her life such as her first day at school, she wanted to capture her first year studying in Liverpool. This 'ode' to her first year began with the pinning of a receipt onto her pin board of the first shopping she did as a student which can be seen in Figure 4.11 on the bottom left hand side.

Her bedroom, then, was a space within which to hold onto memories as well as to explore and capture new ones. Her bedroom space became a 'collage' through which to do this. Among what seemed like constant change in her family life, change that Lisa was resistant to, her bedroom represented a space that didn't have to change; it was hers and it was a space that she said that 'nobody could get into'. In maintaining the consistency in her life that Lisa so craves, she talked about how when she went home to one of her parents' houses in holiday times, she would take a selection of her photographs from her times at university back home with her. For example, she would take back photographs of her boyfriend or of nights out with friends as constant reminders of the good times she is having. She said that this was particularly important when staying at her mother's house. She said: 'when I go home [to my mum's house] I like to have my uni things just to remind me that I'm not going to be under my mum's watchful eye there!'

As discussed in Chapter 3, parental control is something that has historically pervaded Lisa's 'bedroom' experiences, especially those she has in her mother's house, which she concedes as being very different to when she is at her father's house. For Lisa this was the difference between having her 'own room', which she considered she had in her father's house, or just sleeping in the 'guest room' (her actual former bedroom) when she visited her mother's house. Historically, Lisa's

Figure 4.11 A 'display' of Lisa's first year at university

mother had exerted control over what things Lisa could have in her room and that resulted in many 'spatial battles' for her over the years. For example, as discussed in the previous chapter, her mum 'banned Marilyn Manson from her house and she hates a *Clockwork Orange*' so she would not let her have things such as posters related to those things in her room. Her dad, on the other hand, 'didn't care' and let her have her bedroom 'her way'. For Lisa, this meant the difference between having her own space and not having her own space. To be able to make the space look and feel how she wants it to be is what makes that space a 'home' space. Having this freedom also means that Lisa was able to represent different parts of her life in her bedroom, and she speaks of her room in halls, her life 'here' (at university) and her life 'there' at home at her dad's. For example, as discussed above, one of the main artefacts that Lisa had in her room was her collection of photographs that captured both her family life and her current time at university.

Lisa continued to talk about how in addition to her use of photographs other more discreet forms of replication took place too. For example, she has placed particular items brought from home in the same place in her bedroom in halls as her bedroom at her father's house, such as the basket with all her electrical things, like a hairdryer, 'a basket with all my belts in' and 'a basket with all my tights in which came from home – it's like everything has to be separate and it has to be in a similar place'. For Lisa, it was crucial that her bedroom was a space that could be easily replicated from house to house (as it is replicated in halls and at her dad's house). This way, through her bedroom, Lisa was able to maintain a sense of stability and consistency in an otherwise changing life.

The representation of home in halls of residence is not, however, just related to the 'visual' (Kenyon, 1999) as explored through the example of Lisa above, but there are also other techniques used by the young occupants to make their generic bedrooms, their 'containers', meaningful. As Lefebvre has noted:

> Since space is socially produced and reproduced by human activity and association, it is the site of struggle and contested meanings which are created not only by sight, but by smell and other senses – although the visual sense is dominant. (Lefebvre, 1991, p. 76, quoted in Abbott-Chapman and Robertson, 2009, p. 420)

Although this was not something talked about regularly by my participants (despite, as I explain in Chapter 2, the fact that it was a sense that dominated my experiences of young people's bedrooms), on occasions smell was talked about as a way to create a particular atmosphere or feeling in a space, often related to nostalgia and memory. In the case of young people in halls, 'smell' would act as a reminder of home. As one 18-year-old participant explained:

Erin: I did make sure that I took some personal things, you have to make sure you take personal things with you because otherwise it just doesn't mean anything; it is just a room that is empty. Like when you first come in here it feels so hollow, just cold and horrible. But I think when you have been here for a couple of weeks and got all your things out, obviously perfumes and things make it smell like home and put your home bed sheets on but when you first get here it's horrible and it's like 'oh my God why am I here?'

SL: Why do you think smell is an important thing?

Erin: It is because when you go home you go to a friend's and you are, like, God, this smells of you ... anything that reminds you of home, especially if you try and make it a bit more like your parents might do it as well it kind of makes you feel a bit more safe ... like washing powder or anything that smells something like it does at home, like your bedroom or your bathroom, and when you're here it's a bit more the same [as home].

The contested meaning of spaces like halls of residence comes from their multiple occupations and the fact that at the start of most years when new students move into them they are generic, empty, lifeless spaces or, as Erin calls them, 'hollow', 'cold and horrible'. In line of Lefebvre's quote above, the immediate goal of the new occupant is to make the space 'feel like home', feel like 'their space', and this was achieved in a number of ways according to the students that I interviewed. Here, in addition to material objects, Erin talks about smell as an important element in conjuring up feelings of home – the smell of washing powder or the smell of particular perfumes that remind her of people and places that she associated with being in the family home. For Erin, this acts as a great comfort and with familiarities come the feelings of safeness and security that one associates with the parental home. Smell, too, is important in the creation of a particular type of atmosphere in any given space, for example, burning scented candles or incense sticks helps invoke an atmosphere of calmness, relaxation, romance – whatever one is trying to achieve.

The senses, then, work to create a particular atmosphere in bedroom spaces together with the more popular 'visual' elements, discussed above in relation to the materiality of bedroom space. This is most pertinent, I would argue, for young people moving into bedroom spaces outside of the parental home, such as those moving into halls of residence whereby an individual's desire to make that space their own is twofold. First, there is the desire, as discussed above, for a standardised, generic space to feel more like 'their space', to make it feel personal to them and to remove the feeling of alienation from that space as soon as possible. A number of the young students I spoke to talked about how their first few hours at university were spent filling their rooms with their own things to make a connection to home as soon as possible.

The second consideration has to do with what that room represents to other people. In halls of residence individuals' rooms are much more 'open' that they might be in the family home, that is, an open door means other people can drift in and out and it means that you are part of 'the action', you can see what is happening on your floor. In this sense, the contents of the individual's room are very much on display for other people to see and it is often those objects, items and things that will spark off a conversation with a new friend, for example a particular poster or DVD in your collection. While the occupant has the power to 'shut the door', their rooms are likely to be subjected to more exposure to a greater number of people than they have experienced before in their domestic, home environments.

Materiality and bedrooms 4: Consuming in public, mapping onto the private

Thus far, the interplay of public and private spaces in youth culture has been obvious and in this chapter I have explored the ways in which we can understand this interplay through the context of the teenager's bedroom. What has become particularly apparent in conducting this research is the extent to which consumer habits as well as cultural and social interests have shaped in many ways how a teenager's bedroom looks and what it represents. Reflecting back upon the debates raised at the beginning of this chapter with regard to the emergence of youth as a social category within the discourse of youth as 'consumers', it has become increasingly evident that consumer habits are reflected in teenage bedroom spaces. This is not just in the case of 'traditional' activities such as listening to music, but also in what we might describe as more 'mundane' (and collective) activities, such as shopping for clothes. In recent years, it has appeared that clothing is not only an important part of bedroom culture within the context of self-exploration and identity, but that the clothes shops themselves are becoming increasingly represented visually in bedroom spaces. This appears to be done in two ways: first, through the display of the bags from particular shops as well as shop flyers, mirroring the more traditional display of, for example, club flyers; and second, through the layout of the bedroom itself to imitate the interiors of particular shops. Given the novelty of this trend in youth culture very little has been written about it in contemporary youth cultural studies. However, it was an interesting emerging area of analysis in my data.

The examples that I draw on here are from girls, which is unsurprising given that shopping is still largely a female-dominated leisure pursuit, with many of my female participants citing 'shopping with friends' as one of their favourite pastimes. It was not uncommon to see shopping bags from favourite shops 'on display' in bedrooms, such as the 'Vero Moda' shopping bags in Nina's bedroom[1] as seen in Figure 4.12.

Of the store Nina says, 'it looks really expensive but it's not too bad at all; yeah, I really like the carrier bags it makes me want to go in there

Figure 4.12 'Vero Moda' bags in Nina's bedroom

and buy stuff'. As can be seen in Figure 4.12, Nina had a number of carrier bags neatly stacked on the top of her shelf and a larger version of the bag hanging down the side signifying that this is a store that Nina buys her clothes from regularly and it was indeed a shop that she and her friends would frequent. In Figure 4.12 the bag is partially covered but enough of it is revealed to be on display for those 'in the know' (i.e. Nina's friends) and to recognise which shop it is from. The 'classic' paper material and the stripe (reminiscent of the designer Paul Smith) make the item look expensive and desirable, although this is classed as an affordable store for a student. In turn Nina's tastes look expensive and desirable also.

As I suggest above, however, the influence of clothing stores on private spaces such as bedrooms goes beyond objects from the store itself such as carrier bags or flyers, with the interior of stores being mimicked inside the bedroom itself. This was particularly the case for Sonia who, on moving back into her bedroom in the family home after a period

Figure 4.13 A collection of photo frames in Sonia's room

away at university, wanted her bedroom to look like the interiors of Topshop (Figure 4.13). She said:

> I saw in one of the Topshops [sic] they had all these frames down this massive long hallway, and I liked them, so I thought what can I do with all the pictures, because I've got quite a small room so I don't want it to be covered in photo frames everywhere, bordering on crazy old lady! (Figure 4.13)

Charlotte, aged 18, was similarly inspired by shop interiors when thinking about the inside of her bedroom and what she wanted it to look like. In the extract below, Charlotte talks about actively 'copying' the layout of stores such as Urban Oufitters that, like Topshop, have adopted what might be described as a 'thrift store' aesthetic in which the interior is composed of objects and items such as mismatched picture frames of varying designs and sizes, old photographs, eclectic wall paper and fabrics. As she says:

> Charlotte: I'm inspired by different things, like shops and stuff. Like Urban Outfitters, I like all that type of stuff, so try and copy it a bit.

SL: What is it about that store that you like particularly?

Charlotte: Erm, I just like the stuff in it, like the vintage-y home bit, it's nice stuff, like antique-y, even though it's not quite antique, some of the frames and stuff are.

SL: So is it different to other generic high street shops?

Charlotte: Well it's still high street, but it's more like a junk shop isn't it? At the same time it's quite generic and popular, but then it's not, I don't know, maybe because it's American probably, isn't it?

SL: Yeah. Why do you like that junkshop/boutique style?

Charlotte: Erm, I just like the flowers, the floor, the frames, I don't know, I just do.

The merchandise then hangs amongst this eclectic 'thrift store' design with racks of clothes seemingly holding a collection of one or two 'key pieces' inviting customers to discover a thrift store treasure.

Figure 4.14   Sonia's wardrobe door

Back in Sonia's room, the dress, scarves and pashminas hanging on her wardrobe door mimic this 'thrift store' shop interior. Here we see a collection of clothing items, neatly arranged over the top of the door, enticing you to have a look through at all the different styles and patterns. And much like you would see in the shop displays of Urban Outfitters or Topshop, a 'key item' is hung over the front of the scarves (presumably suggesting a versatile dress that can be accessorised with any one of the scarves). Sonia explains:

> I collect pashminas from all different countries I go to and different markets I go to. This one from Prague, this from a charity shop, that's my mum's from the 1940s, they're all from ... that one is from Dublin, I get them when I go on holiday and my family get me them ... I don't mind having them on display, out like that ...

Elements are taken in this example from the Topshop interior that inspired the collection of photo frames in Sonia's bedroom (Figure 4.15).

Figure 4.15   A photo frame decorated with lights

Importantly, while there are obvious outside influences verbalised by Sonia, she also makes it clear that she works these elements into what 'goes' with the space of her bedroom. She personalises this 'borrowed' design by using photographs of family and friends, creating her own collections of things such as the pashminas from trips to various different countries and also with her own artwork as Sonia studies typology as part of her university course. In this sense, she plays an active role in what her bedroom looks like and the extent to which 'the public realm' of shopping seeps into this private world.

Conclusions

While undoubtedly a functional space, a teenager's bedroom is a significant youth cultural site within which a young person is able to articulate his or her identity, be independent and exhibit certain levels of ownership and control. It is a 'container of meaning' within which its content can shift and change in accordance with fluid and interchangeable lifestyles, and in this chapter I have explored some of the ways in which we can understand the objects in teenage bedroom space, be it in the family home or elsewhere. At the beginning of this chapter I suggested that the materiality of young people's bedroom spaces could be understood using a variety of approaches, for example, by drawing on the spatial theory of Lefebvre (1991) to capture the ways in which material goods obtain meaning and the role of space in this construction. I also proposed that in drawing on the post-subcultures approach, young people's use of material goods can be understood using the concept of the 'youth stylist' (Miles, 2000) whereby the focus on consumer goods is not primarily on their symbolic meaning but rather the meaning of those goods to the individuals using them, the context of use and the ways in which they are 'styled' as part of their fluid, interchangeable identities.

I have explored this application in a variety of ways throughout this chapter. For example, I began by revisiting traditional accounts of bedroom culture, namely that of McRobbie and Garber, and critically assessed the meaning of objects in their conceptualisation of teenage girls' bedroom culture. I argued here that in fact the materiality of bedroom space was merely functional and a 'means to an end' in this account, framed within the context of romance. The space within which bedroom culture took place was somewhat detached from the activities that took place within it and there was little sense of an active engagement on the part of the teenage girl in what their bedrooms looked like or with the things in it. Further, there is no real sense of how material possessions really fitted into teenage girls' individual biographies; rather we learn how they fit into a generic romantic biography. While there is some mention of items such as record players in this account, we do not learn anything about the continued significance of these items and how they are styled and restyled into their identities and biographies beyond their teenage years. This is probably because the world of bedroom culture comes to an end once the teenage girl finds her man.

In a contemporary youth cultural setting, consumer goods in bedrooms are made meaningful in a context whereby there is a plethora of choice and a vast array of goods to choose from in making up one's identity and a context within which, in recent times, there has been a reversion of leisure activities back into the home, perpetuated by discourses of the dangerous streets that have been so prevalent in the media. Rose (1999) and Strickland (2002) note the relentless pressure placed on young people to consume, but at the same time, this context of the dangerous streets has arguably pushed parents to consume more too, on behalf of their children, who find themselves having to 'update' the leisure choices available in their homes to keep their children close by. This is complicated by the fact that each choice made is both in reference to a public identity and a private one, with consumer goods being used to 'style' this and thus in themselves becoming what Rose refers to as 'emblems of identity'.

According to my research, objects, items and things in young people's bedrooms are styled with reference to 'age' with young people making choices about the things that they have in their rooms based on, for example, their engagement in the public sphere and the extent to which they participate in it or what the objects and items in their rooms say about their childhood or emerging adult identities. Bedrooms, once generic spaces, are worked upon and 'layered' with the cultural interests of their occupants, thus historicising the space as well as representing current, emerging biographies. Bedrooms can be 'styled' by being changing around and reordering the space, for example in accordance with important transitions such as doing exams whereby the meaning of bedroom spaces needs to change to accommodate studying as well as 'chilling out' afterwards.

Materiality in bedrooms also exists in contexts outside of the family home and I drew upon the example of young people moving into university accommodation to illustrate this. In moving into a new 'home', the process of styling becomes a little more complex. In one way, material objects and items are selected that help a young person to personalise and individualise a standardised, generic space, a space within which they also want to some extent to replicate their bedrooms in the parental home using both visual and olfactory elements to create a familiar context in unfamiliar surroundings. In another way, there is the 'dual' pressure to create a space that is, on the one hand, self-referential but, on the other, a display for others who enter the space. The styling of the bedroom is further complicated when a young person moves out of the family home and then back in again. In this scenario of what has been termed the 'yo-yo transition' (Biggart and Walther, 2006, quoted in Molgat, n.d.), the bedroom needs to be worked upon to make it home again, as explored with the example of Sonia.

Finally, the materiality of bedrooms is not, according to my findings, just limited to the objects and items within them, but is also 'styled' on the stores in which some of these items have been bought. So, for example, bedrooms do not just contain items of clothing, do not just contain carrier bags branded with the stores' name or related shop flyers hanging up on display as emblems of consumption and identity, but also replicate the clothing store aesthetic as well. This in many ways represents the ultimate in consumer styling and brand power when even the space of the private is emulating your style. Further, this could even be considered symptomatic of the relentless consumer pressure placed on young people who are entering these stores on a regular basis. Youth styling thus goes beyond the semiotics of style as utilised by the CCCS. While young people are able to articulate their social and cultural identities through their selection of things in their bedroom, cementing elements of this in a context of instability and insecurity, this is also an example 'par excellence' as Rose (1999) would say, of the public realm seeping into the private worlds of young consumers and their lifestyles, thus becoming enmeshed in the production of bedroom culture.

In the penultimate chapter of this book and leading on from the discussions presented here, I move from the context of the 'material' to the 'immaterial' to consider the role of the media in shaping young people's bedroom spaces. As media rich spaces, bedrooms are spaces of media flows. In using the concept of 'zoning' I present an alternative way to theorise bedroom spaces and their uses by young people.

5
Mediating Young People's Bedrooms: 'Zoning' Bedroom Cultures

Material 'things' in bedrooms are made meaningful in a number of different ways by young people and as I considered in the previous chapter, they acquire their meaning with reference to a variety of contexts that are both unique to the life-worlds of individual young people as well as through discourses of wider 'public' cultures of media, consumption and identity that govern and shaped this materiality. In examining the meaning of things in Chapter 4, I considered the constant interplay of the public and the private realm, concluding that as a 'container of meaning' a young person's bedroom is rarely stable, its variation in content potentially being as fluid and interchangeable as the life of the young person who occupies that space. However, I argued that within this context of flux and change young people use material 'things' in their bedrooms as a way to 'cement' their identities, or elements of it, and make their personal space meaningful, and in many ways more fixed, in what feels like an ever-shifting cultural world, particularly one characterised for young people by a new social media environment.

However, a young person's bedroom is by no means just a space of material possessions and I would like to suggest in this chapter that because a young person's bedroom is a space that is also highly mediated (Livingstone, 2005, 2006), especially through the ubiquity of new media, its status as personal and private can become contested. Ultimately, though, I will argue that privacy and individuality can be achieved when the space is used or 'zoned' (Lincoln, 2004, 2005) by young people, through material 'things' as well as through its mediated elements. In doing this, I explore how the bedroom represents both the fluidity, flux and change of contemporary youth cultures, particularly through the use of new media, as well as the fixing and stabilising of young people's identities through material possessions as I discuss in the previous chapter. In this way, a young person's bedroom can be understood as a web of 'zones' within which there is a complex interplay of public and private, mediated and non-mediated youth cultures, with young people invariably finding themselves floating in between such oppositions.

In considering this idea further, I draw on Livingstone's 'revalorisation' of the private (2005, p. 12) as a binary opposite to the 'public', particularly in discourses around 'boundary blurring'. Livingstone suggests that such blurring is characteristic of contemporary new media cultures but its nature needs to be understood in more sophisticated ways beyond the more prevalent discourses of public as good/positive, private as bad/ negative.[1] Moreover, Livingstone argues that the boundaries that define public and private spheres have traditionally be understood as 'serv[ing] the interests of the cultural and political elite' (Livingstone, 2005, p. 2), an idea that is also evident in the CCCS literature. In her revalorisation, Livingstone proposes that the blurring of public and private boundaries for young people can be understood in a more constructive manner as a series of 'intersections' between the personal sphere and the public sphere (the participation of young people in common culture and social relations), the economy (the penetration of youth cultures by commercial interests perpetuated by cultures of commercialism and individualisation) and the state (governing and regulating the media and young people's uses of them). Young people, then, are not only finding themselves drifting in and out of the 'blur' between the public and private sphere, but are also suspended within the complex 'web' of these intersections in which, on the one hand, they seek their individuality and, on the other, commonality with their peers. These various states of 'in-between-ness' are by no means new in the context of new media as young people historically have always found themselves in 'zones of ambiguity' (Sibley, 1995, p. 34), that is, not quite adults, not quite children, not quite independent, not quite dependent and so on. The media, however, do play a key role in young people's lives as a tool through which to navigate many of these complexities, albeit without an awareness of how their cultural choices are legitimated by them and enmeshed within them. As Livingstone put it:

> Young people use the media precisely to push at, explore and transgress established norms of public and private. They relish the potential of the media to offer flexible tools and the free spaces within which to construct their individuality and relationships. And they are at times naively blind to the power of the media to position

themselves subtly but firmly, according to consumerist pleasures, external cultural prescriptions and powerful interests. (2005, p. 9)

In the two chapters that follow, I wish to explore in more depth the interplay, intersections and convergences between public and private spaces, focusing specifically on the role of the media in bedroom culture. Furthermore, in building on earlier discussions around young people as 'youth stylists' (Miles, 2000) and in referencing the neoliberal context of contemporary media usage, I use the concept of 'zoning' (Lincoln, 2004, 2005) to explore how we can understand young people's bedrooms as creative sites of both consumption and production (Jenkins, 2006; Burgess and Green, 2009), particularly in terms of young people's identity construction and the representation of the self in bedroom spaces.

First, however, in order to contextualise these discussions, I wish to consider the more general usage of the media in the lives of young people and the role that media have played historically in the study of youth cultures more generally. In order to do this, I begin with a brief overview of the rise of the 'young consumer' in the post-1945 period, which is traditionally associated with the emergence of distinct youth cultural groups as I discuss in Chapter 1.[2] Here I aim to set up the context from which contemporary 'media-rich' youth cultures have emerged before I move to focus more specifically on the role of the media in understanding young people's bedroom culture.

Young people, the media and everyday life

As I outlined in Chapter 1, 'youth' as a social category in the UK has traditionally been understood as emerging from the post-Second World War period in which young people for the first time were identified as a distinct social group and as 'consumers' who could be targeted in what would become a distinct 'youth' market. This was a generation of young people without the responsibilities of adulthood and with a 'significant' disposable income that needed to be spent (France, 2007). In his book *Youth in Britain since 1945*, Osgerby explores some of the reasons why post-1945 youth were a particularly notable social group and the context from which youth as a specific market emerged. He suggests that:

In the decades that followed 1945 a range of factors combined to highlight the social 'visibility' of the young, giving British youngsters definition as a distinct cultural entity like never before and convincing many contemporary commentators that post-war youth was palpably different from previous generations of young people. (1998, p. 17)

The combination of factors bringing about the 'visibility' of young people and youth culture, according to Osgerby, included significant changes in the education system, in particular the raising of the school leaving age, which meant that young people in the schooling system were prolonging their move towards adulthood, independence and employment; an expansion in youth- and leisure-related institutions, which highlighted an increased recognition of youth as a distinct group; and the introduction of National Service in the UK in 1948, which meant that for the majority of young men turning 18 years old, a two-year conscription period commenced. Given that at this time the school leaving age was 15 years and the Forces refused conscriptions of young boys under the age of 18, Osgerby notes that this led to 'a period which came to be regarded as an awkward and difficult hiatus' (1998, p. 20), resulting in young men, in particular, being left in a period of limbo, in between education and employment, and becoming 'visible' through their hanging around on the streets.

While many of these societal changes brought about the visibility of young people as a distinct social category, there were also distinct shifts in economic trends as a result of a change in the UK labour market. This, Osgerby argued, 'markedly increased the demand for youngsters' labour, with the consequence of their earning power ... significantly augmented' (p. 22). Further, an intensification of 'lighter forms of pro-duction' over 'heavy industries' (p. 22) based on Fordist style techniques meant an increased demand for young people who were considered unskilled or semi-skilled. As demand for jobs grew, particularly con-sumer goods manufacturing, so did a young person's income. For those young people still living in the family home after leaving school (and for young men waiting to do their two years' National Service), this meant a disposable income available to spend on their leisure time.

France suggests that the rise in what was perceived to be a 'youth market', based on the increasing spending power of the 'teenager' as a young worker, took place at a similar time to a 'market segmentation where industry and advertising moved from trying to understand the ordinary consumer to focusing on the lifestyle activities and consump-tion practices of different social subgroups' (2007, p. 117) with young people particularly in the 1960s being at the heart of a consumer boom and becoming identified as 'targets' for advertising and commercialism

(Miles, 2000). This, in turn, meant that the social category of the 'teenager' was no longer purely a word used to describe a particular period of the life course, but came to stand for 'a particular style of conspicuous, leisure-oriented consumption' (Osgerby, 1998, p. 36). Osgerby cites Laurie (1965) who argued that:

> The distinctive fact about teenagers' behaviour is economic: they spend a lot of money on clothes, records, concerts, make-up, magazines: all things that give immediate pleasure and little lasting use. (Osgerby, 1998, p. 37)

What is clearly presented here is the concept of the archetypal teenager with which we are still familiar as a consumer extraordinaire, always focusing on the here and now, and on those consumer items primarily associated with the spheres of leisure and entertainment. Laurie's quote also highlights the range of goods being manufactured for the teenage market in areas such as music, fashion and style, magazines as well as in the film industry, particularly in the USA when a large number of teen exploitation movies (often referred to as 'teenpics') went into production from the mid-1950s onwards (Doherty, 2002; Tzioumakis, 2006).

During the 1950s and 1960s, however, this form of teen consumption took place primarily in the public realm, rather than the 'private' as had been the case with many of these young people's parents. And while we see in the CCCS writings in the 1970s that this dichotomy between public and private could also be understood as 'gendered' rather than generational (McRobbie and Garber, 1975), until recently the spaces of consumption in youth culture have primarily been associated with the public sphere (for example, as seen in Hall and Jefferson, 1975; Hebdige, 1979; and later Thornton, 1995; Redhead, 1997; Redhead et al., 1997).

There is no denying, as Laurie (1965) testifies above, that 'the media' and their consumption pervade numerous aspects of a young person's life and have done so for a number of years and indeed related markets themselves have been a powerful force in shaping youth cultures. Arnett, in fact, notes that 'in the space of less than a century, all of these media [television, radio, music players, records, CDs] have become a central part of the cultural environment of industrialized societies' (1995, p. 520). Talking primarily about young people in the United States, he asserts that the media are inextricably intertwined into the daily lives of young people in the United States as well as in other industrialised countries and that young people are engaging in a variety of different media on a daily basis (p. 519). Indeed, a report recently produced by Ofcom stated that the average Briton was spending around seven hours a day engaged in media use,[3] be it television, radio, mobile phones or the internet.[4] Arnett goes on to note that young people are indeed 'immersed' in media cultures as a normalised part of their everyday lives, be it through watching television, listening to music, watching films, reading books and magazines and in more recent years spending substantial proportions of time using mobile technologies such as phones and the internet, particularly social networking sites (see also boyd, 2008a, 2008b; Hulme, 2009; Livingstone, 2009) and increasingly at the same time through 'multi-tasking' media, that is, engaging with a variety of media at the same time.[5]

Alongside this rapid change in young people's consumption patterns there has been also a marked shift in youth culture from one seemingly exclusive to the public sphere to one that also incorporates the 'private' realm (Livingstone, 2002; boyd, 2008a). Not only could this be a result of changing perceptions of public spaces (by parents and teenagers alike) as documented in Chapter 3, but also a result of the emergence of a 'youth media' as well as a 'new media' industry, the technologies of which have made public and private spaces increasingly blurred and ultimately interconnected (Miles, 2000; Livingstone, 2002; Osgerby, 2004; France, 2007). France suggests that the label 'youth media' has been adopted primarily because young people have been perceived as being at 'the forefront of the new media "revolution"' and that young people are the 'driving force of social change able to adopt and integrate new technologies in their lives far easier than others' (2007, p. 119). Similarly, in his extensive report 'Life Support: Young People's Needs in the Digital Age', in which a survey was completed by a range of young people aged 16 to 24 years considered to be the first generation who have grown up as 'digital natives',[6] Hulme (2009) notes that the 'hybrid' nature of young people's lives is what in many ways makes this generation of 'digital natives' stand out and as drivers of social change, as France suggests (see also Turkle, 1995; Seiter, 1999; Drotner, 2000; Livingstone, 2009). Crucially, for this generation of young people the offline world is never unconnected to the online world and there is always interplay between the two spheres. As Livingstone suggested, this is also having profound effects on the infrastructure of the domestic sphere in complementing these changing youth lifestyles as well as our everyday lifestyles more generally, with the home 'being transformed into a site of multimedia culture, integrating audiovisual, information and telecommunications services' (2002, p. 1).

To some extent, the argument about youth cultures and shifting spatialities is not new. Willis, for example, argued that the commercial world more generally 'defines the geography of young people's culture' (1990, p. 12), for example in terms of geographical location, social class and 'spending power', suggesting that the shape of young people's cultures shifts and changes. As explored earlier in this book, the public and private distinction in youth cultural discourses has traditionally brought about rigidly 'structured' theoretical accounts relating predominantly to class and, consequently, has rendered specific groups of young people either in the public sphere or in the private. Such accounts have tended to marginalise the voices, biographies, activities and spaces of young people and thus have not always proved useful in making sense of young people's participation in youth cultures today, which are significantly shaped by new media and technology and take place in a different spaces that question 'traditional' notions of public and private space.

'Traditional' bedroom culture and the media

As I established in Chapter 1 since the days of McRobbie and Garber's study on girls and bedrooms 'the media' have played an integral role in the empirical and theoretical understanding of bedroom culture. As I examined in the previous chapter, however, accounts of the relationship between bedroom culture and the media are not without their criticisms. In McRobbie and Garber's account, for instance, the role of the media is necessarily framed within the rather limiting context of a 'teeny bopper culture' and although opportunities 'for both private and public manifestations' exist through engagement in media such as magazines and music, these tend to be limited to 'the postered bedroom or the rock concert' (1975, p. 220). Furthermore, teeny bopper culture is considered synonymous with pop star adoration which, although framed as a sort of resistance to 'authoritarian structures which control the girls' lives at school' (p. 220) and as a form of 'defensive solidarity' (p. 221), ultimately places the teenage girls' interests in pop music at the superficial level of 'poster-gazing', thus rendering the teenage girl a rather passive consumer.

In considering further the relationship between the media and bedroom culture, McRobbie's analysis of *Jackie* magazine in 1991 serves as a now classic example through which one is able to ascertain the perceived relationship between (in this case) the reader and the text and how one might make sense of the ways in which different media texts contribute to the production of a bedroom culture as meaningful cultural 'space' to those engaging in it.[7] In her analysis of *Jackie*, McRobbie drew upon a set of ideological codes, informed from the outset by a dominant culture of 'femininity'. Through the coding of *Jackie*, McRobbie aimed to demonstrate how (heterosexual) 'womanhood' and 'girlhood' (1991, p. 84) was 'mapped out' through the popular teen media and 'mapped on' to the lives of their young teen readers:

> Addressing themselves solely to a female market, their [teenage girls' magazines] concern is with promoting a feminine culture for their readers. They define and shape the woman's world, spanning every stage from early childhood to old age. (1991, p. 83)

This 'map', according to McRobbie, was one that was essentially 'closed' in the sense that the uses of teenage girls' magazines, such as *Jackie*, were predominantly dictated through their pages with little room for interpretation or adaptability by the teenage girl in the 'real world'. In this sense, then, McRobbie identified a set of 'codes' operating in *Jackie* that, she argued, enforced this structured femininity. These codes were the 'code of fashion and beauty', the 'code of personal life', the 'code of personal and domestic life' and the 'code of pop music' (p. 94), all functioning within the dominant 'code of romance' and each a stepping stone of being able to 'fight to *get* and *keep*' your man (p. 101).

The code of personal life as represented by *Jackie*'s problem page 'Cathy and Claire' was presented in a 'dialogue' type of format whereby its female teen readers were invited to participate in a 'chat' about their problems with Cathy and Claire who were presented much like 'big sisters'. However, as McRobbie demonstrated, in actual fact this was a highly edited forum which meant that 'dialogue ... was not so open-ended' (p. 108). 'What appears on the page itself and what, as a result, constitutes a problem is wholly in the hands of the editors' (p. 108). While common problems were established and repeated in various issues of the magazine (generations of girls would experience the same problems), the teenage girl was by no means encouraged to deal with these issues with her friends where she would have to admit to 'not knowing things', but rather alone and in isolation and as a 'secret ritual carried out in the privacy of the bedroom' (p. 121). As McRobbie states, 'frequently letters begin, "there's nobody I can talk to about this"', which conjures up an image of a writer alone in her bedroom, 'like the housewife trapped at home', and 'the solution likewise revolv[ing] round the individual alone, not on girls organising together' (p. 109).

This image of the teenage girl in isolation not only in her bedroom but also in terms of communicating with her friends about problems and seeking advice seems a far cry from the 'culture of communication' of which the contemporary young 'digital native' is supposedly part. While, indeed, as we have seen in previous chapters, the bedroom is a place to find solitude, to escape and be alone, it is also a space that is interconnected with other spaces through various media forms. What we read from McRobbie's analyses is a rather one-dimensional, one-way flow of media cultures ending with the lonely teenage girl, although, admittedly, teenage girls' bedrooms in the early 1970s did not have the extent of connectivity with other spaces that they have had in more recent times.

In *Jackie*, the 'code of fashion and beauty' is the one that predomi-nantly 'commodifies' adolescent femininity. As McRobbie writes, 'the central concerns of fashion and beauty are the care, protection and embellishment of the body with the use of clothing and cosmetics' (p. 117). Further, however, she remarks that

> fashion and beauty are not merely concerned with the material fact of clothing and 'servicing' the body. As commodities, they are cul-tural signs and one of the qualities of these signs lies in their ability to look fixed and natural. (p. 118)

In fact, McRobbie notes that in their advice on make-up *Jackie*'s advisers suggest that 'naturalness' and supposed 'effortlessness' are highly attrac-tive to girls' male counterparts, while heavy, brash make-up or 'in your face clothing' are an instant turn off, a sign of aggression and being 'unfeminine' (p. 118).

In many ways, such 'maps of meaning' commodified 'bedroom culture' by default and, according to one of my research participants who was a teenager at the height of *Jackie*'s popularity in the 1970s, its working-class readers were in many ways 'priced out' of the market in their pursuit to be like a *Jackie* girl; despite *Jackie* advocating the purchase of cheap products, the maintenance was still expensive (not to mention ongoing) for the young teenager with perhaps only pocket money to spend or limited income from a part-time or low paid job. As Nicole, the above mentioned research participant, 44 years old, states:

> She always seemed to have plenty of disposable income and she was also ... I tell you what I suppose I also did feel, that I could never have looked like those girls anyway, because they were still a form of model ... they weren't models but a form of model, so their make-up is always right, the clothes they wear are always right and I always

felt like, you know, I was always the one in primary school whose socks were never up! Mine never stayed up and that sort of defined me, I never felt smart like a *Jackie* girl, they were somebody else, they weren't me ...

McRobbie notes that such issues with regard to the cost of a teenage girl's 'self-beautification' were recognised in the problem pages of 'Cathy and Claire', albeit fleetingly, and often without a solution as to how to deal with this issue. But such hindrances should not necessarily 'halt' a girl's pursuit for perfection as she will need to do something about it 'as best as she can through the use of cosmetics *available to her* as commodities on the open market' (p. 122; my emphasis). This has also been noted in Steele and Brown's (1995) study of adolescent room culture and the media in Tasmania. Specifically, they found that many of their female participants would buy magazines to get advice and tips on clothing and make-up and while the girls identified the importance of both, this was in the context of knowing that ultimately the 'commercial' look presented was by and large unobtainable. As one of their participants, Audrey, who was 14 years old, noted:

> I think that they use these beautiful people to sell their products because they want fat old ladies sitting at home with curlers in their hair watching the soaps to think that if they buy Loreal's [sic] 10 day formula they'll end up looking that beautiful. I think that that's really stupid because, for one, I know perfectly well that I don't look like Sybil Shepard and Loreal's [sic] 10 day formula's not going to change that. (Steele and Brown, 1995, p. 564)

What is understood by McRobbie, however, is the image of the teenage girl as a 'slave' to self-beautification, embroiled within an industry that relied on her being the 'constant consumer'. McRobbie points out, for example, that:

> Fashion depend[ed] on its consumers wanting to be up-to-date; so, for example, the sweater is advertised for autumnal walks; but the language of fashion indicates that it is not for *all* autumnal walks but for *this* season's rambles in the country. (1991, p. 118)

So while the teenage girl is seemingly operating her right to 'choice', this is practised within highly structured youth marketing strategies which, in the main, render the teenage girl rather passive. This passivity too is coded, according to McRobbie, within pop music. While acknowledging that the teenage girl did make 'active' choices over what she listened too, the 'code of pop music' was essentially framed within the context of femininity, she argues. McRobbie states that in *Jackie* 'the musical side of pop is pushed into the background and is replaced instead with the persona of the pop idol' (p. 126).

For McRobbie, the role of pop music in *Jackie* is not presented as an alternative leisure activity open to the teenage girl, as an alternative cultural pursuit (for example, one in which they are encouraged to 'create their own music' [p. 126]). Rather, pop music is seen as another opportunity for the teenage girl to 'indulge her emotions but this time on the pop-star figure rather than the boyfriend' (p. 126). This is another form of 'coercion' for the teenage girl who is encouraged not to live out her sexual and emotional development 'in public' where there is the persistent threat of her being seen as 'easy', a 'tart' or a 'slag', but enables her to live out the romantic relationship in a fantasy world created through the pages of a magazine. This is a 'safe space' for her to do this and a space in which she is able to make mistakes without anyone else knowing about it. She does not place herself in a position of vulnerability. Further, as McRobbie notes, pop stars in *Jackie* are constructed in such a way that they 'are dreamy, successful and to be adored in the quiet of the bedroom'. The meaning of pin-ups hinges, then, 'on the *unequal* relationship between the adoring fan and the star looking down on her' (p. 127).

In her discussions of *Jackie* magazine as a 'map of meaning' through which the teenage girl could follow her leisure pursuits of essentially 'finding her man', McRobbie emphasises the critical role of the teenage girl as an *individual* engaging in *personal* pursuits as an essential part of the teenage girl's leisure career. In doing this, the site of the teenage bedroom is acknowledged throughout and 'assumed' to be the ideal space within which to engage in these personal pursuits, even though it is not taking on a central role as *the* female teen space. For McRobbie, the privacy that such a space affords (although this would be compromised if girls shared bedrooms with siblings) complements the isolation required for the teenage girl as she 'trains up' to be a wife and a mother, allowing her to experiment with hair, clothes and make-up in various styles without the threat of being judged either by her friends or potential boyfriends.

The contemporary bedroom, however, while housing many of these activities for teenage girls and boys alike, is by no means limited to such pursuits and is indeed a more dynamic space where the young person is at the forefront of their cultural pursuits as well as navigating their way via multiple consumer markets and contexts. In the following section, I consider some of the more recent accounts of bedroom culture and the more dynamic ways in which the media are, essentially, woven into these cultures. Where these accounts largely differ from earlier ones is that they attempt to understand a young person's emerging sense of self within a wider context of youth culture beyond the home, something that was not considered to a great extent in McRobbie and Garber's account.

'Contemporary' bedroom culture and the media

In their study of adolescent room culture and the media, Steele and Brown explore how young people use the media as integral to their identity construction and to their social worlds (1995, p. 551). In a similar vein to traditional youth subcultural studies, Steele and Brown argue that young people 'appropriate and transform media messages and images to help them make sense of their lives' (p. 551). While cultural artefacts were appropriated by subcultural members in traditional accounts, the media, more contemporarily, are understood as a key site from which young people draw as part of their everyday cultural lives. From the band posters, to music lyrics, to the health advice in the pages of a magazine, in terms of individual identities and one's own way of making sense of the world, to their more collective identities and peer-related cultures, the bedroom is a key site within which the media can be appropriated and transformed by individuals.

Steele and Brown's research highlights the many ways in which the media have become embedded into the everyday, ordinary lives of young people. Importantly, in their study, young people's use of the media is never static and the ways in which they draw on them in the construction of their identities is circuitous and governed by young people's lived experiences, both inside and outside of the home (p. 557). This means that as young people encounter different social and cultural experiences, their media practices shift and change accordingly. What this suggests, then, as Hall (1990) has argued, is that a young person's identity is never complete but always under construction and a work in progress (cited in Steele and Brown, 1995, p. 558). As I suggest in the previous chapter, a young person's bedroom can be under construction in much the same way, reflecting its young occupant's experiences, particularly when it comes to what it represents as a space of identity. In a wider context, and again as I suggest in the previous chapter, the 'under construction' state exists for young people in society beyond the bedroom, and has partly resulted from the contemporary culture of risk and uncertainty, which has driven young people to seek out more stable spaces of identity. The bedroom, I have argued, offers this space and allows elements of their identities to become more 'fixed' and permanent (for example, through their material possessions as part of their personal identity spaces). In exploring the notion that young people's identities are always being constructed, Steele and Brown develop what they refer to as the 'Adolescents' Media Practice Model' (p. 551), a circuit model that, they argue, helps to make sense of the complexities of media practice for young people in their bedrooms as a continual process of 'selection,[8] interaction,[9] and application' (p. 551).[10]

Unlike McRobbie's analyses of *Jackie* magazine which construct the teenage girl as a consumer of media texts within the context of romantic femininity and engaged in a fantasy world alone in her bedroom, the Media Practice Model aims to capture 'the continuous process of cultural production and reproduction that characterises everyday life' (p. 556). Contrasting the 'vacuum' created in bedroom culture for teenage girls by *Jackie* magazine, young people's usage of the media, according to Steele and Brown, is typified through 'the moment to moment interface between media and teenagers who come already armed with a sense of how the world is' (p. 567). The Adolescents' Media Practice Model can, they argue, capture the 'lived experiences', of young people as they happen, thus suggesting that there is not simply one model of 'bedroom culture' that 'fits all'. Instead, bedroom cultures exist in their plurality and are unique to each and every teenager based on a range of contextual factors. Such a conceptualisation also enabled Steele and Brown to capture the life stories and emerging biographies of teenagers, not only through their discussions with them but also through the content of their bedrooms. The role of the media in this study is crucial in the making of youth identities and in the presentation of them in spaces such as their bedrooms in which artefacts (for example, posters), while still prevalent, are not only there as displays of teenage fantasies (although this still plays an important part). Rather, the media function as inspiration and for 'emulation' purposes, while also being crucial parts of the ongoing construction of the self and self expression (p. 568).

While Steele and Brown focus on the ways in which young people use their bedrooms as a space in which to mark out their changing identities and to capture their changing use of the media, Larson (1995), whose article appeared in the same issue of the *Journal of Youth and Adolescence* as Steele and Brown's paper, argues that young people's uses of the media are influenced by the spaces available to them within which they can engage with them. Further, he argues that young people's *experiences* of the media differ greatly depending on the spaces in which they use them, in both the public and private realms. Ultimately, he argues that 'it is in their solitary bedroom lives where media has some of its most significant functions, where public and private are woven together' (p. 536).

Using the specific examples of television and music and drawing on a psychological approach, Larson notes that relatively little attention (at least until 1995 when his paper was published) had been paid to the private contexts of young people's engagement in media such as music, and that most youth cultural studies had explored the role of music as part of 'public' subcultures and identities (for example, Hebdige, 1979).[11] However, Larson argues that in fact young people engage more fully in media practices when they are on their own rather than with their friends and peers and that their uses of solitary spaces are deliberate. Thus the paucity of literature on young people, music and private space seems rather out of kilter with how young people actually engage in media practices. In his paper, Larson explores the solitary use of music by young people in their bedrooms, particularly in relation to the stresses and strains of everyday life and the multiple identities of young people that, according to Larson, can be 'real', 'desired' or 'feared' (p. 535). In some ways, Larson's argument is reminiscent of McRobbie and Garber's conceptualisation of bedroom culture inasmuch as the imagination of other identities beyond the real one can be indulged in the bedroom and this can be further intensified through the use of music (although the type and sound of music is important for Larson's participants rather than just the teeny bopper elements of poster-gazing that are key for McRobbie and Garber's girls). Larson argues that the media are a key resource through which images and realisations of alternative identities are drawn. Music is also a key resource in 'real' identities, that is, in the search for what Larson describes as the 'authentic' personal self (p. 536) while television, Larson argues, is used by young people when they wish to 'turn off' from their selves and their lives for a short time.

What Larson does in his study that differentiates it from McRobbie and Garber (1975), McRobbie (1991) and Steele and Brown (1995) is that he uses 'age' as a conceptual framework through which to explore the notion of bedroom culture and the role of the media within it. 'Age' (quantified in his study as 'pre-adolescence', 'adolescence' and 'adulthood') is, he argues, a crucial indicator of media use in spaces such as bedrooms with 'pre-adolescents' spending less time in their rooms than 'adolescents' who are experiencing what may be considered much more 'fragile' and 'fragmented' identities and thus demand more private time (p. 538). As he writes:

> Adolescents *deliberately* use solitude for personal reasons and for the cultivation of the private self. I think the bedroom door is guarded vigilantly by adolescents because this private self, this self that they experience as 'more real' is tentative, fragile and thus highly vulnerable. (p. 541; original emphasis)

This search for privacy and solitary time, in turn, Larson argues, impacts on the ways in which different media technologies are engaged in by young people in their bedrooms. This might not necessarily be a choice made on the basis of wanting to be 'alone' but about having the choice to watch the programmes they want to and to engage in a 'more personal viewing experience' (p. 543) away from the rest of the family. Related to this, Larson suggests that listening to music in the bedroom is a way to 'indulge' the moods and feelings of the adolescent, for example, if they are feeling low or 'depressed' (p. 545) or reflective, as McRobbie (1991) and Steele and Brown (1995) also highlight. Larson argues that 'solitary music listening serves for more than just demarcating separation from parents' and that 'it is a context for self-exploration' (p. 544) and recalls how one of his female research participants sat alone in her room listening to 'soft rock and sometimes thinking about boys' (p. 545) or another girl sitting in her room and asking herself 'why does everyone else have a boyfriend and I don't?' (p. 545). For Larson, these uses of the music in the bedroom make the latter a 'fantasy ground for exploring possible selves' (p. 547).

What Larson's and Steele and Brown's studies highlight is the integral role of the media in the lives of young people, especially those experiencing their teenage years. Moreover, the bedroom is noted in both studies as being integral to young people's experiences and uses of the media, particularly in relation to their emerging identities, which at around this age become uncertain, fragmented and unsettled. Steele and Brown propose the Adolescents' Media Practice Model as a framework through which to capture the circuitous nature of young people's media use, while Larson argues that young people's uses of the media are intrinsically related to developmental changes and the desire for more privacy and solitude.

'Zoning' young people's bedroom spaces

In her revalorisation of the private (2005) Livingstone argues that the notion of boundary blurring is characteristic of new media cultures. In youth culture, then, when young people are constantly moving in and out of different media spaces across multiple spheres (the public, the private, the virtual), they often find themselves in this 'blurred' space where they find they do not quite fit neatly into one element of culture or another. This is part of the process of exploring one's emerging adult identity when eventually that 'fitting in' starts to become a little easier. As I mentioned earlier, this notion of not quite 'fitting in' is a classic debate in youth studies (see for example, Erikson, 1968; Griffin, 1993; Furlong and Cartmel, 2006; France, 2007) and indeed many of these studies are devoted to the exploration of how young people negotiate this 'fitting in' in various contexts and cultures. I would argue that the concept of 'zoning' is one way in which we may be able to make sense of the ways in which young people use private and personal spaces, such as their bedrooms, as sites within which they seek to work out and negotiate their own personal 'fitting in'. As a theoretical framework, 'zoning' enables us to explore how young people negotiate their way through the 'blurring' between different spheres through the cultural choices they make and the contexts in which they make them. In addition to this, and in accordance with Livingstone's notion of 'intersections', 'zoning' can capture the ways in which young people negotiate their relationship to the public sphere, their social relations, the tensions and struggles between their individualised media use and broader commercial interests, and the regulation of their personal private spaces, not just within the context of the family (as explored in Chapter 3) but also in relation to wider media cultures.

'Zoning' also captures young people's engagement in both 'old' and 'new' media. As I will demonstrate later on in this chapter, different media zones can be opened and closed through a young person's media practices, for example, when they choose to watch television, read a magazine, listen to some music, read a book, text on their mobile phones, check Facebook on their laptops, play on their games consoles or, as scholars such as Baker (2004) and Kearney (2007) argue, produce media (such as 'zines' or mix tapes). Not only does 'zoning' capture media-related practices, it is also a useful tool through which to see how the spaces in which these activities take place operate simultaneously with these practices, a theme that I have explored throughout. So while the visible, material elements of the space are integral to young people's experiences of bedroom culture, so too are the invisible flows of communication and information. In using the concept of 'zoning' one can explore how a young person's bedroom is both a container of meaning and a portal of communication, how it is a space of permanency and impermanency, of the physical and the virtual, how it is a blurred space through the use of new media and of clarity through material objects, how it is a space that is always 'under construction'.

The space of a young person's bedroom as a collection of 'zones' shifts and changes according to who is occupying that space, and so does the engagement of young people in particular cultural practices. As Larson (1995) argues, the intensity with which young people engage with the media, most significantly with music, is much greater within the private realm of their bedrooms than in other rooms in the house or with friends and peers. He argues that such a form of music listening is more 'authentic' and meaningful in this context as the music can be used according to moods, feelings, emotions and so on. Similarly, as I explore in Chapter 3 and I have explored elsewhere (Lincoln, 2004), the bedroom can become a social space, shared with friends, siblings, peers or partners and thus the ways in which the space is used in this sociable context will change accordingly. Different 'zones' will have different significances depending on who is occupying the space, but ultimately the media are embedded in all of these zones and the interactions that take place within them, as Brown and Steele have argued, in relation to young people and youth cultures more generally.

Young people use 'zones' as a form of spatial 'mediation', for example if they wish to create a specific type of atmosphere or mood, a 'sensuous and emotional ethos' (Malbon, 1998) in their bedrooms. As I discussed in my earlier work (Lincoln, 2004), bedrooms are often used as a 'sequel' to a night out within which a small group of people who have been out together may hang out, 'coming down' from the night's partying. In that paper, I gave the example of Leila, aged 16, and her friends who, on returning to one of their bedrooms after a night out, would put on 'mellow' music, adjust the lighting in the room using lamps and fairy lights as opposed to a main ceiling light, recreating the dim lighting of a pub or a club. They would also drink alcohol, smoke and talk about the night's events thus combining the visual, aural and olfactory elements of bedroom spaces. As I also noted, this social gathering in the bedroom does not necessarily remain within the room's four walls, but can 'seep out' into other (bedroom) spaces. This can be done, for example, through the use of the mobile phone on which to talk or text to other friends or partners or, as I explore more fully in the final chapter, through social networking sites such as Facebook and Twitter when the night out is transferred back into the home, then out again into the public realm through the virtual, for instance, when photographs of the night's events are posted on a Facebook page and 'tagged'.[12]

'Zones' invariably 'blur', overlap and integrate (Lincoln, 2004, 2005). However, contemporary youth cultures within which new media are intrinsically embedded are not simply shifting, movable entities that are at the disposal of young people, rather youth cultures are cross-cut by a series of intersections as Livingstone (2005) suggests. For example, as I have explored primarily in Chapter 3, young people's bedrooms are regulated and governed by both inside and outside forces. They are regulated by parents and the dynamics of the household, regulated when the space is shared, regulated by access to different types of technologies, by the activities that take place within them (and outside of them) and by the content of the rooms themselves. Furthermore, bedroom spaces are not removed from the wider commercial and consumer cultures within which youth cultures operate, and this can be detected even in the smallest details of the space, for example, through the display of a gig ticket or a club flyer, through the choices of magazines and of music. Further still, while young people today are growing up in a culture of individualisation within which their chain of experiences is unique (Roberts, 2009), the hunt for the 'authentic' self is constantly infiltrated by pervading cultures of 'broadcasting yourself' (Burgess and Green, 2009) and social networking that demand a constant 'updating' of one's status and thus identity. Such pressures, perpetuated by peer groups (and experienced by parents also) pervade bedroom cultures in other ways too, for example through the changing around of posters on the bedroom wall, having a wardrobe of latest trends and styles of clothing (objects that themselves can sometimes be on display, particularly in girls' bedrooms as I note in the previous chapter), playing the 'right' music, especially if the room is inhabited with friends, and even having the most up-to-date technology, be it a mobile phone or the latest games console. The culture of updating, then, exists both inside the physical bedroom as well as in what could be described as the virtual bedroom (Hodkinson and Lincoln, 2008) in the context of sites such as Facebook, themes that I explore in the final chapter. In the rest of this chapter, I discuss 'zoning' in action in young people's bedrooms, drawing specific attention to the role of the media, although this is, of course, inextricably linked to the context in which bedroom cultures exist and the young person experiencing this.

Zoning in action 1: Transforming space

As explored in previous chapters the 'typical' content of both young males' and females' bedrooms tended to be similar and organised according to the practicalities and limitations of the space, especially in relation to the size and dimensions of the room. For instance, all bedrooms contained a bed with most also containing a desk, a dressing table or a surface on which health and beauty products were placed, shelving, a wardrobe and other types of storage for clothing. The furniture in bedrooms was not necessarily fixed (although halls of residence are an exception to this where there are often rules and regulations about furniture not being moved around), but was moved around for a variety of reasons. These reasons included: creating space to work towards important exams, creating a divide between two sides of a bedroom when the room was shared or moving the furniture around when a room was being redecorated or having some kind of 'renovation'. As I have argued, often this changing around is related to specific ages and related transitions or perhaps when an older sibling moves out and a new, better bedroom becomes available to move into. Typically, though, there were clearly designated areas for particular activities in the bedroom, for example an area with a bed to sleep in, a dressing table to get ready in front of, a shelf containing books or items related to music such as CDs or a stereo or a docking station for an iPod or MP3 player. However, while these seemingly designated areas were visible, it was also clear that one would often 'seep' into the other, for instance, particular items from one area of the bedroom finding themselves in another part of the room or even objects from other areas of the house ending up within the confines of a young person's bedroom (Lincoln, 2004). Zones could also invade each other 'aurally', most commonly through playing music at various volumes and using different technologies, depending on the intensity of sound one wishes to achieve and the level to which the young occupant seeks privacy (for example, in using a set of headphones, the musical listening experience is intense and the noise of the household in which the listening takes place can be completely zoned out, depending on the volume). Music can be played loudly too on a stereo system, achieving more of a personalisation of the space, marking out one's territory and exclaiming through sound 'this is my space'. The high volume of music is a common annoyance for parents and often other siblings too, with the 'thudding' of the bass infiltrating other rooms in the house. I explore the role of music later on in the chapter.

To illustrate further 'zoning in action', I draw on two examples below from my research data. The first is a discussion of Nina's desk

(Figures 5.1 and 5.2). Nina was 20 years old and living in halls of residence in her first year at university. Her desk, fixed in a specific place in her room, was used as a main 'holding' point for many of the activities that took place both inside her bedroom as well as outside of it.

What is particularly interesting about the example of Nina's bedroom is that her organisation of it and the arrangement of physical 'zones' within her room in halls of residence was done with much deliberation and with the intention of recreating her bedroom back at home with her family as much as possible. In discussing this, Nina said:

> like I wanted it to be like it was at home, like that has to be there and that there because, like when I first came, I wanted to have my teddies and cushions there for it to look the same as home, that was quite important to me. It's the same kind of size, the bed's on that side of the room and the doors at the side not at the back and then I have got like a cupboard and my desk at the end, so it's a similar

Figure 5.1   The left hand side of Nina's desk

Figure 5.2   The middle of Nina's desk

layout really. I had my wardrobe and stuff piled on top of my ward-robe and some shelves ... I think it was so hard when I moved in I wanted to make it look like home and have brought the same linen with me. Like Mum wanted to buy me all new stuff but I wanted to bring my home stuff with me I wanted it to look the same, like all the same boxes and things just so that like it looked like home.

As Nina says above, the physical arrangement of her bedroom in halls of residence mimics the arrangement of her bedroom in her family home, which was fairly easy to achieve given that the dimensions of the room were similar. However, this home bedroom simulation was fur-ther achieved through the materiality of her space, summed up in her desire to bring with her the bedding that she had in her old bedroom to university, rather than replacing it with new linen, as her mother had suggested. For Nina, the familiarity of such items (for example in terms of how it feels on the skin, its smell, the association of pattern of the fabric with home) means that in a rather banal, generic space like her room in halls, she is able to recreate elements of a familiar and comfortable environment in which she feels herself and sufficiently 'at home'. This is particularly important given that it was the experience of moving away from home (a difficult transition for Nina), living independently and being in a big city (Nina had moved to Liverpool from a small Yorkshire town).

As I have argued in the previous chapter, the visible display of material possessions can 'cement' elements of a young person's identity, particularly pertinent in times of transition, change, risk and uncertainty. Nina's arrangement of her bedroom is testament to this. Additionally, her choice of photos, postcards, pictures, etc. make a statement to those who enter into her space, which is particularly important when trying to make a good first impression. However, as we shall see, her new life at university means that the use of her bedroom as a space of zones shifts and changes, opens and closes all the time, and in line with the new lifestyle that Nina has adopted, whereby she is studying, socialising with new friends and experiencing many aspects of independence, while at the same time maintaining connections with her family, friends and loved ones back at home. New media play a central role in this complex of relationships and are central to Nina's experiences of a bedroom culture that is part of her new life at university.

The small dimensions of Nina's room in the halls of residence and the fact that this is a space within which she lives out many aspects of her everyday life (for example, the bathroom is en suite, she sometimes eats in her room, she does work for university, hangs out with her friends, spends time with her boyfriend) make this dwelling experience somewhat different from living at home where, she said, she spent much less time in her bedroom and more time in other rooms such as the living room or kitchen with her sister or parents. Given the fixed location of furniture in her halls of residence room and given the number of activities that take place within it, the space has had to become multi-functional. What is captured in Figures 5.1 and 5.2 are the ways in which, across her desk, typically associated with studying and homework, there are distinct 'zones' visible, providing a useful visual example of how 'zoning' works 'in action' more generally in young people's bedroom cultures.

In my earlier work I have argued that there are significant elements of McRobbie's 'coding' of bedroom culture that remain useful when applied to a contemporary setting, particularly those that capture the everyday, mundane uses of the space. For example, the 'zones' on Nina's desk can be identified as a 'fashion and beauty zone', a 'leisure zone' and a 'doing [university] work zone' (Lincoln, 2004, pp. 103–4), with the presence of a mediated, communications zone represented by a mobile phone and laptop (not pictured). In using her desk as a 'hub' for all the main activities she partakes in on a daily basis, Nina is able to easily access and 'glide' through various aspects of her bedroom life, as well as her social and cultural life more generally. Her desk, then, visually represents more generally the instantaneous and 'of the moment' nature of contemporary youth culture when access to it in public, private and virtual spheres is at one's fingertips.

Figure 5.1 shows a common arrangement in a young woman's bedroom. The left hand side of the desk serves as a 'dressing table' chosen because it is close to the plug sockets thus ensuring that electrical equipment, namely a hairdryer and hair straightening irons, are always plugged in, the switch down and ready to use at any moment, reflecting the typical lifestyle of a student. On the desk, just above this electrical equipment are a number of products associated with 'fashion and beauty', laid out ready for days at university and nights out on the town. These items include a lipstick, eyelash curlers, dry-in shampoo, hairspray and various lotions for the hands, face and body. Next to the hairdryer and straightening irons are a cosmetic bag and hairbrushes, again neatly set up and ready to use. In her framing of the 'fashion and beauty code' (p. 117) through adolescent femininity in teenage girls' magazines such as *Jackie* McRobbie argues that such items are not simply about 'servicing the body' (p. 118) but are cultural signs held within a discourse of beauty that dominates that of banal consumerism (p. 120). For McRobbie, the consumption of such beauty-related goods in the quest for constant self-improvement should not be made obvious (p. 122), but are part of the 'beauty work' of the teenage girl who will inevitably find herself housebound (p. 124). What we see in Nina's case however, is a deliberate, visual display of such products that in many ways are there to 'service' her body, but the pursuit of beauty is not an end in itself in this bedroom space.

Clearly Nina's life is different from that of the *Jackie* girl portrayed in McRobbie's discussions and this is visually represented by her photo clock that is next to her fashion and beauty 'zone'. Photographs play a crucial role in Nina's bedroom, as reminders of home but also as visual depictions of good times with her new friends at university. They were stuck on her walls in neat horizontal arrangements, on the side of the wardrobe as well as in frames located in various places in her room. In the photo clock pictured in Figure 5.1 are images of nights out with friends, photographs of Nina with her boyfriend as well as photographs of family members: her life beyond the four walls of her bedroom and within the public sphere and all the things that, McRobbie argued, a teenage girl was isolated from in her bedroom.

The objects and things in bedrooms are not to be understood one-dimensionally, but as objects that can take on different, even multiple meanings at different times of the day, and a display of beauty products and cosmetics as seen in Nina's room is an example of this. While the items are used as part of a 'beauty' routine practised on most days of the week, the use of them has different meanings in different contexts and different levels of 'social labour' (p. 77) and so transforms them. For example, the application of make-up for a day at university or work is likely to be less elaborate than that for a night out. The products are used in conjunction with what activities Nina is going to be undertaking and is preparing for. Similarly, as I discuss above, other 'things' in bedrooms such as those used to create particular types of mood can also take on spatio-temporal meanings, for example the selection of music (as I discuss in more detail below) or lighting that can be adjusted according to the mood desired (for example, the lighting when trying to read in a room that is a bit dark is different from the lighting used to create an intimate, romantic environment). Importantly, then, objects and things in bedrooms become 'zoned' in different ways, depending on their use, by whom and when.

In Figure 5.2, the area on Nina's desk leading on from her 'fashion and beauty zone', we can see the merging and overlapping of what can be understood as 'leisure' and 'work' zones. This is depicted through the fashion magazines (*Cosmopolitan*, *Vogue* and *ASOS*) that are slotted within a pile of papers and notes laid out in preparation for exam revision. The magazines are a temporary distraction from studying for Nina and are placed in easy reach should a short respite be in order. Additionally, they give her ideas about the latest trends and fashions but Nina prefers to buy clothing from cheaper stores such as Vero Moda, the carrier bags from which she hung as a display in her room. As I discuss in the previous chapter, when asked about why she liked this particular store so much Nina commented on how the clothing looks really expensive yet is affordable. Additionally, the bags pictured in Figure 4.13 are highly appealing to Nina who expressed her desire to buy things from the store when she sees one. On the windowsill, above the pile of revision papers is a framed photograph of friends from school. The photo is placed in such a position that it can be seen by Nina while she is studying, if she needs a bit of inspiration or if she is feeling reminiscent about home. The photo provides a touch point of familiarity and serves as a legitimation of her identity and biography in a time of new experiences and change. On the right hand side lies Nina's mobile phone, always on and always in reach allowing her to have instant communication with the outside world of her friends and family, be it through texts or through phone calls ('if it's more personal stuff, we would call each other up'). Her phone here represents wider themes in contemporary youth culture, such as the continuous interplay of public and private (Livingstone, 2005), of sociality and solitude (Larson, 1995), of the multiple activities (Hulme, 2009) being undertaken or organised constantly as she drifts through multiple worlds. Switching off the mobile phone would mean instantly shutting of this access to friends and peers creating an uncomfortable feeling of being 'out of the loop' and 'isolated', not part of a network of friends and activities.

The mobile phone, in turn, is within inches of Nina's laptop (not pictured here, but caught in the reflection in the window in Figure 5.2), from which she has access to the internet. This means that she has access to social networking such as Facebook and instant messaging services such as MSN, as well as access to different types of information related to her studies. For Nina, as with many young people, having instant communication to a variety of people through a variety of means is essential and allows her to maintain multiple relationships in various different aspects of her life, an issue I discuss further in the final chapter. By using a small lamp next to her laptop Nina can create a 'tranquil' feeling in her room, especially when studying. This, she explained, was a form of 'shutting out the rest of her room' as well as other, noisy, rooms in the halls of residence, a form of 'zoning', through visual elements in her room, also enabled and intensified through her use of new media where she accesses other 'personal' spaces such as her Facebook page.

The second example I use here is a discussion of Evie's dressing table (Figure 5.3). Evie was 16 years old, living at home with her mother and father and sister aged 12. As I discuss in the previous chapter, Evie, who was an 'A' level student, was very much into music, both listening and playing, and proclaimed herself to have rather eclectic musical interests and tastes that did not always go down very well at school. As she says:

we don't have any gothic people in our sixth form, I guess if we did then I suppose it'd be us, but we're not really, maybe a little bit alternative, I dunno, it all kind of goes on your music taste doesn't

Figure 5.3   Evie's dressing table

it? That's the way people look at it, our group, really we're the geeks, to be honest!

As I discussed in the previous chapter, Evie uses her bedroom as a space within which to 'display' her musical identity, visually representing her eclectic tastes, for example through her collection of gig tickets stuck onto her wardrobe doors, between which her dressing table sits.

Evie's dressing table (Figure 5.3) shows a space devoted to 'fashion and beauty' as was the case with Nina's desk, that is similarly 'ordered' in terms of its organisation. Here we can see make-up and make-up brushes on display (rather than packed up in a cosmetics bag) alongside skin products and contact lens solution and moving across the dressing table to a container of hairbrushes in the right hand corner, next to hair products and accessories. Under her desk hangs a pair of hair straighteners, easily accessible and plugged in ready to use. Also on Evie's dressing table are two jewellery boxes. All of these items are then placed in front of a large mirror and there is a chair to sit on. In the mirror one can see the reflection of another 'zone', this time one of sleep and relaxation, with the bed scattered with cushions that Evie has made herself.

As discussed in Chapter 4, Evie's room is in many ways a 'music haven', representing many of her eclectic tastes, interests and hobbies. These interests are clearly represented alongside her 'fashion and beauty zone' and, as is the case with Nina's clock with the photographs, may act as reminders of good nights out (for example as displayed through the gig tickets) but are perhaps also reminders to herself of her identity as it is emerging; an identity, which, as I mentioned above, is also characterised by some form of resistance within the context of her school and her peers, particularly in relation to what she described as her 'eclectic' music taste. These tastes are represented and styled within her bedroom by the 1960s 'peace' imagery, beads and pendants hanging from her wardrobe cupboard door, the miniature glitter ball and fairy lights reminiscent of the 1970s hanging inside the frame of the dressing table area and the gig tickets (that demonstrate attendance at shows by old and new bands), serving as legitimations of her identity that are not necessarily displayed to peers, but can safely be displayed in the privacy of her own bedroom.

In these images, then, one can see the ways in which a young person, and in these examples, young women, organise their space in accordance with the activities that take place within their rooms and how 'zones' fade in and out of significance all the time depending on what is in the room, who and at what time. Nina's desk offers a useful, visual example of the ways in which different 'zones' integrate and merge and how physical and mediated 'zones' are necessarily 'blurred' into one another in bedroom space. As in the examples above, the role of the media is crucial in the formation of identity and in the understanding of bedroom zones working as part of the space which is, essentially, a portal of communication with the outside world, especially as young people get older and gain greater independence. Through media-related objects and items, different zones within the bedroom can be folded and unfolded instantly, and the young occupant can dip in and out of a variety of activities, whether education- or leisure-related, at any moment when the technology is available to them. What is also clear in these examples is how more 'traditional' zones interact with contemporary ones and how these remain a standard part of a young person's space, lest we should forget that it is, first and foremost, functional.

While there were exceptions to this (for example Nicole, aged 18, took a less ordered approach to her fashion and beauty zone, preferring

Figure 5.4   The sink in Richard's room

instead to 'throw' everything in a drawer in her bedside cabinet), the creation of a distinct 'fashion and beauty' zone, as seen in both Nina's and Evie's rooms, was evident in many of my young female participants' bedrooms. Variations of this appeared in young males' bedrooms too, particularly those occupying rooms in halls of residence that arguably require the production of some sort of space like this by default, especially if there is no separate bathroom. For instance, in Richard's room in Figure 5.4 we see a sink being used for functionality rather than for aesthetic appeal.

Zoning in action 2: Background and foreground zones

While the girls discussed above laid their 'fashion and beauty' zones out in such a way as to be practical and functional as well as aesthetically pleasing and an integral part of their bedroom space, the products 'on display' in Richard's room (Figure 5.4) that are literally spilling out of the toiletry bag, alongside a toothbrush, toothpaste, a scrunched-up flannel, razor, deodorant and a couple of skin care products, appear separated from the rest of his space that is dominated by his interests in music. Indeed, in comparison to Richard's 'music zone' in Figure 5.5, which shows a space set up for multiple musical pursuits as well as other new media interactions (for example, a stereo system, a laptop, a recording box, iPod, keyboard, amps, guitars and mobile phone are all visible), the sink represents functionality and necessity rather than pleasure and enjoyment; a space that is used only when necessary, rather than engaged in for any length of time, which was often the case with my female participants who would spend time getting ready for nights out or (like Sara and Natasha in Chapter 3 who experimented with clothing and make-up). I would argue, then, that this is a 'background' zone in Richard's bedroom space and that it only becomes a significant part of the space when it is necessary.

Figure 5.5 shows a specific area in Richard's room that is dominated by new technology, mostly related to music (as he says, 'I don't have use for a TV at the moment really'); the rest of his room is also organised and decorated according to his musical interests, which was also the case in his bedroom when he lived at home with his parents. Richard

Figure 5.5   Richard's music zone

was in his first year of studying music at university, played instruments (mainly the guitar, although he could play the trumpet too) and was in two bands, so music played an important role in his life. In his room, the majority of posters on his wall were music-related (Gorillaz, Kings of Leon, Jimi Hendrix and a local Liverpool jazz band called the Marley Chingus Quartet, the poster of which had been ripped down from the venue in which he had seen the band). Richard had also stuck up sheet music that he had to learn as part of his studies. As he said, 'I've got loads of sheets of guitar music to learn, so rather than sit here spending 10 minutes looking for them, they're just here. I suppose it's meant to help make me do it too, it hasn't worked yet though!' Richard also had four guitars and a mandolin in his bedroom, causing him to comment on the decreasing amount of space that he had for anything else that then tended to end up being put into a cupboard (for example clothes, books and cooking equipment). Richard said 'it does look kind of messy in this room, but it's mainly because I haven't got enough room for all my stuff ... so I've had to kind of create space'. The creation of space, as can be seen in Figure 5.5 is achieved through the piling up of pieces of kit and music-related items (for example, as seen with the stack of CDs piled on top of the stereo system, the papers sitting on top of the recording box and so on). The creation of space was also achieved through the use of guitar racks which enabled Richard to carefully store his guitars while taking up the minimum space possible. Richard went on to comment that even though his room appeared messy, his space actually had to be 'quite organised' in order for him to be able to access his musical equipment, ensure it did not get damaged and be able to find his things easily.

But by far the most 'musically intense' zone in Richard's bedroom is on his desk, the uses of which cross both into his work and his leisure 'zones' as well as into wider social and cultural realms through technologies such as his laptop (with internet access) and his mobile phone. Richard would spend the majority of his time sitting there and, as he said, 'I am surprised I haven't got a suntan on my face yet!' given the amount of time spent there, in front of the window. As mentioned earlier, everything on the desk is within easy reach for Richard and enables him to access different zones using different technologies. His guitar amp was also placed next to the desk, enabling him to 'plug in' when he needed to. In comparison with Nina's room there is practically nothing 'nostalgic' on display in Richard's room (for example, family photos or any other visual markers of his life before university such as childhood toys, as found in Nina's room). A small number of photographs, however, do exist, and these are to be found on Richard's laptop or those posted on Facebook, for example of nights out, gigs that he had played and trips with friends before coming to university:

> I've got photographs on things like Facebook, on my computer that I had before I came up. I've looked through a few times, but nothing else from home ... parties yeah, a few pictures of my old band – I'm talking about music a lot aren't I? Well we did some quite memorable concerts – well, gigs I mean – erm, and a few days out as well, erm, school trips, we went, when we went to places with my friends, we went to France one year ...

Again the context of his photos is very much music-driven, but rather than being visible all the time, Richard prefers to 'actively' find and look at them, opening and closing the 'zones' within which these images exist when he wants to. The technologies in Richard's 'music zone' are interlinked and he has also used a number of extension cables in order to ensure the equipment is either on all the time or can be easily switched on when needed without having to swap plug sockets, find the right cables and so on. It is of utmost importance to Richard that this space is instantly accessible and that he can immerse himself in his music zone in an instant, either consuming it through listening to music or producing it when he plays his guitars or uses his recording box. Additionally, other networks of communication are opened up through access to social networking sites such as Facebook where Richard can chat with friends from back home or at university although he did have a preference for phone calls if there was something that he wanted to discuss with his friends, hence the mobile phone is also in easy reach.

Music as a youth cultural form, 'zoned' in and out of bedroom spaces in different ways and to varying degrees is often dependent on what is going on in that space, as I suggested earlier. Objects and items relating to music are also meaningful in bedrooms and, as Brown and Steele also note, their role in the fabric of young people's bedroom space tends to be extremely significant. In the final part of this chapter, then, and as part of exploring the concept of 'zoning' further as an alternative theoretical approach to understanding youth cultures in private space, I consider how bedroom spaces are 'mediated' by the everyday presence and uses of music, outside of the material objects associated with it, and other forms of media, such as television and the internet. In doing this, I aim to establish the integral role of the media in the construction of bedroom culture, not just by those young people who have an avid interest in music, as discussed earlier in this chapter, but in the more mundane, everyday cultural and social lives of young people. Ultimately, I explore how the media 'resonates' at different levels, at different times and with different meanings, returning to themes such as the role of young people's social relations, consumption and individualisation and regulation that I have begun to address in previous chapters.

Zoning in action 3: Music and media zones

Music can be considered as a medium that can transform bedroom cultures, enabling mundane spaces to become 'dynamic and social' (Lincoln, 2005, p. 399). As explored previously in this chapter, music has played a central role on the construction of bedroom culture, an argument also put forward by McRobbie and Garber (1975), whether this be within the wider context of a 'teeny bopper culture' (whereby we see a rather passive teenager engaging superficially through 'poster-gazing' and the worship of the pop idol) or a more dynamic usage of music (where teenagers choose and select on the basis of their emotions, motivations and activities both inside and outside the home). Larson (1995) argues that age plays an important determining factor in how music is used in bedrooms and the extent to which music is a part of bedroom culture. He argues, for example, that young people's media habits tend to shift from visual to aural media, particularly as they move towards adulthood. For instance, watching television, a popular activity in many young people's bedrooms, whether it be purposefully watched as part of a routine or as a form of background noise or just a familiar 'flicker' on the screen that is secondary to other activities going on in that space, becomes less important with music taking on a more signifi- cant role. This, Larson suggests, is for a number of reasons, including: young people's preference for the solitary experience of music listening, the easy fit of music with other activities, and music's ability to be an emotional motivator that can conjure up different feelings, fantasies and scenarios when listened to. McRobbie (1991) makes a similar point in her examination of the 'code of pop music' as discussed above, as does Willis who argues that music is used by young people to 'create and mark off cultural and personal taste' (1990, quoted in Larson 1995, p. 542) and that a young person can 'read [themselves] into a song and temporarily inhabit its identities' (p. 542) and that as a media text music 'speaks' to young people far more successfully than television tends to do (young people relate more closely to the lyrics of a song than the plot of a television show).[13] Music enables young people to explore their identities and experiment with different genres; it is listened to as a solitary pursuit, as Larson suggests, but also as a social pursuit whereby the space of the bedroom becomes transformed into a social zone.

I first introduced James in Chapter 3 who, on reaching 16 years of age, had undertaken a 'major transformation' and 'renovation' of his bedroom, shifting what he described as a very childlike space into one that he considered more 'mature' and representative of his current interests in 'music, films, girls and sport' as well as of his teenage social position, relationships and leisure pursuits. The most significant change that he had made was the addition of a graffiti wall: an aspect of his room that James said his friends found 'very cool', was highly original and not something usually found in a bedroom. It made his room stand out from his friends' rooms. Discussions with James about his room had been particularly interesting because he was so vocal about this transformation and recognised that this change to his private and personal space was representative of a broader shift from his childhood to his emerging adulthood in both his private and public life. For example, when talking about his 'new' room he explained that if I had visited a few months earlier, I would have seen things in it from his childhood, which had now been removed as part of the renovation of the space. As James put it: 'I thought it looked babyish for my age'.

James had 'zoned' his bedroom in accordance with what he classed to be 'childish' possessions and what items should and should not be visible in his room. For example, he identifies the stuffed toys, 'things' hanging from the ceiling, the absence of posters, the colour of the room and its lighting as indicators of a younger, '12 year old' person's room, rather than of a more mature '16 year old'. In his 'new room' the stuffed toys had been replaced with pieces of technology (a television, stereo system, iPod, games console), posters had been put up onto the walls, as well as an array of photographs, postcards and flyers, all referencing different aspects of his social and cultural life, as I explain in more detail later on. What these changes represent first and foremost is James' frequent engagement in leisure activities and cultural pursuits in the public sphere and how this public life that he is increasingly leading is constantly referenced in the personal realm of his bedroom. The technology represents different communications and connects with the public sphere, while the posters, flyers and photos flag up his participation in public life as well as his active social life.

The room had also been repainted a dark shade of blue (what could be described as a bold, 'manly' colour compared to the more childlike yellow, affirming his awareness of his masculinity and confidence in

Figure 5.6   James' music zone

this) and instead of using the central ceiling light, James had bought a lamp so that he can create a more calming, ambient atmosphere in his room, especially at night, and complementing the main activities that took place in there, namely computer game playing, reading and listening to music as well as hanging out with friends or having girl-friends round. James claimed that he was unlikely to change his new room significantly in the future after the renovations, but rather he was more likely to 'just add to it. Cinema tickets on the wall, things that I like'. For James, his newly renovated space represented a more stable, long-term emerging adult identity, one that he wanted to invest in and build upon, rather than dramatically change in the future. As James stated 'I've stamped my personality all over it'. Indeed James had 'styled' a meaningful space (Miles, 2000) to represent him, to 'mark out' his identity at the age of 16, to his friends, his family as well as himself as a site of 'self-reference' (Rose, 1999), which was extremely important to him because he was starting to experience changes and uncertainties in his life. For example, James used to play a lot of sport, especially football and tennis, but had recently given up a lot of it because he had exams to prepare for and so needed to use his spare time for revision.

At the same time, his social life with his friends had become far more active as they had begun to go to bars and clubs at the weekend as well as spending time in each other's homes, especially if there was a 'free house' (no parents at home). On the 'free house' nights, James and his friends would get together, listen to music and have a few drinks, for example they would often drink beer or vodka. As James explained, 'I'm just happy to have 3 beers, not drinking to get drunk' although he explained that they would drink vodka if they 'wanted a good night'. As is clear, James is being exposed to a whole realm of new experiences that legitimate his desire to have a space that clearly marks out who he is. His use of his bedroom was very much related to the time of day, who was or was not in the house and what else was going on in his life. As he explained, 'the more free time I have, the less time I spend at home'. For example, if he was at home during the week, he would spend more time downstairs 'in the afternoon', with early mornings, evenings and nights spent in his bedroom if he was not going out or if it was a college night. James would spend time both alone in his room and with his friends and did not mind either. In fact, he said that 'everyone has days when they prefer to chill out and have time on their own'. When he has this time on his own, James chooses to listen to music, watch television or read, as well as play computer games, although his console had broken and he had to do this round at a friend's house, which means that he was playing less and doing other things in his room more. All of these pursuits open up different zones within James' bedroom, be it through a television programme, through the interaction of a computer game (particularly if played live and online) or through the fantasy worlds created by the imagination when reading a book. However, more complex examples of 'zoning' emerge when James talks about music in his bedroom.

James said that he 'liked music' but that there was 'no specific genre' that he was interested in; he just liked to listen to different things. On his bedroom wall there were posters of the bands Bloc Party (whom James had seen play live, although one of his friends 'fainted and got crushed' so he did not enjoy that gig very much), Gorillaz and a local band called Day for Airstrikes, representing some of the bands that he currently liked. James explained that he had first started listening to music at around the age of 9 or 10 years when he said that he began to relate more to music and he started to become more adventurous and curious about the types of music that he listened to. As he put it:

I was about 9 or 10 I started to get into music. You start to relate to music and understand a lot more and broaden your horizons, expand to a lot more. I got an iPod when I was around 15.

James had an iPod music collection of around 4,600 songs. This 'virtual' collection, he claimed, represented his broad music tastes more accurately than his 'physical' collection of CDs, a collection that was much smaller and, according to him, '[didn't] reflect [his] tastes, but what [he] bothered to buy'. James downloaded a lot of his music or burned CDs borrowed from his friends that he would then upload onto his iPod. As he said: 'I download a lot of music for free'. James would then link up his iPod to his stereo, featured in Figure 5.6, so that he could play his wide selection of music through his good speakers. For James, the quality of the equipment that he used in his room to play music was important and he explained that in making his room a place to relax and chill out in, he had bought 'the best TV and stereo I could afford'. Having the best that he could afford was important to James because his room was no longer just a space to 'play' as it had been when he was younger. Now it was a space in which he 'lived': 'It's the best [the TV and stereo system] because it's my room and I wanted to have the best that I could afford because I'm living in it.' So rather than just a space of 'play' as had been the case when James was a child, he was now using his bedroom to study in preparation for exams, to hang out with his friends, to relax and 'chill out' when he felt he needed some time away from studying, from his family, to listen to music, read, play computer games and so on. 'Living' in his room, which, for James, means using the space as an integral part of his everyday life rather than just for 'play' has meant a significant financial investment in the space and he used money from part-time work to buy technical equipment for his room (for example, his stereo and television), while other items such as the games console had been a gift for his birthday from his parents. Given that his bedroom had become a much more social space in which his friends would hang out, the brand of the equipment purchased was no doubt important, with his friends 'checking out' the quality of the equipment and the sound of his stereo system. In addition, knowing what is the best equipment for your money gives James extra kudos and 'cultural capital' (Bourdieu, 1989), especially amongst his group of male friends who are into the music listening experience, as I explain below.

When James hooks up his iPod to his stereo system, old and new technologies merge to give him the best music listening experience he can achieve. Simply connecting the iPod from the stereo means that James can 'zone' his musical listening experiences to achieve a highly personal and private listening experience (Bull, 2005) that no one else in the house can hear, through a set of headphones. In having this option, James can use music to complement his moods and what he is using his space for (for example doing college work, playing computer games and so on). If he just wants to relax he can 'put the iPod on shuffle and listen to new, good music, also then I'm going to sleep. I also use the 360; put it on shuffle and play.' The use of his iPod, then, whether linked to the speakers or through headphones, gives James (remote) control of his listening. This is useful if, for example, he is listening while in bed and he doesn't have to get up to change the music or switch it off. He has numerous tracks that he can flick through if he is in the mood to listen to something specific, or by using the 'shuffle' feature on the iPod a soundtrack can be created for him. His substantial music 'collection' is also useful when his friends are round. In a collection of songs of such a size it would be difficult not to find some music that all of his friends would like. Furthermore, James and his friends would often hang out on a Friday and Saturday night in each other's bedrooms, each with their iPods flicking through each other's collections. As James said, 'all my friends have their iPods and we all put them on "random", so that we can listen to new songs and check them out if we like it'.

Here, then, is 'zoning' in action in James' bedroom through the medium of music. James and his friends congregate at one of their houses and hang out in one of their bedrooms in which they usually play some music. When they get together, they usually all have their iPods with them and are 'plugged in' to them with their headphones, although just in one ear so that they can listen to the music and can speak to each other at the same time. During the course of the evening their iPods get passed around so that they can listen to each other's collections and potentially discover new tracks, bands and artists. At first, James explained, when the iPods are passed round they are on 'random'. This way, little concentration is needed to flick through artists, albums and songs and, rather than being aurally cut off from each other, the boys are able to dip in and out of a selection of songs as well as engage in conversation. It is only when they hear a track that they like that they may then listen to other tracks by the same artist, or 'check it out' later on the internet and download it. A number of 'zones' are in play in the bedroom in this scenario. First, it is the main music zone of the bedroom itself in which the boys gather. Music is selected from James' iPod for whoever wants to listen to something or otherwise it is left to play on 'random'. Zones within zones are created when the boys plug into each of their iPods, zones which are mobile and can be passed around. Each of the music zones created by each iPod are opened and closed accordingly and as the boys engage in conversation. These zones can resonate at different levels, depending on what else is going on in that space. In addition, at the same time the boys can be playing on a games console, texting on their mobiles or checking Facebook, opening and closing other mediated spheres of media and communication. In terms of this experience of listening to music in bedrooms, zones are by no means static. They are primarily controlled by the boys as they listen to and share music and are shifted in and out of accordingly.

The boys' 'zoning' music in the example above and their musical interactions are by no means engaged in 'freely' by them, but take place within what Livingstone (2005) identified as a set of intersections which govern their everyday social and cultural lives. For instance, their musical practices in this example fundamentally intersect with the public sphere, not least in the sense that the boys, who are all part of a wider peer group, are changing their iPod content frequently; updating, changing and deleting its content in line with their changing preferences, the emergence of new music and the exchange of tracks between friends on a regular basis. As James' music collection on his iPod attests, having access to a broad range of music means that there is always likely to be music that friends coming into his room or listening to his iPod may wish to listen to, which may be outside of James' specific preferences and tastes (despite his claims that as yet, there was not a specific type of music that he preferred to listen to and that he liked different bands at different times). On the one hand, there is the pressure to have common interests with peers, for example in relation to music preferences, as well as common interests in film, televisions shows, console games and so on, while at the same time developing individual tastes and preferences that may be represented in bedroom spaces, as with Evie in earlier examples. Indeed, James' display of posters of bands such as Bloc Party does at least flag some specific interests, even if this poster might not stay on the wall for very long. As James says, on listening to the music of his peers on his iPod, he will then often go and locate the track online. He does say that a lot of the music he downloads is for 'free' suggesting the use of illegal downloading sites but, on occasions, James will buy music as well. Either way, there is a continuous pressure to keep this collection 'moving' in terms of its content; to have new things for his friends to listen to, to add new tracks from their iPods and to have a sufficiently large collection of music to accommodate the range of tastes of those coming into his room. This is as well as being able to accommodate his individual changing tastes, moods and feelings that influence the way in which he listens.

In addition to this, the experiences of listening to music in bedrooms and representations of musical tastes in these spaces are also subject to a series of regulations and controls. In some ways it can be argued that music listening in private spaces such as bedrooms is regulated by who is occupying this space. Indeed, as I have explored with the examples of Lucie in Chapter 3, as well as Evie and James in this chapter, musical preferences shift and change depending on who is occupying that space, whether a group of friends are hanging out there or whether listening is a solitary experience (one that Larson [1995] argues is a more 'authentic' representation of the listening preferences of teenagers). Temporal aspects are also important, as I have suggested above, for instance, the type of music played can depend on whether the occupant is doing college work in their bedrooms in the daytime, requiring music in the background, or whether they are using the space to get ready for a night out at which point music to 'get you in the mood' is played, often at a higher volume so that the music becomes a focus point in the bedroom (Lincoln, 2004). The sound of the music then 'spills' out into other areas of the house, with parents and siblings complaining when the music is played too loud.

Music is also a way of 'regulating' shared bedroom space with its occupants stating their claim over the space using the volume on the stereo system and music as an aural statement of domination, as was the case with Chloe, aged 12 (discussed in Chapter 3). The question of who was going to play their music was a constant source of argument and fighting because having control over the stereo system, the iPod and the music playing signified the dominance of one sister in the space over another. As Larson argues, turning up music signifies that 'I exist. I have my own tastes and they are different to yours' (1995, p. 542). Additionally, Chloe found it embarrassing to have her younger sister's music playing, especially when she had friends over and wanted to spend time in her bedroom. Rather than do this, however, she will play her own music in another room.

The types of music that young people can listen to is sometimes regulated by parents, for example some of my younger female participants stated that their mothers would sometimes question their listening to artists whose lyrics are often explicit. Lisa, aged 18, said that her mum 'banned Marilyn Manson from her house' when she was younger, not allowing her to listen to the music or to display posters of the artist in her bedroom, while other parents were more lenient. Natasha, 13 years old, said that her mother did not stop her from listening to particular bands or artists who use explicit lyrics, although she did ask her not to play the music in the presence of her younger brother: 'my mum doesn't approve if it, but she doesn't mind me listening to it [Eminem], just that I shouldn't listen to it when my brother is around'. So Natasha's listening experiences are restricted by the presence of her brother which means that she either listens to her music at a volume where it cannot be heard in other rooms or she uses a portable music player such as an MP3 players or an iPod, so that it cannot be heard at all or she selects other music to listen to so that she can listen to it without getting into trouble with her mother.

Conclusions

Young people have to negotiate their way constantly through these various intersections within which they often find themselves caught in the 'blur' between the public and the private. While, on the one hand, they seek out their individuality and independence through their engagement in social and cultural activities, both inside and outside of the home, on the other, they live out their everyday lives in constant negotiation of different contexts of control and regulation, again both inside and outside the home. The concept of 'zoning' is one way in which to explore how spaces such as bedroom capture the ebb and flow of these negotiations, both as a physical space and a mediated one. In this chapter I have considered the role of the media in both traditional and contemporary accounts of bedroom culture, all of which emphasise the extent to which the media are embedded in it as well as in young people's everyday lives more generally. In critiquing the role of the media in McRobbie and Garber's concept of bedroom culture (1975) as well as McRobbie's coding of it (1991), I have presented a theoretical approach to the study of young people and bedroom culture that, I have argued, captures the dynamics and flow of young people's bedroom spaces, which are constantly 'under construction', and enables a study of the space that mimics the nature of contemporary youth culture that is constantly evolving and changing. At the same time, I have also argued that young people use media 'zones' in their bedrooms as markers of their identities, both as individuals and as part of a wider peer group, and that much like the physical space of the bedroom as explored in the previous chapter, the media can be used as a way to 'cement' elements of a young person's emerging adult identity. In the final chapter, then, I continue to explore the theme of identity construction and the representation of the self, while further exploring the complex interplay and intersections (Livingstone, 2005) between public and private spaces in the lives of young people. In doing this, I focus specifically on young people's uses of social networking sites as an extension of personal and private spaces such as their bedrooms and argue that such spaces can be understood as 'virtual bedrooms' (Hodkinson and Lincoln, 2008; Robards, 2010).

6
Mediating Young People's Bedrooms: The 'Virtual Bedroom'?

I could put the effort into MySpace or Facebook but I'd
rather go out. (James, 16 years old)

Young people's bedrooms are not just physical spaces within which their
identities can be represented but they can also be understood as 'mediated' spaces within which there are continual and complex interactions
between young people and physical, virtual, public and private spheres.
It is within the interactions of these spheres that young people often
find themselves suspended and in a perennial state of 'in-between-ness';
in the 'blur' of the many boundaries created between these spheres. In
the previous chapter I utilised the concept of 'zoning' (Lincoln, 2004,
2005) as a way in which to understand the uses of personal and private
spaces such as bedrooms by young people as spaces within which the
boundaries of public and private are inherently blurred and within
which the negotiation of these boundaries is done. As I have argued,
young people commonly find themselves suspended in this 'blur' and
thus use 'fixed' physical spaces such as their bedrooms as spaces within
which to authenticate and legitimate their identities, or at least some
elements of them, in a world of risk and uncertainty.

As I explored in the previous chapter, the role of the media in bedroom spaces, as argued, for example, by McRobbie and Garber (1975)
and McRobbie (1991), has historically been one that renders their young
(female) occupants passive, for example as articulated by McRobbie in
her application of 'codes' to teenage girls' bedroom culture whereby
an ideology of femininity is understood to be 'mapped on' to teenage
spaces and constructed by media such as the teenage magazine *Jackie*.
However, McRobbie does acknowledge the fact that despite this dominating discourse of passivity, the teenage girl is ultimately active in her

media choices, at least in making a selection over what magazines she will read, what music she will listen to and so on. In fact, as McRobbie notes, the teenage girls represents one of the most lucrative media markets and this market is one that primarily relies on young women consuming specific media products (1991, p. 6).

In a contemporary context, we see a far more dynamic and active use of the media by young people who, against a backdrop of neoliberalism (Rose, 1999; Livingstone, 2005) are able to 'select' from a vast array of media products and content and through a variety of different outlets (Hendry, 1983, 1993; Howard, 1998; Tapscott, 1998, 2008; Abbott-Chapman, 2000; Bovill and Livingstone, 2001; Livingstone, 2002, 2005; Buckingham, 2007). Typically, too, young people engage with multiple media and cultural outlets at any one time (Miles, 2000; Muggleton and Weinzierl, 2003; Reid-Walsh and Mitchell, 2004)[1] and with a variety of purposes (Hulme, 2009),[2] and this is particularly true of young people transiting throughout their teenage years, as Larson (1995) and Arnett (1995) have suggested. This is what Hulme refers to as the 'hybrid lives' of young people (especially those between 16 and 24 years old) who, he suggests, engage in a 'seamless network of communication, information, entertainment and sharing' (2009, pp. 3–4).

In the previous chapter I referred to Livingstone's 'revalorisation of the private' (2005, p. 12). Livingstone proposes that, in contemporary society, the blurring between public and private spheres through new media can be understood as consisting of three 'intersections', each of which impacts on the others. These intersections are: the public sphere, the economy and the state. As I have discussed in that chapter, young people find themselves caught in a web of these intersections and in a process of constant negotiations of boundaries that they cannot always quite penetrate. In working their way through these intersections, young people also find themselves caught between the demands for commonality with peers as well as hunting out the 'authentic', in their own individual worlds. Often the two clash and contradict and, invariably, young people 'float' between these two states, finding that their identities are always 'under construction', not least because of the shifting and changing consumer markets from which their identities are constructed. As I also explored in Chapter 5, young people find themselves caught in a constant flow of information and communication through their interactions with new media; a flow that is also constantly shifting and changing. Building upon earlier discussions, in this chapter I argue that young people's engagement with new media, and especially with social network media as the prime arenas of communication in contemporary society, forces them to 'oscillate' between what Mallan (2009) has described as 'authentic' and 'deceptive' identities on and offline. More specifically, I explore the idea that as a result of the negotiations that young people undertake in relation to the intersections proposed by Livingstone whereby public and private boundaries become blurred, young people actively seek out and use bedroom spaces as sites of their 'authentic' and 'true' identities over those created through social networking sites such as Facebook. This is because identities created in social media can be considered 'deceptive' inasmuch as they are created with a public in mind and within the constraints of various pressures (peer, commercial, parental). To this extent, then, such spaces have also been described as types of 'performance' space, akin to Goffman's (1959) proposition that in the presentation of the self people manage those identities that others readily see, and those that they do not.

I explore below how, in working through the intersections of the public sphere (for example young people's social and cultural relations), economy (youth cultures as commercial entities) and state (regulation and governance of new media) as identified by Livingstone, young people's identities are in a permanent state of uncertainty and compromise and thus, private spaces such as bedrooms, as I have demonstrated, become important spaces of identity markers, both visual and mediated. I have argued with Hodkinson elsewhere (Hodkinson and Lincoln, 2008) that, in many ways, young people's uses of social networking media are an extension of their personal and private space and that the ways in which sites such as MySpace and Facebook are being used by them do bear close resemblance to the ways in which young people use their bedrooms as personal identity spaces. As I argue below, while indeed there are numerous ways in which online personal spaces such as social networking sites are analogous to physical personal spaces, young people describe the selves presented in the spaces such as their bedroom as a 'truer', more authentic representation of them. Furthermore, such spaces have become even more important in the context of new media that is characterised by continuous self-exposure alongside the relentless pressure to always 'update' one's online profile.

Young people, then, have very specific ways in which they are using these virtual environments, which highlights the complex interplay of multiple public, private and virtual realms. Further, as Hulme (2009), Livingstone (2009), boyd (2007), Robards (2010) and others have noted, new media have become so embedded in the everyday lives of young people in the western world that are considered an intrinsic, 'natural' part of their everyday life, space and culture. Hulme, for example, argues that the internet is one of the first spaces young people go to to communicate with others and where they feel 'a sense of purpose and control' (2009, p. 4). He uses the term 'digital natives' (p. 4) through which to identify a generation which, he claims, is 'fundamentally different' from previous generations (who are often referred to as 'digital immigrants') in their use of communication technologies.[3] Hulme suggests that:

> They [16- to 24-year-olds] have grown up with digital communications and have different expectations and needs in terms with how they engage, converse and expect information to be presented. (2009, p. 4)

Robards (2010) argues that because of such complexities, unique to this generation, there is a need for ongoing research into young people's life online, particularly in relation to the use of social networking. Through their study, he argues, we are able to further understand the dynamics of young people's use of such 'personal' spaces (p. 10) that sees them constantly engaging in complex and multiple negotiations, for example, in terms of their identities, their social network patterns and 'friends', the regulation of 'private' spaces as well as their uniqueness of use of virtual worlds. In doing this, we are able to explore even further the importance of the 'private' realm in the lives of young people as significant – and complex – cultural and social spaces, which, as I have suggested so far, is still a comparatively under-researched area in youth cultural studies. This series of complex and multiple negotiations, of course, also takes place within the private space of the teenage bedroom. In this sense, a 'bedroom' metaphor has in some cases been applied as a way to account for young people's uses of various personal and private spaces online (Hodkinson and Lincoln, 2008).

Using spatial metaphors

The use of spatial metaphors in describing youth cultural activities is of course by no means new and in the context of young people and communication technologies 'private' and personal spatial metaphors have previously been applied, although primarily to what are now considered 'older' forms of internet communication. For example, Brown et al. (1994) Chandler and Roberts-Young (1998), Walker (2000) and Reid-Walsh and Mitchell (2004) are mainly concerned with individual web pages, while Hodkinson (2007) and Hodkinson and Lincoln (2008) are concerned with weblogs or online journals, which, although still popular, have been largely overtaken by social networking sites such as MySpace and Facebook as the primary online spaces through which young people are communicating with one another.

In these studies, however, it has been suggested that when considering the uses of web pages or online journals by young people, the 'bedroom' metaphor provides a useful theoretical framework. This is because it allows one to make sense of young people's use of online spaces as a 'virtual version' or extension of their actual bedroom, as a site of identity, a personal space and a private 'social space' (Hodkinson and Lincoln, 2008). Importantly, such analogies have been drawn from young people's own descriptions of their uses of these sites. For example, in the case of Hodkinson and Lincoln, users of online sites such as LiveJournal, a diary-like application in which users reflect 'upon their everyday experiences, thoughts and emotions' (2008, p. 27), would often talk about such spaces as sites of ownership and control using the analogy of their bedroom. In describing her LiveJournal page, Kate said that 'It's like being given a room – and you can furnish the way you want and paint it the way you want – and you make it your room ...' (p. 34). Kate draws on the analogy of a room to explain how her LiveJournal page starts out as a simple and generic format and layout, and is personalised and made unique through its 'furnishing'; its decoration through, for example, 'a range of images, symbols and background designs symbolic of different facets of [her] identity' (p. 35), much as a generic, four-walled bedroom space would be.

More recently, and in considering the use of social networking sites, Pearson applies the 'glass bedroom' metaphor, which she says is drawn from 'informal suggestions' by SNS users and helpfully captures the nature of private space as negotiated by users of social networking spaces:

> The metaphor can take a number of forms, but at its core it describes a bedroom with walls made of glass. Inside the bedroom, private conversations and intimate exchanges occur, each with varying awareness of distant friends and strangers moving past transparent walls that separate groups from more deliberate and constructed 'outside' displays. The glass bedroom itself is not an entirely private space ... it is a bridge that is partially private and public, constructed online through signs and language. (Pearson, 2009)

In contributing, then, to the need for constant revision that Robards (2010) stresses above, in this chapter I revisit the bedroom metaphor theme that I first explored with Paul Hodkinson in 2008 and explore this specifically in the context of social networking sites, namely Facebook and MySpace, which have been identified by my participants as the key online spaces within which they engage.[4] In accordance with my earlier discussions, I explore the ways in which young people's uses of social networking reveal the 'multiplicities' of their bedrooms, identities, performances, privacy and technology, as Robards (2010) suggests, as well as the complexities of their 'hybrid lives' (Hulme, 2009, p. 3) that sees them constantly connecting to both their physical and virtual worlds. Additionally, I focus upon the ways in which my participants drew upon the bedroom metaphor themselves, particularly when reflecting upon issues of identity construction and in light of the negotiations that young people face in the blurring between public and private spaces. In doing this and reiterating the importance of physical 'private' spaces in the lives of young people, I argue that in many ways their engagement in social networking sites has led them to rethink, to some extent, the significance of their bedrooms in conjunction with their life online and as sites within which they are able to 'pause' elements of their identities in an otherwise ever-changing, constantly 'updated' media world.

In doing this, I draw once again on a number of the themes already explored throughout this book. For example, I consider how young people's uses of social networking sites can be understood as sites of identity (and additionally sites of 'performance', as suggested by Pearson [2009] and others), how, like bedrooms, social networking space can be decorated by young people 'stamping' their identities on them, as Hodkinson and Lincoln (2008) suggest and as I explore in previous chapters, and how this is an ever-evolving process. Importantly, I draw on the ways in which young people themselves articulate different identities in different private and personal spaces and how they 'assess' such spaces in terms of what they consider to be the display of their 'true selves', the 'authentic' experience of identity construction and display (boyd and Ellison, 2007; Mallan, 2009; Sveningsson, 2009), drawing as in previous chapters on my argument that such spaces offer a context in which young people are able to 'cement' elements of their identities in a culture of 'risk' and uncertainty. Alongside this, I explore how such sites, like bedrooms, can be understood as 'transitional' spaces (as illustrated in bedrooms in Chapter 4) and how young people's uses of virtual spaces such as social networking sites can be marked out or 'hierarchical, as Robards (2010) suggests, through age and through the transitions young people are experiencing (for instance in reference to education).

I also consider how, like bedrooms, social networking sites are sites of often complex regulation and control of privacy for young people who are primarily in control (albeit with some limitations) of who 'enters' such spaces and who participates in them. Finally, I consider how such spaces as an extension of the teenage bedroom are important sites or 'portals' of communication and interaction with the outside world, capturing the constant interplay of virtual and physical spaces and the constant 'zoning' in and out of different private spaces and social networks that make up a young person's social and cultural life.

Virtual bedrooms as 'identity spaces'

As we have seen in the previous chapter, the role of media in the construction of youth identities has been crucial in the understanding of youth cultures dating back to the post-1945 period, whether in terms of the negative portrayal of young people through newspapers, magazines or television or in terms of the use of the media by young people as forms of cultural expression through which a dissatisfaction with the dominant hegemonic forces could be articulated.

Popular music is a good example of such a medium, considered in much of the youth cultures literature as a way through which young people could metaphorically and physically mark out their identities, for example, through their allegiance to particular subcultural groups as differentiated from dominant mainstream society, a form of 'boundary marking'. Christenson and Roberts (1998) argue that the use of popular music for this type of boundary marking could be done both collectively and individually:

> Popular music at once expresses, creates, and perpetuates the essential 'us–them' distinctions that develop between groups, and not just symbolically. Whether played by groups in public places or by individual teens in upstairs bedrooms, music stakes a powerful territorial claim. Indeed, it may be the most highly charged 'No trespassing' sign in adolescent society. (quoted in Druits, 2008, pp. 58–9)

I have demonstrated in previous chapters this 'territorial claim' in action in the context of a young person's bedroom when, for example, music is played loudly with the intention of it being heard in other rooms in the house by other members of the family as well outside in the street when there is literally an overspill of 'private' music consumption in bedrooms into more public domains (Lincoln, 2005). I have also demonstrated how this form of boundary marking works in relation to the materiality of bedroom space as discussed in detail in Chapter 4 whereby young people articulate their ownership of space through the objects and items to be found in their rooms.

This boundary-marking strategy does not, however, just work in relation to the claiming or 'territorialising' of particular spaces, but also works in relation to the teenagers themselves seeking out and claiming their own identities, identifying their own social and cultural boundaries. For young people, it has been argued, this is a notoriously difficult thing to do because the concept of identity tends to be one that is very porous and is a movable feast in those turbulent teenage years of self-discovery. For example, Sibley refers to this period as an 'ambiguous zone', whereby a young person finds themselves 'oscillating' between what appear to be clearly defined boundaries of childhood and adulthood:

> Adolescence is an ambiguous zone within which the child can be variously located within the child/adult boundary and can be variously located according to who is doing the categorising. Thus, adolescents are denied access to the adult world, but they attempt to distance themselves from the world of the child. (1995, pp. 34–5)

Music (as well as other media forms), then, has traditionally been understood within the context of youth culture as offering young people a way in which they are able to express their identities. Additionally, the role of the media more generally can be understood as offering young people more than just a mode of 'expression' in regard to the territorialisation of space or the articulation of personal identity. In much of the girls' culture literature, for example, the role of the media has been celebrated as offering young women in particular not just sites through which their identities can be expressed but sites within which identities can be 'performed' (Bloustien, 1998; Baker, 2004; Harris, 2004a, 2004b; Kearney, 2007; Druits, 2008) or, as Frith proposed, allowing an individual to experience the 'self in process' (1996, p. 109) given that the identities of young people are in constant flux and always being evaluated and revised reflexively, as Goffman (1959) suggested.

A number of scholars exploring contemporary youth identities have drawn on Goffman's notion of the 'presentation of self in everyday life' (1959) as an analytical tool with which to explore aspects of the postmodern self and identity (for example, see Chandler and Roberts-Young, 1998; boyd, 2007; Buckingham, 2007; Abbott-Chapman and Robertson,

2009). For Goffman, the foundation of this notion was the concept of 'dramaturgy', which is based on the perspective that all human actions are in some way a type of 'performance' (1959, p. 28) and that this 'performance' is shaped by a variety of factors, such as where it is taking place and who the audience is. Goffman conceptualised what he called 'front' and 'back stage' performances. Of 'front stage' performances he says:

> It will be convenient to label as 'front' that part of the individual's performance which regularly functions in a general and fixed fashion to define the situation for those who observe the performance. Front, then, is the expressive equipment of a standard kind intentionally or unwittingly employed by the individual during his performance. For preliminary purposes, it will be convenient to distinguish and label what seem to be standard parts of the front. First there is the 'setting' involving furniture, décor, physical layout, and other background items which supply the scenery and stage props for the spate of human action played out before, within and upon it. A setting tends to stay put, geographically speaking, so that those who would use a particular setting as part of their performance cannot begin their act until they have brought themselves to the appropriate place and must terminate their performance when they leave it. (1959, pp. 32–3)

Despite this concept being over fifty years old, it is still considered to have much currency in understanding human interactions and, although not without its criticisms, has received a renewed interest, particularly in the context of young people and the internet in more recent times (for example, see Brown et al., 1994; Chandler and Roberts-Young, 1998; Crowe and Bradford, 2007; Hodkinson and Lincoln, 2008; Pearson, 2009) as well as in the context of teenage bedroom culture (see, for example, Abbott-Chapman and Robertson, 2009). Goffman's 'front stage' and 'back stage' analogies work well in the context of young people, particularly when trying to make sense of their uses of public and private spaces, although they do not necessarily help to make sense of the 'multiplicity' of youth spaces within which we potentially see a number of performances being undertaken at any one time.

For Goffman, 'front stage' performances are regulated by the social and cultural constructs of 'public' spaces and there is a system of codes and conventions that regulate these spaces within which the 'performance' takes place. The individual 'performs' accordingly and, additionally, the performance is 'standardised' within those conventions. In his reference to the materiality of the setting, Goffman suggests that the objects and items to be found 'front stage' are largely those 'fixed' by the geography of the space and, accordingly, we 'perform' in a specific way, dictated by that space. Goffman argues that we play up to the setting of the 'performance', are ultimately in control of the 'performance' and may modify it accordingly, and then once the 'performance' is complete we leave the setting only to engage in other 'performances' in other spaces. Conversely, 'back stage' the 'performance' becomes regulated by the codes and conventions of the 'private' realm within which the individual has arguably more control, for example, over the material setting and thus over his or her performance to an audience (or not) of his or her choosing. This, one could argue, allows for the presentation of the self in a more authentic fashion, in that it is one that is seemingly freer of the codes and conventions to be found in 'front stage' spaces.

However, drawing on Goffman's work within a contemporary youth context of social media, Pearson argues that there is a collapsing of front and back stage whereby the boundaries of public and private space are increasingly blurred. This means that potentially elements of a public front stage performance may seep into a back stage performance and vice versa, as she demonstrates through the 'glass bedroom' metaphor (2009). Additionally, as Robards (2010) in his discussion of Pearson (2009) suggests, the notion of the audience also changes as it may be one that is primarily imagined and, alongside that, the setting and performance becomes imagined too. Further, I would suggest, in social networking sites such as MySpace and Facebook there is an interplay of both the 'real' and the 'imagined' audience. In reference to Facebook, in particular, 'friends' are largely those acquaintances with whom one is already friends in real life, which suggests that, in this respect, there is a 'real' audience in this virtual setting. However, more typically on sites such as MySpace, 'friends' are less likely to be made up of 'real life' friends and, as boyd points out in her discussions of the significance of 'top 8' on MySpace, 'friending' becomes a numbers game, even a popularity contest, representative of the young users' status which then forms the 'backbone for networked participation' (boyd, 2006).

In a world of 'look at me!' (Orlet, 2007; Mallan, 2009), of participatory culture and self-exposure (Jenkins, 2006; Burgess and Green, 2009), the concentration on the presentation of the self and on spaces of 'performance' and identity for young people has, arguably, never been greater. Abbott-Chapman and Robertson, who draw on Goffman's front stage/back stage analogy in their discussions of teenagers' favourite places, argue that for many young people choosing a 'performance space' is often defined by the ways in which they wish to express their understanding of the boundaries of a particular space. So, for example, they suggest that certain spaces, such as the home, might be considered a 'representation of inter-generational power relations' (2009, p. 419); thus teen spaces within the home may be marked out as different from the spaces of parents or siblings and articulated through their decoration and through their use.

Social network media as extensions of bedrooms

So far in this book, discussions of 'marking out' of identity spaces have largely focused on the interplay of public and private spaces and the levels of independence that such marking out affords. For example, in Chapters 3 and 4 I explored the ways in which a teenager's curiosity for and interaction in cultural and social life in the public realm goes hand in hand with a perceived increased independence (for example being allowed 'into town' with friends and no parents). This suggests that their identity in public space (the front stage) in some ways eclipses their identity in private space (the back stage), which is often considered to be the 'experimenting ground' in terms of their identity construction. As this becomes more stable, their identity performances shift somewhat into the public realm. However, while the public realm seemingly affords greater status and markers of independence for a young person, there is by no means a complete separation of the public and the private realm as spaces of identity and there is, of course, an interplay between these spheres as I have argued in the previous chapter. Hall suggests:

> The actor's subjective perceptions and meanings of physical space are in constant interaction and re-formation because space, like time, is culturally defined, with perceptual and physical boundaries related to action. (1969, quoted in Abbott-Chapman and Robertson, 2009, p. 420)

The meaning of a bedroom, as with many other spaces in a young person's life, is often highly subjective and the meaning of that space to them is constantly changing and gaining new and different meanings. How they perceive the meaning of those spaces is wrapped up in a number of complex, often ambiguous, layers and is part of the 'web' within which a young person holds a precarious position in society as neither children nor adults working their way through a series of 'intersections' (Livingstone, 2005), as explored in the previous chapter. Their uses of these spaces, too, demonstrates their conceptualising of 'boundaries', particularly between public and private life and when these boundaries may be crossed, defiantly or not, or become blurred. 'Boundary crossing' is not merely a physical manoeuvre from one space to another but is also a metaphorical manoeuvre and new media and communication technologies are playing a key role in the reformulation of cultural and social boundaries for young people. As Abbott-Chapman and Robertson suggest:

> Cultural understandings of 'free time' and 'free space' are rapidly changing. Because use of ICT creates new subjectivities as interactive tools, web 2.0, web 3.0 and now web 4.0 enable users to explore ideas and test theories of self in constantly changing spaces. These help to increase 'confusion and incoherence in our sense of space and time, in our maps of places where we live, and in our ideas about the times in terms of which we organize our lives' – confusions and distortions that are expressed in post-modern pop culture. (2009, p. 422)

Abbott-Chapman and Robertson suggest that new communication technologies have brought about a reconceptualising of 'the subject' by young people whereby they experience multiple identities which, they argue, can be understood as 'interactive tools' through which they are able to engage with multiple, ever-changing social and cultural spaces. In other words, their multiple subjectivities allow them to interact in a variety of different spaces often at the same time. Similarly, Mallan argues:

> When young people construct profiles on MySpace or participate in blogs or play video games, they actively construct shifting social positions to interface with the global reach of a distributed network. These subject positions are not just ontological states, but inevitably entail a politics of visibility both at the personal level and at the level of the technological infrastructure. (2009)

In drawing on the 'bedroom' metaphor (for example, Pearson's 'glass bedroom'), one is able to explore the notion of multiple and shifting subjectivities in the context of young people using social networking sites such as MySpace and Facebook. In Pearson's metaphor, the walls of the bedroom are made of glass. Inside the four glass walls, she suggests, 'conversations and intimate exchanges' take place (2009), and those who are inside the glass bedroom will be aware that there are friends, acquaintances, etc., passing by the bedroom walls in some way all of the time (afforded entrance through 'friending', as boyd, 2008a and Robards, 2010 would argue). The walls, despite being made of glass, give some sense of the separation from the outside world and an additional sense that, theoretically, with the metaphorical bedroom door shut, the conversations taking place within the bedroom cannot be heard by those outside it. However, the glass walls afford some level of visibility, which may be outside the control of the occupant, unless they were to draw a metaphorical curtain over the glass walls which would privilege complete invisibility or privacy. Nonetheless, the glass material used to construct the walls does not assure complete privacy over the space. As Pearson says, drawing on Goffman, there is a blurring of the front and back stage; of public and private. So how do young people negotiate the complexities of using multiple personal and private spaces online and offline, particularly in relation to privacy, as well as manage their ever-shifting subjectivities that adapt and change in accordance with the context of each space?

In exploring this question, I draw on research data collected in the later stages of this research project between 2007 and 2009. In the original study, conducted in the early 2000s, there were very limited discussions of the use of the internet generally and virtually no discussions of what is now termed social media. Since the mid-2000s, however, there has been an explosion in the uses of social networking sites,[5] which led to a series of questions in addition to those concerned with the traditional bedroom, and which were based around young people's uses of online personal and private spaces. This stage of the research involved ten young people, four males and six females, between 16 and 24 years old, which, coincidentally, is the age classification drawn on by Hulme (2009) in his discussions of the 'digital native', the first generation to have grown up with the internet. My participants included both those still at school and those studying at university, and while there was some diversity in terms of the sample including young people from both working- and middle-class backgrounds, all of my participants were white and British growing up in the north of England. Therefore, the discussions below are to be considered as explorative, considering the notion of 'bedroom culture' beyond its traditional definition and potentially setting up a context for more research to be conducted into the notion of the virtual bedroom as young people's engagement in online spaces evolves.

As Livingstone (2005), boyd (2008a), Robards (2010) and others have argued, a young person in contemporary times is embroiled in a rather complex and sophisticated process of shifting social positions. These shifting positions in the context of personal and private spaces, such as bedrooms and social networking sites, are dependent, Pearson (2009) suggests, on a 'politics of invisibility', whereby there are levels or 'hierarchies' of privacy that are constantly being negotiated. For example, young people who are now considered to be multi-site users in terms of their social and cultural lives are very adept at navigating multiple 'interactions' online (Hulme, 2009), be it interactions with friends in networks, with various identities or with issues of privacy as they constantly drift across the boundaries of public and private life.

Discussions with my participants revealed that young people themselves are by no means oblivious to this complex series of negotiations and in some cases demonstrated a real awareness of this constant shifting between the public and the private, particularly when thinking about how their uses of social networking sites might in some way be considered an extension of their 'physical' bedroom space:

SL: Did you kind of see [social networking sites] as an extension of your personal space?

Charlotte: MySpace was more like that, 'cos you could change the layout and background how you wanted it and put music on it whereas Facebook isn't really like that, everyone has the same layout.

SL: What did your MySpace page look like?

Charlotte: It had all vintage frames and vintage wallpaper and some songs but I can't remember, I used to change them. But with Facebook you can't. You can change your photos and I do that and my profile picture.

The first thing to note here is how 18-year-old Charlotte's discussions resonate with Pearson's (2009), Mallan's (2009) and Abbott-Chapman and Robertson's (2009) suggestions that young people are engaged with constantly shifting and changing subjectivities. What Charlotte reiterates here in her discussion of social networking sites as 'extensions' of her bedroom space is the importance of being able to change the layout of one's pages, despite the restrictions that might be set by the site (for example, Facebook pages follow a uniform and generic layout, and therefore each and every page can only be personalised through the text and images uploaded). MySpace, on the other hand, as Charlotte notes, affords a greater engagement in making the space one's own and making it unique in relation to other people's pages. What is clear, though, is her desire to be able to update and change her profiles.

Second, the layout of Charlotte's MySpace page described above mimicked the decoration of her bedroom space in which she had a number of vintage-style photo frames of varying shapes and sizes covering one of her bedroom walls creating a vintage type feel to her bedroom (further marked out with the placement of three flying ducks on another wall). When I asked Charlotte if this was a conscious 'mapping' of one space to another she replied 'I don't think it was deliberate'. Despite Charlotte talking on a number of occasions about her using photographs, particularly on Facebook, and how she liked to change them and upload new ones capturing a constant process of updating and upgrading of an online identity, this appeared to be a comparatively more 'static' experience in her physical bedroom (Hodkinson and Lincoln, 2008) within which she also had a number of photos displayed of family and friends as well as a number of empty frames that she had not yet put photos in. Charlotte said that she had not done this because 'I just don't want to put any photo in, I want to save it for a good one and then I'll change them [the old photos in frames to new photos]'. Similarly, some of the photos in frames around her bedroom had photos in that she had not got round to changing or she had left up because she liked the picture (for example, a photograph of her with her ex-boyfriend on a holiday together of which she says 'I like that one so I thought I'd keep it up').

Charlotte's use of multiple versions of her own personal space is in this instance defined by 'immediacy' that appears to be quite different depending on which space her photographs are being displayed in. When being displayed on her Facebook profile, for example, photographs such as those used for her profile picture have to be updated regularly – photographs are an identity 'currency' that needs to be quickly and regularly changed and exchanged, a theme I explore in more detail below in relation to young people's posting on Facebook pages. The ease of use of the Facebook interface, in particular, means that uploading a photograph is quick and easy and can even now be done through mobile phones and pretty much at any time if one has access to the internet. This is as opposed to taking a photograph, printing it off and then putting it into a frame on display in the physical bedroom and means that the photos she selects for her profile can be made from an array of photos uploaded to the site which are easily interchangeable.

Like Charlotte, Richard, 18 years old, talked about decorating his MySpace page and had a similar reticence to Charlotte about the customisation of this page as an extension of his physical bedroom space but again referred to the desire to change basic elements considered by him as important identity markers such as music (representing current tastes and interests in particular bands and artists – a key use of MySpace) and photographs (for example, those of nights out, profile picture, etc.):

> I tried it a couple of times, to customise it, but I don't really have the patience for it, so I did it once, I think. I don't really put my stamp on things too much, apart from you can add music to your profile, sometimes I change that, and the pictures I'd put up. I don't do a lot of typing on there though ... I don't do the small talk thing.

Richard's practices highlight the varying levels of 'identity' work undertaken in the regulation of different social networking spaces (Robards, 2010). For example, he talks about how the work involved in creating and maintaining a MySpace profile particularly was rather time consuming and meant that he would use just the very basic functions of his page to maintain some sense of a continuously 'up-to-date' representation of his self. By just changing 'markers' such as music and photos (and much like changing posters around in a bedroom) Richard is able to maintain his profile and keep it 'current'. This issue of rather labour-intensive 'maintenance' of MySpace is reiterated by Sonia, aged 22:

> I think Facebook is more geared to ... I don't know, I don't think it's the ... MySpace you could do a bit more and represent yourself more like changing your wall and stuff, but I think that might be a bit fussy and people's pages take ages to load whereas on Facebook everyone's page is the same, you actually know who's adding you because you see the full name, but on MySpace you can call yourself what you like.

For Sonia, the representation of herself on her MySpace profile is more akin to the ways in which she uses her bedroom. Its format, she suggests, affords more room to be creative and to personalise one's profile making it unique and marking out the profile as 'her space'. For example, Sonia is able to change the background 'wallpaper' of her profile, as one might change the colour of the bedroom walls or the posters and pictures that adorn them. The 'stuff' Sonia refers to is in relation to, for example, the use of music that can be uploaded (a feature not found on Facebook), photographs and 'badges', and emotions reflecting mood which all go some way to personalising the page further and which lend themselves to a culture where the desire to 'ever change' and update is rife. However, this ability to decorate one's profile in elaborate ways does not necessarily lend itself to the 'immediacy' aspect of social networking and the desire to be able to access and check such sites in a moment. Sonia suggests that one of the flaws of MySpace is the time it takes to upload some people's profiles, an unwelcome feature that stalls a sense of immediacy associated with such sites: that your profile is available at the click of a button and you are instantly connected. The generic format of Facebook makes it less 'content heavy', and more user friendly, enabling her to connect with friends quickly which, for Sonia, is the main purpose of Facebook.

Drawing on the metaphor of the bedroom once again, what we see in the above discussions is what Hodkinson and Lincoln (2008) refer to as both practical and symbolic control of social networking profiles in the maintenance of online identities. However, in the context of social networking both practical and symbolic control are influenced by issues of usability and temporality. This suggests, then, that the extent to which young people engage in the production and maintenance of an online profile relies on easy access and simplicity of use. Like bedrooms, online profiles are designed to be spaces that young people can 'access' with ease and the contents of which can be changed or updated with similar ease, although this is somewhat complicated through the desire to constantly have and view updated profiles in maintaining one's online presence. This typically captures yet again the tensions of 'in-betweenness' that young people encounter as they move through to adulthood and, as Mallan suggests, that oscillation between various states is also now characteristic of young people's activity online:

> Young people's engagement with online communities and SNS oscillates between opposing states of exhibition and inhibition, self-exposure and self preservation, authenticity and deception. (2009)

The oscillation between authenticity and deception as noted here by Mallan, and by Sessions (2009) elsewhere, is an interesting one in the context of the 'virtual bedroom' and is a theme that my participants spoke of in their discussions around their uses of social networking sites as 'private' domains alongside the more traditional 'private' domain of the bedroom. In those discussions, a number of the participants identified different forms of 'self-presentation' within these two realms with a number of them suggesting that their 'physical' bedrooms were what they considered to be spaces that allowed for a 'truer' (in the words of Lisa, aged 18) or the more 'authentic' representation of their 'real' selves. This was because unlike the 'glass bedroom' metaphor of social networking where the glass walls mean people can 'peer in' at any time and the interior of which can potentially be seen by a large number of people (as with MySpace) or accessed by a sometimes large number of friends,[6] the concrete walls of the actual bedrooms did not allow all the above to happen.

However, as we have seen in previous chapters, it is not possible to claim that traditional physical bedroom spaces are purely spaces for the exploration of the occupant's own self-identity; they too are spaces that can be seen by other people, especially by family or friends. Because of this, then, it can be argued that such spaces are always to some extent 'on display' to others and for others and the young occupant is likely to be mindful of this in relation to the look of their bedroom and the things they have on display within it. This is particularly pertinent for older teenagers who may encounter moving into bedroom spaces outside of the home, for example into halls of residence, where the display of identity for others to see becomes a crucial 'starting point' in the creation of friendships and associations. As I explore in Chapter 4, the selection of 'things' from home to go on display in this new space is crucial – not only as markers of the things that a particular individual likes but also in terms of having reminders and memories of home.

This form of displaying for others by young people in private spaces relates in some ways to Bourdieu's notion of 'cultural capital' (1989) as certain items, objects and things (for example, posters or flyers) found in teenagers' bedrooms are there as 'signifiers of cool' (Danesi, 1994), visible signs of being 'in the know' or being au fait with the latest music or film trends without necessarily liking those things very much or considering them to be playing a key role in who they are (Lincoln, 2004). Such 'things' may hold rather superficial value, a form of symbolic exchange and currency to a young person rather than a value that is meaningful and that would be associated with a more 'authentic identity', what they consider to be a more genuine version of themselves. A number of my participants identified this 'superficial' version of identity as being more akin to their use of social networking sites, where, they argue, there is more pressure to engage in forms of display that represent a certain 'coolness' rather than a real statement of 'this is who I am'. For example, Lisa, 18 years old, says:

> In my room I don't care with what's here, I don't even care, I don't know ... that I've got pants, that I've got a High School Musical

calendar – it's not me but I don't care that it's there, it's a practical thing, I couldn't get rid of it … Always on Facebook and MySpace I'm very careful of what I say so that I don't get called an Emo or I don't get called whatever, just so it doesn't look that way, but in my room I don't care …

…………

I think that my room is the more 'natural' me …

In addition to this, Erin, 18 years old, says:

I think it's all a bit fake in a way because everyone is trying to make themselves look the best of what they are and I just don't think it's, it's very, I mean, if you have been chatting to someone that you have known for years then it's a bit different than if you're having a bit of a gossip. I think it's hard to be yourself on it unless you have known someone for so long …

Another 'temporal' aspect is drawn upon here by Erin who demonstrates this oscillation between the 'authentic' and the 'deceptive'. She suggests that interactions with people who are simply social networking friends rather than real-life friends who one has known for some time can be rather 'fake', a performance through which you can present yourself in any way that you choose and, as Erin suggests, presenting 'the best of what [you] are' rather than presenting one's real self as you would when interacting with people who are your friends in real life. Some further analogies can be made to the context of the traditional bedroom, as the caution Erin practises in using sites like Facebook is similar to that which would be practised in her interactions with friends in the private space of her bedroom and it is unlikely that she would use this as a space to interact with people that she does not know too well – it is a space to share with friends.

This authentic/deceptive oscillation not only works at the level of the individual in marking out their personal, social and cultural interests but also works at a more communal level in that their profile or 'personal' spaces exist as part of a wider social network of which their friends and peers are also part. It could be argued, then, that there is a network of 'peer pressure' that operates around individual profiles that places its young user in an 'in-between' position. An example of this 'peer pressure' on social networking sites is in relation to Facebook where there are a number of 'groups' that one can join covering a vast array of social and cultural interests as well as many being rather random and arbitrary. In joining any group you are able to find out about different events, activities, nights-out, etc. organised by those groups. A young person may join such a group, not because they are particularly interested in it but because their friends are part of it and it ensures that they are not left out of this particular social loop; there is pressure to stay connected to those networks of which one's friends and peers are part. The groups that one joins are then displayed on their profile page, so the individual would be associated with that group (which would also be displayed on the 'newsfeed' page for all your 'friends' to see) and it becomes a virtual marker of their Facebook identities.

Photo displays and 'tagging'

As we have seen in previous chapters, photographs play a key role in the construction of a young person's identity in their bedroom spaces, often being seen as worked upon displays of family and friends, instigators of treasured memories, representations of nights out and parties, mementoes and reminders of 'home'. Photographs contribute significantly to the uniqueness of a teenage space and are items that both remain fixed symbols and capture the ever-changing identities of a young person. In the context of social networking photographs are just as important sources of identity display and, as some of my participants have demonstrated in the discussions above, are one of the main things that need to be updated and changed regularly on one's profile.

Photographs on sites such as Facebook are a prime example that highlights some of the multiple and complex issues around identity, performance and privacy that young users have to negotiate constantly and also captures well the interplay of public and private life in social networking spaces (Lenhart and Madden, 2007). Below is a discussion with Lisa, 18 years old, that encapsulates many of these complexities:

SL: And have you got lots of photographs on your Facebook?

Lisa: Yeah, I've got absolutely loads, but if I'm on a night out and I take my camera, no one is allowed to see or delete the photos and they all go on Facebook.

SL: Right, OK.

Lisa: No matter what. You can end up with, one night I ended up with like 200 photos from one night out and they all went on and everyone got tagged in every photo they were in. And there were some attempts to un-tag them but they weren't coming off, and there some hideous ones of me but they were part of that night, they had to be there kind of thing.

SL: Yes, yeah. So why do you think that's so important to you?

Lisa: I think it's down to my lack of ability to delete things again. Like when I went to America I took 1000 photos, I was there for two weeks and took 1000 photos and videos and I wouldn't delete any of them.

SL: Yeah?

Lisa: I only chose selected ones to get printed, but they're all there on CD, there's like 4 CDs. But I couldn't delete any of them 'cos they're all; they all meant something, part of that.

As explored in Chapter 4, Lisa is an avid collector of photographs and her bedroom was covered in photo collages that included photographs of both family and friends. Lisa considered her bedroom space to be the place within which she 'documents' her ongoing life and, at the time of her interview, this was her life in the first year at university. In Chapter 4, Lisa talks about how she is a 'hoarder' and does not like to throw anything away and that any item or object, from a shopping receipt to a demonstration banner, can tell a story about her life and her experiences as they unfold.

This ethos is very much carried into Lisa's world of social networking, a space which she describes as being heavily populated with all sorts of applications, text and images. In the discussion above Lisa talks specifically about how, on nights out, she documents the whole evening by taking photographs, then, as soon as she arrives home, she uploads the images onto Facebook. In many ways, Lisa goes for the most 'authentic' representation of the night possible in her claim that there is no editing process with the photographs before they are put on display. She says that, even if there are particularly awful photographs of herself, she will not edit them out of the 'album' of that evening out. Lisa, in addition, is keen for her 'friends' to further experience and share the evening's events and she embarks on the process of 'tagging' whereby all of the people featured in the photographs will be named.[7]

The ability for anyone to 'tag' others on Facebook is often considered to be a form of 'privacy invasion' given that the controls over one's profile as a personal and private space are somewhat displaced. If a person is 'tagged' in a photograph, then the application of the tag will appear in the newsfeed that is accessible to all of one's friends and then to friends of friends if a comment about a photograph is made, thus showing up on friends of friends' newsfeeds. This then becomes a very complex process for the individual to manage and compromises to some extent the display of identity on such sites. As Erin notes below, because a user is aware that 'privacy' on Facebook is not necessarily assured because of functions such as 'tagging' this often leads to rather 'fake' representations of the self through a profile constructed in the knowledge that it may be seen by those other than one's friends:

> I don't know, I find it really, I don't know, like having my photo taken, I don't like that side of it especially on Facebook because you can tag people, I hate it. I just think that if I wanted to tag I would, I don't want to see that. I don't know, I think most of it is public; I don't think there is much of it that is private, you can decide who your friends are but people can still look at it. I like using it to speak to my friends and it's nice to see photos of everyone. (Erin, 18 years old)

Photographs on social networking sites are also important markers capturing the interplay of public and private life and representing different 'performances' in different domains. For example, in his study of young people, drinking cultures and the news Nicholls suggests that:

> Social networking sites have become an important element of drinking culture among many young people. In particular, the uploading and 'tagging' of photographs taken during drinking sessions is commonplace. (2009)

In previous work, I have suggested that the bedroom is a space which acts not only as a 'prequel' to a night out with friends, as a space used to get ready for the night's events but also one that acts as a 'sequel', as a space within which to hang out with friends after a night out, to chill out, drink, smoke, listen to music, talk about the night's events, etc. (Lincoln, 2004). In expanding upon this, the social networking site can be understood as an extended domain of the bedroom also to be used as a sequel space as it is a space within which to further 'relive' the night's events through the uploading of photographs and perhaps through 'chatting' through Facebook or other messaging services with friends about the night out they have just had (as the example of Lisa above demonstrates). Through the use of social networking sites, a mediated form of post-night out socialising may still take place but does not necessarily require the physical participation of friends; rather their virtual participation. So through Facebook those friends who have shared a night out may post photographs on their pages that are then open for comment by other 'friends' on the site, who may comment on each other's 'walls' on the night's proceedings, perhaps chat using the chat facility embedded into the site, gossip about the night's events, arrange other nights out and so on.

The concept of immediacy is again pertinent here, particularly as posting photos of a night out can be done as soon as one gets home (and even before that), creating a sense of being 'virtually there' again. Photographs of nights out with friends can be selected and posted within moments of gaining access to the site, and through the mobile phone could even be uploaded on the way home. These are memories that are quickly shared, because once a group of friends embark on another night out those photos will be replaced by new ones, while the old ones will become 'archived' on one's profile page, much like the historical layering discussed in Chapter 4 in relation to the materiality of bedroom spaces.

However, not all of my participants used Facebook in such ways and in fact in a number of cases they were rather vocal about their dislike for such forms of display use:

I find it a bit weird, not just, you know, how certain people use it to put pictures up and show what they're doing and show them in a certain way. (Lucie, 20 years old)

Yeah well, I don't put too many things up [on Facebook], but other people do, and you know how they can tag you? So a lot of the time I spend seeing what photos are up there, and proof checking to see if they're suitable! It's good to be on the same pages as others, if I need it, I mean I'm not against it either so I might as well reap the benefits. (Richard, 18 years old)

What these comments suggest, then, is that the uses of social networking spaces in such ways mean that 'friends' are engaging in a form of 'self-surveillance' where one is forced to constantly check one's profile to see, for example, whether or not they might have been tagged in a photograph and, if so, what the photograph depicts – as Richard says 'proof checking to see if they're suitable' to be displayed on his Facebook page. This could be done for a number of reasons, for example, some of Richard's 'friends' on Facebook are family members and this is also a way to keep the representation of his self 'in check'. So while, as is the case with Richard, one may not be in the habit of uploading photographs or populating one's profile with other images, texts and applications, it is still of paramount importance to remain regularly logged in so as to be able to check that your online profile is as you wish it to be and not infiltrated by others, for example, through tagging. This, then, requires some level of identity management, even if it is not an identity being created by the owner. This too demonstrates some of the complexities in managing social networking spaces as personal and private spaces and is perhaps another reason why a number of my participants should consider their physical 'traditional' bedrooms as the spaces within which to display their 'real' and 'authentic' selves. In a few cases, this leads to an almost complete resistance to social networking sites, whereby participants dismissed them as a 'waste of time', a crude form of self-promotion and marketing rather than a genuine alternative space of identity and 'performance' favouring real time with their friends: 'I'm not that typical, it feels like a waste of time, I don't see the point of advertising myself and I'm not a techy freak' (James, 16 years old). However, others more typically spoke of their use of social networking sites as a sort of necessity and 'peer pressure' because it is a space that is used by their friends. For example, Laura says:

> I had MySpace and Facebook, but now I just use Facebook. More people use it. I tried to get on MySpace the other day but I couldn't remember the password, I don't know it's just no one uses it anymore...

Her choice of social networking site is not made on the basis of which site she considers to be the most useful to her or the site within which she feels most comfortable displaying aspects of herself and her evolving identity; rather, her choice is made on the basis of what everyone else is using. In the quote above she demonstrates how very quickly sites become redundant when networks of friends stop using them to the point at which she can no longer remember her password. This is similarly echoed in the quote below when Charlotte talks about how there has been a gravitation to Facebook as the main social networking site through which her friends are communicating. As noted in Sonia's comments earlier, the ease in the usability of Facebook is identified as being a reason why the site overtook MySpace as the site used by her and her friends:

> [Facebook] is the one that everyone's on now, so if you're going to contact people, well ... MySpace was easier to use, but once you've been on Facebook and then go back to MySpace, it's tried to have all the things that are on Facebook and it's got quite complicated now ... none of my friends use it either ... (Charlotte, 18 years old)

Virtual bedrooms as 'transitional' spaces

Robards (2010) argues that there is a hierarchical aspect to social networking sites and that there is a notable process of young people 'moving' through the social networking ranks. This is an aspect also noted in my research, but one that I prefer to consider as a 'transitional' process rather than a hierarchical one, as the latter represents a more fluid process by which young people move through spaces. I suggest this as an alternative approach because the participants in my research articulated their use of various social networking through their age rather than rank, status or 'coolness' of the site, although the last also had some bearing on their choice, as this quote from Lisa, 18 years old, demonstrates:

> I like Facebook because it's more mature for social networking, you can be more mature, like with uni and the events on it and stuff, but I prefer MySpace because you can have music on it and choose your background ... I prefer the set-up on MySpace but *'university people have Facebook'* ... that kind of thing.

The emphasis on *'university people have Facebook'*, while indeed tinged with sarcasm, demonstrates that there was clearly pressure on Lisa to switch from using MySpace as her main point of communication, which she clearly prefers and the layout of which complements her lifestyle more favourably, as discussed above, to using Facebook as the main site through which to communicate. This, she considers, is a more 'mature' site and one that in many ways mimics university life and its numerous social and cultural networks. Going to university as a key transition was used in a number of instances by my participants as a 'turning point' in their use of social networking spaces, with many of them shifting from MySpace to Facebook. As Richard, aged 18, demonstrates:

Richard: I used MySpace before, but I stopped using it in kind of mid-2008. I still sometimes listen to music on it.
SL: Why did you stop using it?
Richard: Erm, I prefer the interface on Facebook and it seems to be more aimed at university graduates really, and now students as well. Recently some people that are still at school are using it. It's nice to be able to keep the friends in your own age group, with MySpace it gets a bit out of control, people that I don't really know and talk to.

Going to university affords a different type of communication for Richard whereby keeping in touch becomes more important than the number of 'friends' he has, something that is very important on MySpace (boyd, 2006), which, he says, tended to 'get a bit out of control'. Being able to communicate with friends (who are real-life friends) becomes more important when moving away as the use of social networking sites replaces the regular face-to-face contact that a young person would have had with friends at school. To this end, sites such as Facebook, as noted by a number of my participants, were often used in place of other social networking sites such as MySpace when such a transition occurs:

> I've got a MySpace and I use Facebook now. I used to have a MySpace when I first got to uni because everyone had one and I only have it now because 2 of my friends won't go on Facebook for some reason, so I use it to speak to them ... I think Facebook is a bit more mature, like as much as social networking sites can be ... (Sonia, aged 22)

As Sonia demonstrates, to some extent there is a form of peer pressure to be on the most popular networking sites and that, in that instance, being at university is synonymous with having a Facebook profile, as Lisa describes earlier. In the quote above she, like Richard, discusses the differences between 'having' and 'using' different social networking sites which, while demonstrating her familiarity with different sites, also demonstrates her transition from one site to another (the transition from Bebo to MySpace to Facebook was noted by several of my participants). This shift from one space to another can be understood as some sort of 'electronic trail' of her social networking experiences and how her uses of such sites work in accordance with the relationship with her friends in real life. So, for example, she says that she only really checks her MySpace account because two of her friends still use it, whereas Facebook is her main point of contact with all her other friends. Her MySpace page, then, has become purely functional rather than a maintained identity space. Richard's use of Facebook was similar and, as he noted, he had stopped using MySpace a couple of years earlier and had replaced it with Facebook.

Even if a young person is not currently using the most popular sites, such as Facebook, there is still an understanding that once away from the parental home it will be a necessary tool through which to keep in touch with friends:

> I had a Bebo and I could get into it [Facebook], but it's just getting started [becoming popular among his friends] and there's no

need ... When I leave home I might set it up as a way of keeping in touch with friends. (James, aged 16)

In this sense, then, it seems that certain social networking sites are becoming synonymous with particular stages in a young person's life, with the uses of different sites being associated with being younger or older. This is articulated by Lisa with reference to her older brother and her desire to have the same social networking spaces as him, to be considered part of 'his generation' as well as to annoy him by being part of his 'world':

Well, I had a MySpace originally 'cos my brother had one, he's older than me, he's 23 so 5 years older than me, so he had a MySpace because his generation had a MySpace sort of thing ... So I got one to annoy him more than anything, which I never used and deleted. Then I got Bebo because you could make quizzes like 'how well do you know me' and you could write like, you could paint on walls and stuff on it, then MySpace I had for quite a while 'cos you can choose your background, I had jellybeans for quite a while which someone once told me looked like ecstasy pills and I was like 'thanks'!! (Lisa, 18 years old)

Given Lisa's desire to decorate and to highly personalise her bedroom, sites such as Bebo and MySpace did in many ways appeal to her more than Facebook because they were sites that she could play around with in terms of their content. As she notes in reference to both sites, she likes the intricacies of resources such as the games applications and being able to play around with different backgrounds on MySpace. But as she notes in an earlier quote, there was some pressure when she moved to university to 'graduate' to Facebook (alluding to Robards' concept of hierarchies) because, ultimately, although she preferred sites such as MySpace there were considered less mature and were not identified as a key communication space.

Reflecting back on previous discussions whereby we see the teenage bedroom as an integral space for young people as they move through a series of transitions, the above examples have much to say about the integration of social networking sites as personal and private spaces into young people's transitions. First, social networking sites appear to become embedded into transitions such as leaving home to the point at which the use of particular sites such as Facebook is seemingly becoming synonymous with the leaving home experience as a number of my participants note above.[8] It seems that a student who is not on Facebook will not have the same networked experiences of their peers should they choose to opt out and that joining such sites is something that they do by default when they move away. Second, transitional processes can be experienced through social networking sites much as they are experienced within the space of the bedroom, for example when used by teenagers undertaking important exams. Social networking sites provide the space to accommodate a new lifestyle and new interests and can be 'built' and moved around as such to reflect these new interests, much like the space of the bedroom. Third, as I demonstrate in the final section of this chapter, social networking sites, often used within the confines of the bedroom, are portals of communications for young people. Given that Facebook in particular is largely made up of 'friends' who exist in real life (boyd, 2006), such spaces offer young people the ideal way through which to stay connected to friends and family back at home as well as becoming a part of various university networks using the same site. As we have seen in previous discussions in Chapters 4 and 5, this is what might be referred to as a kind of 'oscillation' between two social worlds, the connection to which is in the hands of the individual. In some ways, then, a young person can experience transitions without necessarily having to leave the private domain of their bedrooms – they can always be connected.

Finally, what is evident here is the interplay between identity and communication. On the one hand, such sites are about representing the self in a virtual public domain as argued earlier in the chapter (Mallan, 2009; Pearson, 2009), but they are also about interacting with friends, suggesting that some form of privacy may be afforded because primarily the young person is in control of his or her profile (boyd, 2008b; boyd and Hargittai, 2010). A presence through social networking sites such as Facebook is primarily done through interaction on those sites and this is evident through the use of mainly images and text. The posting of photographs of nights out, for example, demonstrates a participation in public life that is crucially important in the university years. Posting also shows a continued dialogue with one's network of friends as they comment upon the images, post a message on the 'wall' or communicate through the instant messenger facility. The ability to 'tag' 'friends' in photographs, however, while contributing to this dialogue, does also compromise the extent to which one has control over such personal spaces complementing Pearson's 'glass bedroom' metaphor in which, to reiterate:

Inside the bedroom, private conversations and intimate exchanges occur, each with varying awareness of distant friends and strangers

moving past transparent walls that separate groups from more deliberate and constructed 'outside' displays. (2009)

In some ways, then, the use of photographs in virtual social networking spaces is similar to the display on a teenager's bedroom wall as this
is a 'worked upon' display and one that will change often according to
the social and cultural activities going on in a young person's life. As
noted above, however, the selection of photographs that appear on an
online profile may not be chosen with the precision with which those
in the bedroom are selected; the constant updating of images is crucial
to maintaining an identity and presence on such spaces. Mallan (2009)
additionally suggests that this selection is also done through a consideration of who the display is for and this will differ according to the
context of this display.

Finally, the use of such sites complements the transitions that a
young person is experiencing in real life, rather than replacing them,
and this is a transitional experience that is in many ways enhanced
through the use of new communication technologies and through
social networking.

Bedrooms as 'portals of communication'

Nina, who was 20 years old and lived in halls of residence, talked about
the ways in which her uses of Facebook mimicked the social relationships she used to have with her best friends when they all lived at
home. In many ways, this social networking site was being used as a
'replacement' of face-to-face interactions while still maintaining those
elements that we might associate with a group of friends hanging out
in their bedrooms:

> Like me and my friends really because we have a constant network
> where we will just go around writing stuff that we have been doing
> everyday; it's more like a diary where we tell each other what we have
> been doing and my sister is usually online later so I'll chat to her.

She continues:

> We just talk about what we have been doing ... but because we all
> went [to university] this term we were really bad at keeping in touch
> and it got to like Christmas and we were like 'oh my god' we have so
> much to tell each other. So we have set it up on Facebook so that we

chat in the evenings; so we just say what we've been doing in the day, how work has been going, how work is and how our families are.

There are a number of interesting issues in this use of social network sites that are reminiscent of a bedroom culture and which can be related to the concept of 'zoning' discussed in the previous chapter. The space of the bedroom is important for Nina as a 'portal of communication'; it is the space that she uses on the evenings she arranges to 'get together' on Facebook with her old school friends from home. Nina alludes to the analogy of a diary when she talks about the types of things that she and her friends talk about when they 'get together' online to chat; so, for example, they will exchange rather mundane, cathartic stories about what has happened in their day, much as they would with each other in real life. Like the use of online journals such as LiveJournal (Hodkinson, 2007; Hodkinson and Lincoln, 2008) the 'conversation' was limited to a small number of friends, who, in Nina's case, are her five closest friends from home. In relation to 'zoning' in a young person's bedroom as explored in the previous chapter and within which we are more likely to find that diaries are hidden away in memory boxes and for personal use only, this private 'zone' has been opened up to include close friends. In relation to more traditional forms of communication technologies, Nina and her friends' interactions are also like a phone conversation.

Replicating this conversation online via social networking means that Nina can talk to more than one friend at a time; it does not cost anything, unlike a phone call each night, and it also means that the girls can join in the conversation as and when they can. Much like the example of Dean and his friends discussed in Chapter 3, because the girls are separated geographically and all have different things going on in their lives, social networking sites such as Facebook allow for ease of accessibility and 'dipping' in and out when one can. As Nina goes on to explain: 'Emma hasn't been on it for a while because she's been really busy but she will catch up in a couple of days' time.'

As I have explored in the previous chapter, bedrooms are portals of communication in other ways too, the flow of which is 'zoned' according to who is in that space and what activities are taking place within it. The flows of communication within that space are multiple too, for example communication is achieved through the objects, items and things in a young person's bedroom, read in different ways by the young occupant themselves, their friends and peers, family members and so on. The physical, visual aspects of the bedroom itself are crucial in the construction of the young occupant's identity and capture the shifts and changes that are always 'under construction'. Layered upon and around this physical construction are mediated sites of communication, the invisible flows of which ripple through the space of a bedroom with different mediated spaces being opened and closed at different times. However, as Livingstone (2005) argues, in opening and closing these different flows, young people are, on the one hand, engaging with a tool that offers them flexibility and space within which to explore their identities, cultures and relationships, while, on the other, she argues, they may be 'naively blind' to the power of that media they are engaging with in terms of the lifestyles of consumption they present to them and construct for them. Yet what my data have shown is that in a post-modern age of flux and change dominated by cultures of 'risk', uncertainty, instability and fear, young people seek out, perhaps more than ever before, those spaces that can offer them some form of stability and I have suggested in this book that their bedroom is one of those spaces. This is particularly the case given that the contemporary context of social media is defined by constant shifting and movement that keep those very spaces 'alive', while traditional personal and private spaces such as bedrooms offer a context in which to stabilise one's identity, permanently or not. So while the analogy of the bedroom is one way in which to explore young people's uses of social networking sites, it is not the case that one space replaces the other. Indeed one is an extension of the other, but each with distinct functions in representing who a young person is.

Conclusions

It is clear from the above discussions and the accounts of other scholars working in the area of young people and social networking media that an analogy with the traditional private and personal space of a young person's bedroom is a useful way of exploring young people's engagement in social networking sites as identity spaces (Brown et al., 1994; Chandler and Roberts-Young, 1998; Hodkinson and Lincoln, 2008; Pearson, 2009; Robards, 2010). What many of these accounts suggest is that the notion of a bedroom culture should not be understood as a singular model that is applicable to a range of youth contexts, but that elements of bedroom culture are taken by young people themselves in their articulation of the use of such spaces, much dependent on what is going on in their lives at the time. And much like their use of bedrooms, this use may constantly be in flux. This suggests, then, that there are indeed pluralities of bedroom cultures (or multiple bedrooms as Robards [2010] suggests), the experience of which are both highly personal as well as 'networked'. What can be learnt from this is that the social and cultural lives of young people in much of the western world are complex, highly fluid and inter-penetrable and they are indeed what Hulme (2009) has referred to as 'hybrid'. Given this and particularly given the rapid changes in communications technologies shaping our social world, continued discourses around young people's use of them are vital.

Conclusion: Youth Culture and Private Space

Whatever the extent of young people's uses of private spaces such as their bedrooms or social networking sites, they are without any doubt integral to their everyday lives and to their youth cultures as I have demonstrated throughout this book. The physical space of the bedroom provides young people with a place of refuge and escapism, exploration and experimentation, an island to be alone in or a hub from which to connect and communicate with friends and the outside world. It offers a space within which a young person can explore and express their identities and figure out who they are at any given moment in time. Importantly, it is a space that evolves and changes in accordance with young people's experiences as they move towards their adult years.

While youth cultural studies have largely focused on young people occupying public spaces such as the street, the youth club, the night club or the music gig, the 'private' realm of youth cultures, for example those housed in domestic spaces such as the teenage bedroom, have been under-researched in comparison, as significant sites of youth culture and identity. As I have argued, there are a number of reasons for this, not least those related to methodological problems and issues and ethical dilemmas faced in merely entering the private and personal realm of the domestic. What I have attempted to demonstrate is that in order to understand young people's private spaces as youth cultural spaces, a range of methods, particularly those that draw on the methodological tradition of ethnography, can be adopted to enable the researcher to 'get inside' these highly personal and private spaces. To this end, I have argued for an approach to the study of bedroom culture that does not only incorporate more traditional ethnographic approaches such as in-depth interviewing and observation but also more contemporary ethnographic methods, namely those drawn from visual and sensory ethnography. I argue that these approaches are highly appropriate in studying bedroom culture because they enable the researcher to capture the visual and sensory experiences of contemporary youth cultures that are lived out not only in the public sphere, but also within the realm of the private. Further, there is a constant interplay between these two spaces through which young people use social media such as social networking sites as a way to connect to and engage in both spheres.

This constant interplay within which young people find themselves in a process of relentless updating, revising and inventing their 'identities' and which occurs within the contexts of globalisation, neoliberalism, and 'risk' suggests that young people are in fact becoming *less* connected to physical spaces. However, I have argued that as personal and private identity spaces, bedrooms are in fact becoming *more* significant to young people who find themselves caught up in the daily push and pull of media and consumption cultures. Indeed, as I have demonstrated in the final chapter of this book, many of my research participants described their bedrooms as a space in which they can live out and display their 'real' and 'authentic' selves, away from the pressures and exposure that are part and parcel of life on social networking sites. So while one can draw similarities between young people's uses of their physical bedrooms and social networking sites such as MySpace or Facebook, as I have demonstrated, these are quite different as spaces of youth identities. However, it can be argued that in fact bedrooms too are sites of multiple identities, not least because young people's interests and experiences change all the time and this is often captured in bedrooms themselves, and because bedrooms are also hubs within which, through new media technologies, the multiple spaces and 'zones' through which young people live out their social and cultural lives can be accessed, all from this one room. In this case then, the teenage bedroom is a 'hub of communication' in which a young person is physically located, but through technologies such as the mobile phone and the internet can also be virtually located elsewhere and in multiple locations at any given time.

As I note above, in a digital age in which identities can be convoluted or mendacious, challenged or compromised, the physical space of the bedroom takes on a renewed significance for young people. In exploring this further, I argue that the materiality of young people's spaces provides a rich tapestry within which the history of their emerging identities is woven. As a response to the rapidity of contemporary life and the neoliberal context of 'relentless consumption', I suggest that the 'things' found in young people's bedrooms may usefully be understood as identity 'anchors'; that is, meaningful things that represent and remind a young person who they are, temporarily 'pausing' or 'cementing' their sense of self when this is constantly being questioned. As I have demonstrated in Chapter 4, moving things around in the bedroom is particularly significant for young people, when, for example, they are experiencing important transitions such as undertaking exams or leaving home or even moving to another bedroom in the house when an older sibling moves out. This is often a complex process in which a young person makes definite statements about growing up, represented through the process of, for example, getting rid of things related to 'childhood' that no longer represent a more mature self and replacing these things with gig tickets that represent a social life, and one beyond the domestic sphere. Importantly, this continues to adulthood as youth identities are perceived to be always 'under construction' and thus, the space of the bedroom is always, in some way, evolving.

To explore this evolution further, and particularly in the context of post-subculturalism, I have proposed the concept of 'zoning' as a conceptual tool with which we can explore the interplay of different cultural spheres and contexts in young people's lives. The concept of 'zoning' that draws on McRobbie's 'coding' of teenage girls' bedroom culture, enables us to make sense of teenage private spaces both as physical entities and as spaces within which other 'virtual' and 'mediated' spaces, such as social networking sites, are opened and closed all the time. Through 'zoning' we understand how young people negotiate the interplay between physical, material spaces as well as virtual, mediated immaterial spaces as they are used when spending time alone in their bedrooms as well when socialising in them with friends, family and peers. The concept of 'zoning' allows us to unpack the complexities around these negotiations that see young people working their way through various forms of regulation and control both inside and outside of the home.

Importantly, the concept of zoning not only helps us to make sense of the interplay of these different spheres that influence young people's lives, it also enables us to further understand how young people are positioned in relation to cultures of the family, education and work, the media and consumption, cultures that young people have to navigate, often meeting intersections that invariably place them in a position of vulnerability and uncertainty.

Which (bedroom) door to open next?

It is hoped that this book has gone some way to address a theoretical gap in current youth research and that I have demonstrated the importance and significance of the realm of the private in the lives of many young people today. I argue strongly that this realm needs further attention and in this respect, there are a number of themes that have emerged from this research that could be usefully explored in the future.

I recognise that the findings discussed in this book in relation to young people and bedroom culture do, by and large, focus on cultures of consumption, and indeed this is a criticism of my work as well as work by others, such as Brown and Steele (1995) and James (2001) taken up by scholars such as Kearney (2007). Kearney argues that young people's bedrooms should not just be understood as sites of consumption (or as what she terms 'non-productive spaces' [p. 126]), but that given recent advances in new technologies (and the associated social and cultural worlds of self-broadcasting and user-generated content), domestic spaces, or more specifically bedroom spaces, should also be considered as significant sites of media *productivity* in the lives of young people.

While I would dispute that bedrooms as spaces of consumption are, by default, 'non-productive' (particularly in the context of my arguments about bedrooms as spaces that are worked upon, constructed spaces within which young people's identities are most certainly produced and reproduced using a variety of sources and techniques – isn't the compilation of music to create individual soundtracks on an iPod a form of production?), I agree that it is important that young people's bedrooms be further researched as sites of media production and this is particularly relevant given that we now have a generation of young people who have grown up with new technologies and social media, as Hulme (2009) argues, and for whom media production is an integral part of their lives and interactions both inside and outside the home and in multiple virtual spheres. I would suggest too, then, that it is now timely to explore further how young people are growing up both online and offline in tandem, through multiple social and cultural spheres, contributing further to explorations of the often complex interplay between physical and virtual private and personal spaces, alongside public spaces that are significant in young people's lives and identities.

As I was completing this book, a new television show was being aired on the BBC's children's channel CBBC. The series, entitled *I Want My Own Room*, used the tagline: 'kids take control of a room in their house and re-design it anyway they choose'.[1] In the series, a large number of the young participants chose to redesign their bedrooms, creating what they perceive to be their 'fantasy' and 'dream' bedroom spaces. Perhaps the fact that the UK's biggest broadcaster chose to commission such a show, targeted at young people who are no doubt engaged frequently in 'spaces' of social media, is at least some testament to the continued significance and relevance of bedrooms in the lives of young people today.

What the commissioning of this series in 2011 also demonstrates is how young people's bedrooms can represent the 'ultimate' in bringing the outside in, a major theme that runs throughout this book. And although, as I suggest above, studies of bedroom culture to date have been criticised for their focus on consumption, I would argue that there are still aspects of consumer culture that can be explored in such spaces. For example, many previous bedroom cultures studies, including my own, have drawn on common and traditional leisure pursuits such as playing and listening to music, an activity that manifests itself in both material and virtual aspects of young people's bedroom cultures. However, other 'traditional' popular leisure activities such as shopping have not been so readily explored. As I have suggested in Chapter 5, my research revealed some very interesting findings with regard not only to young people's consuming behaviour, for example in relation to buying clothes, but also in relation to how clothing and the shopping experience became part of bedrooms as markers of identity. Clothing was often 'on display', especially in girls' bedrooms, and in many cases items had been styled in such a way as to capture the essence of the shop from which it was purchased.

This is interesting in a number of ways. For example, while many young people may cite films, television programmes or music (as is the case in *I Want My Own Room*) as influential in the decoration of their bedrooms, a small number of my participants cited actual shop interiors as influencing what their room looked like. This is potentially an interesting development in studies of bedroom culture in that here is a mapping of the 'physical' onto the 'physical', made achievable in the cases of my participants by the 'thrift store' ethos that shops such as Urban Outfitters model themselves on and whereby buying 'second hand' makes achieving the look seemingly affordable and thus easy to replicate and recreate. This also demonstrates that while this is another 'seeping' of consumer culture into young people's spaces, this time through clothing, the articulation of its meaning in each individual bedroom demonstrates the importance of them as spaces of 'youth styling' (Miles, 2000). In their bedrooms young people can draw on the wider public cultures within which they engage, but draw on them in ways that personalise that space.

As I have explored through this book, private spaces such as bedrooms are far from simple, functional spaces in which a young person just sleeps and stores his or her 'stuff'. As spaces of youth culture, bedrooms can be complex and the unravelling of their meaning requires not only paying attention to the wider spheres and contexts within which such spaces exist, but also to the individuals who occupy and use those spaces. As I suggest in the introduction to this book, the uses and arrangement of private and personal spaces such as bedrooms can be utterly predictable in a number of ways, but in many others they are unique to each and every young person who occupies such a space – whether shared or not. And as young people continue to engage in new and social media in many aspects of their everyday lives, I believe, more than ever, that we should keep the bedroom door ajar and continue to explore what may seem very traditional spaces compared to those of new media because bedrooms continue to capture so clearly the lives, transitions, experiences and cultures of the young people who occupy them.

Notes

Introduction

1. My reference to young people and teenagers throughout this book is restricted to those living in the western, developed world. I acknowledge that the discussions in this book are by no means applicable globally or universally.

1 Exploring the Private in Traditional Youth Cultural Theory and Beyond

1. For Kearney (2007) the term 'room culture scholarship' refers specifically to adolescent bedroom culture (p. 130). I use this term similarly throughout the book to refer to young people's bedrooms and those scholars who study them.

2 Researching Young People's 'Private' Space

1. This quote was from an interview that filmmaker John Hughes gave in *The Chicago Herald Tribune* following the success of his now classic teenpic *The Breakfast Club* (1985).
2. According to Ponterotto (2006) the two lectures given by Ryle were entitled 'Thinking and Reflecting' and 'The Thinking of Thoughts[:] What is La Penseur doing?' They were published in Ryle (1971).
3. Paul Willis' work *Learning to Labour: How Working-Class Kids Get Working-Class Jobs* (1977) is often noted as one of the few exceptions to this as Willis undertook extensive ethnographic work to complete this study.
4. Some of the empirical work Bennett critiques includes Hall and Jefferson (1975) and Hebdige (1979).
5. For example, in relation to the context of the research, working with groups of friends and adopting research activities that mimic the participants' social and cultural interests are both techniques that afford more power to the participants (for example, see Baker, 2004).
6. This age limit applies to the UK context as other countries apply different age criteria.
7. It should be noted that there may be other entry requirements in place, such as a club membership, that have to be negotiated or approved before access can be granted.
8. When conducting my fieldwork I always wore casual clothing, for example jeans, T-shirts and trainers rather than formal styles of dress such as a business suit in order to further put my participants at ease, dressing in similar ways to them (and indeed this is clothing I was more comfortable in) and 'signalling' through my clothing the informality of the research process. I also tried to maintain informality through the use of small, discreet notebooks

(rather than, for example, a clipboard) in which to take notes, although this was somewhat compromised by the use of a digital Dictaphone (while small, it needed to be placed centrally in the room to pick up the discussions as clearly as possible). Indeed, as I note later in the chapter, after a while the participants paid little attention to the equipment (and I tried to just glance quickly at the equipment to check it was working and recording) and I made it clear the use of a Dictaphone was so that I could listen back to our discussions and could avoid having to take notes as we spoke; its very presence dictated more formal elements of the research process. Additionally, as part of the consent process, I was required to inform the participants about how the information recorded would be used and stored. This arguably added another layer of formality to the process.

9. Beverley Skeggs (1994) discusses a similar issue in her ethnographic work with women as they move through and beyond the education system given that her research sample amounted to 83 participants.

10. On a few occasions, when asked if it would be OK to do the interview in the bedroom, the participant would suggest another room, for example the living room or kitchen. The reason given was usually that their bedroom was too messy so they didn't want to take me in there. I was never really sure if they had been told to say this by their mother or whether it was a decision they had made. Interestingly, the couple of times this did happen, it was with male participants.

11. Although my participants had a general idea about what my research visits would entail, what we would talk about and that the visits would take place in their bedrooms, I did not explicitly refer to the 'room tour'. This was because although inevitably there may have been some pre-arrangement of their bedroom by my participants before my visit (often based on demands from parents to tidy up in preparation for my visit), I felt that placing an emphasis on talking about specific things in their rooms may have made them select particular items to talk about and to remove others. In understanding how young people use their bedrooms, I felt it was important to see those things that are significant and meaningful to them at the time as well as those things that are simply 'there' having had some significance in their younger years. In being able to observe this, I could capture the 'historical' layers of bedroom space and the changing and shifting meaning of the space as shaped by its contents. Additionally, I did not want my participants to feel that their rooms were being compared in any way, a concern raised by my university's ethics committee.

12. A number of the female participants had what they called 'memory boxes' kept in a drawer, a cupboard or under a desk, mostly hidden away. The boxes contained things like photographs or what the girls would describe as 'random' items such as coins or stamps, small toys or objects given to them by family members, friends, boyfriends or girlfriends, as well as things like birthday cards or Valentine's Day cards from old boyfriends, notes written between friends, postcards and so on.

13. Kearney (2007) critiques the existing body of 'room culture scholarship' and argues that much of this work is concerned with the consumption of music rather than its production. More broadly, she proposes that bedrooms can be spaces within which young people 'make media' (see also Harris, 2004b; Piepmeier, 2009).

14. This argument has been explored more fully in the creative audience methodologies literature, for example see Gauntlett (2007) and Horsley (2005).
15. In my pilot study written up as my MA thesis entitled 'The Socio-Spatial Configuration of the Teenage Bedroom', Manchester Metropolitan University, Manchester, UK, 1999, I asked four of my female research participants to keep diaries of the activities that they did in their bedroom over a two-week period. The results were disappointing because while the girls attempted to undertake the task, they confessed to finding it hard to complete. This was because when in their bedrooms, the girls would be doing a number of different things at any one time and this was too difficult to record while trying to remain 'natural', doing what they would normally do. Getting them to think and record in such a way distorted their everyday activities and so did not provide an accurate representation of their social life-worlds.
16. Another important factor that should be noted was time. Much of the data presented here was completed for my PhD and so the research was conducted during a one-year period. Therefore, there was limited time to try and test alternative strategies with the participants to enable them to take the photographs themselves. Had I had more time, I would indeed have pursued this before deciding to take the photographs myself.
17. Interestingly, we learn very little about the setting of the interviews from the content of McRobbie and Garber's essay 'Girls and Subcultures' (1975) and only a little more in future revisions of the same essay (McRobbie, 1991, 2000).

3 The Role of Private Space in Contemporary Youth Culture

1. For example, the teenage bedroom might be the place where a teenage girl gets pregnant. Rather abruptly her adolescence comes to an end and a life of adult responsibility ensues.
2. 'Tweenies' is 'set in a playschool and deals with dilemmas, challenges and issues common to very young children, such as squabbling with friends, or not owning up. Storylines provide a non-threatening context within which such issues can be discussed and resolved simply. These characters move like real children; they laugh at the same things they do; sing the same songs; play the same games and see the world in the same way' (www.bbc.co.uk/cbeebies/tweenies/).
3. An American R&B artist and lead singer of the band Dru Hill famous for their hit 'thong song'.
4. The 'gatherings' tended to involve 'music, barbeques and things like that' according to Adam, 15 years old.
5. 'Sharing' a bedroom was quite unusual in middle-class families, although in the case of David, he was one of three children with his youngest sister being aged only 8 at the time of the interview.
6. I witnessed this on a research trip to Natasha and Sara's house as described in Chapter 2.
7. Positive activities was a buzz-phrase for the previous Labour government which aimed through initiatives such as 'Every Child Matters' and 'Find Your

Talent' to ensure young people's leisure time was more structured, particularly in the context of 'cultural activities'.
8. The primary codes included the codes of 'romance', 'fashion and beauty', 'personal life' and 'pop music.'

4   Young People, Bedrooms and Materiality

1. Vero Moda is a young women's contemporary fashion store established in 1989 in Scandinavia that now sells its products in stores in over 45 countries; http://www.veromoda.com/#/company/history (accessed 15 October 2010).

5   Mediating Young People's Bedrooms: 'Zoning' Bedroom Cultures

1. Livingstone draws on Habermasian notions of 'the public' as: 'routinely construed positively while "the private" represents threats, danger and loss' (2005, p. 12).
2. Osgerby points out that although the post-1945 period is marked out as a 'turning point in the development of British youth culture', subcultures, 'youngsters', and a degree of disposable income were identifiable before this time, for example, in the nineteenth century (1998, p. 17). See also Savage (2007) for a detailed account of teenage and adolescence before this time.
3. 'Ofcom report highlights "multi-tasking" media users', http://www.bbc.co.uk/news/technology-11012356 (accessed 19 August 2010).
4. Reported on the BBC News, available at http://www.bbc.co.uk/news/technology-11012356 (accessed 1 November 2010).
5. 'Multi-tasking media usage' was highlighted in Ofcom's annual communications market report (see note 3).
6. The term 'digital natives', according to Hulme, 'represents a group which have grown up with the internet and mobile phone who are fundamentally different from previous generations in the way they seek information, engage, interact and entertain themselves' (2009, p. 2). Hulme's report was commissioned by Youthnet.
7. *Jackie* was a best-selling weekly teenage girls' magazine published by D. C. Thomson and Co. in the UK between 1964 and 1993.
8. Selection refers to 'the process of choosing which media to engage in from an ever-changing selection' (Steele and Brown, 1995, p. 558).
9. Interaction refers to 'the cognitive, affective, and behavioural engagement with media' and the cultural meanings that are produced from this interaction (Steele and Brown, 1995, p. 558).
10. Application refers to 'the "concrete ways" in which young people use the media in their everyday lives', how they become an established part of their daily lives and routines (Steele and Brown, 1995, p. 559).
11. There are, however, a number of studies that explore individualised, personal listening practices, for example, see DeNora, 2000; Bull, 2005; Lincoln, 2005.

12. 'Tagging' is the process of attaching a person's name and (if they also have one) Facebook profile to an image posted on the site.
13. While my findings support such claims with a number of participants identifying music as a key component in both the use and decoration of their bedrooms, it should be noted that the culture of television watching has changed significantly in recent times, not only in terms of 'how' we now watch (for example, television viewing is increasingly 'on demand' and individualised rather than scheduled) but what technologies we watch television programmes on. For example, the television set is less popular with young people who can watch in a more 'mobile' fashion on their laptops and on their smart phones. It would be very interesting to explore in more depth the ways in which these new forms of television watching reshape young people's experiences of bedroom culture, if indeed they do.

6   Mediating Young People's Bedrooms: The 'Virtual Bedroom'?

1. See also the findings of Ofcom's report (2010) in 'multi-tasking' media users, http://www.bbc.co.uk/news/technology-11012356 (accessed 19 August 2010).
2. Professor Michael Hulme was commissioned by Youthnet.org to produce a report entitled 'Life Support: Young People's Needs in a Digital Age' (2009). The study was undertaken by the Future Company with 994 respondents between 16 and 24 years old and also drew on research conducted by the Social Futures Observatory at Lancaster University, UK. The main focus of the report is on how young people seek advice online and how they assess its credibility but it also considers how young people communicate using digital media, how they present themselves online and how young people deal with issues of safety.
3. See in particular *Safer Children in a Digital World: The Report of the Byron Review* by Dr Tanya Byron and commissioned by the (now decommissioned) Department of Children, Schools and Families (2008, p. 208) which cites Prensky (2001) as one of the critics who first used the phrase.
4. It should be noted, however, that MySpace is a more or less redundant social networking site today, with Facebook and Twitter dominating the social network media sector.
5. Statistics published at http://www.socialmediatoday.com/SMC/206771 cite Facebook as dominating the US market share of hits at 45.90%, while MySpace comes in third place (after YouTube) with11.79% of the share. In the UK according to http://www.netimperative.com/news/2010/june/top-10-social-networking-websites-uk/?searchterm=None Facebook again dominates, followed by Twitter, then MySpace (accessed 1 June 2010).
6. According to Facebook statistics a user has 130 'friends' on average http://www.facebook.com/press/info.php?statistics (accessed 25 October 2010).
7. Tagging is a function of Facebook that allows you to 'tag' the faces of people who are your Facebook friends and thus creates a link to their profile that can then be viewed, depending on the privacy settings in operation.

8. Indeed the site's creator Mark Zuckerberg invented Facebook in 2004 along with fellow students Eduardo Saverin, Dustin Moskovitz and Chris Hughes as a tool through which Harvard college students were able to communicate across campus through the creation of online profiles.

Conclusion: Youth Culture and Private Space

1. www.bbc.co.uk (accessed 12 January 2012).

Bibliography

Abbott-Chapman, J. (2000) 'Time Out, Spaced Out', *Youth Studies Australia*, Vol. 19, No. 1, 21–5.

Abbott-Chapman, J. and Robertson, M. (2001) 'Youth, Leisure and Home: Space, Place and Identity, *Leisure and Society*, Vol. 24, No. 2, 485–506.

Abbott-Chapman, J. and Robertson, M. (2009) 'Adolescents' Favourite Places: Redefining the Boundaries between Public and Private Space', *Space and Culture*, Vol. 12, No. 4, 419–34.

Arnett, J. J. (1995) 'Adolescent's Use of Media for Self-Socialisation', *Journal of Youth and Adolescence*, Vol. 24, No. 5, 519–33.

Arnett, J. J. (2004) *Emerging Adulthood: The Winding Road from the Late Teens through the Twenties* (Oxford: Oxford University Press).

Atkinson, P., Coffey, A., Delamont, S., Lofland, J. and Loftland, L. (2001) *The Handbook of Ethnography* (London: Sage).

Atkinson, P., Delamont, S. and Housley, W. (2007) *Contours of Culture: Complex Ethnography and the Ethnography of Complexity* (Lanham, MD: Altamira Press).

Back, L. (2005) '"Home from Home": Youth, Belonging and Space', in C. Alexander and C. Knowles, C. (eds.), *Making Race Matter* (Basingstoke: Palgrave Macmillan), 19–41.

Back, L. (2007) *The Art of Listening* (Oxford: Berg).

Baker, S. L. (2004) 'Pop in(to) the Bedroom: Popular Music in Pre-Teen Girls' Bedroom Culture', *European Journal of Cultural Studies*, Vol. 7, No. 1, 75–93.

Banks, M. (2001) *Visual Methods in Social Research* (London: Sage).

Barnard, H. (1990) 'Bourdieu and Ethnography: Reflexivity, Politics and Praxis', in R. Harker, C. Mahar and C. Wilkes (eds.), *An Introduction to the Work of Pierre Bourdieu: The Practice of Theory* (London: Macmillan), 58–85.

Beck, U. (1992) *Risk Society: Towards a New Modernity* (London: Sage).

Becker, H. S. (1963) *Outsiders: Studies in the Sociology of Deviance* (New York: Free Press).

Bennett, A. (1999) 'Subcultures or Neo-tribes? Rethinking the Relationships between Youth, Style and Musical Taste', *Sociology*, Vol. 33, No. 3, 599–617.

Bennett, A. (2000) *Popular Music and Youth Culture: Music, Identity and Place* (Basingstoke: Palgrave Macmillan).

Bennett, A. (2002) 'Researching Youth Culture and Popular Music: A Methodological Critique', *British Journal of Sociology*, Vol. 53, No. 3, 451–66.

Bennett, A. (2010) 'Re-Evaluating the Post-Subcultural Turn', *TASA Sociology of Youth Thematic Group Newsletter*, 9–12.

Bennett, A. and Kahn-Harris, K. (2004) *After Subculture: Critical Studies in Contemporary Youth Culture* (Basingstoke: Palgrave Macmillan).

Berger, J. (1984) *And Our Faces, My Heart, Brief as Photos* (New York: Pantheon).

Bloustien, G. (1998) 'It's different to a mirror "cos it talks to you": Teenage Girls, Video Cameras and Identity', in S. Howard (ed.), *Wired Up: Young People and the Electronic Media* (London: UCL Press), 115–34.

Boden, S. (2006) '"Another day, another demand": How Parents and Children Negotiate Consumption Matters', *Sociological Research Online*, Vol. 11, No. 2, http://www.socresonline.org.uk/11/2/boden.html (accessed 12/06/08).

Bourdieu, P. (1989) *Distinction: A Social Critique of the Judgement of Taste* (London: Routledge).

Bovill, M. and Livingstone, S. (2001) 'Bedroom Culture and the Privatization of Media Use', in S. Livingstone and M. Bovill (eds.), *Children and their Changing Media Environment: A European Comparative Study* (LEA's communication series, Mahwah, NJ: Lawrence Erlbaum Associates), 179–200.

boyd, d. (2006) 'Friends, Friendsters, and Top 8: Writing Community into Being on Social Network Sites', *First Monday*, Vol. 11, No. 12, http://firstmonday.org/issues/issue11_12/boyd/index.html (accessed 06/11/10).

boyd, d. (2007) 'Why Youth (Heart) Social Networking Sites: The Role of Networked Publics in Teenage Social Life', in D. Buckingham (ed.), *Youth, Identity, and Digital Media* (Cambridge, MA: MIT Press), 119–42.

boyd, d. (2008a) 'Taken out of Context: American Teen Sociality in Networked Publics' (PhD thesis), www.danah.org (accessed 11/10/09).

boyd, d. (2008b) 'Facebook's Privacy Trainwreck: Exposure, Invasion and Social Convergence', *Convergence*, Vol. 14, No. 1, 13–20.

boyd, d. and Ellison, N. (2007) 'Social Network Sites: Definition, History and Scholarship', *Journal of Computer-Mediated Communication*, Vol. 13, No. 1, http://jcmc.indiana.edu/vol13/issue1/boyd.ellison.html (accessed 21/09/10).

boyd, d. and Hargittai, E. (2010) 'Facebook Privacy Settings: Who Cares?' *First Monday*, Vol. 15, No. 8, http://firstmonday.org/htbin/cgiwrap/bin/ojs/index.php/fm/article/view/3086 (accessed 29/01/12).

Brake, M. (1985) *Comparative Youth Culture: The Sociology of Youth Cultures and Youth Subcultures* (London: Routledge & Kegan Paul).

Brown, J., Dykers, C., Steele, J. and White, A. (1994) 'Teenage Room Culture: Where Media and Identities Intersect', *Communications Research*, Vol. 21, No. 6, 813–27.

Buckingham, D. (2007) *Introducing Identity in Youth, Identity and Digital Media* (Cambridge, MA: MIT Press).

Bull, M. (2005) 'No Dead Air! The iPod and the Culture of Mobile Listening', *Leisure Studies*, Vol. 24, No. 4, 343–55.

Burgess, J. and Green, J. (2009) *YouTube: Online Video and Participatory Culture* (Cambridge: Polity Press).

Burgess, R. G. (1982) *Field Research: A Sourcebook and Field Manual* (London: Routledge).

Burgess, R. G. (1991) *In the Field: An Introduction to Field Research* (London: Routledge).

Búriková, Z. (2006) 'The Embarrassment of Co-Presence: Au Pairs and their Rooms', *Home Cultures*, Vol. 3, No. 2, 99–122.

Chandler, D. and Roberts-Young, D. (1998) 'The Construction of Identity in the Personal Homepages of Adolescents', http://www.aber.ac.uk/media/documents/short/strasbourg.html (accessed 10/02/06).

Chaney, D. (2004) 'Fragmented Culture and Subcultures', in A. Bennett and K. Kahn-Harris (eds.), *After Subculture: Critical Studies in Contemporary Youth Culture* (Basingstoke: Palgrave Macmillan), 36–48.

Christie, H., Munro, M. and Rettig, H. (2002) 'Accommodating Students', *Journal of Youth Studies*, Vol. 5, No. 2, 209–35.

Clarke, G. (1981) 'Defending Ski-Jumpers: A Critique of Theories of Youth Cultures', in K. Gelder (ed.), *The Subcultures Reader* (London: Routledge, 2nd edn. 2005), 169–75.

Clarke, J. and Jefferson, T. (1976) 'Working Class Youth Cultures', in G. Mungham and G. Pearson (eds.), *Working Class Youth Cultures* (London: Routledge & Kegan Paul), 138–58.

Coffey, A. (1999) *The Ethnographic Self: Fieldwork and Representations of Identity* (London: Sage).

Coffey, A. and Atkinson, P. (1996) *Making Sense of Qualitative Data: Complementary Research Strategies* (London: Sage).

Cohen, S. (1972) *Folk Devils and Moral Panics* (London: MacGibbon and Kee).

Cohen, S. (1991) *Rock Music in Liverpool: Popular Music in the Making* (Oxford: Oxford University Press).

Coles, B. (1986) 'Gonna Tear Your Playhouse Down: Towards Reconstructing a Sociology of Youth', *Social Science Teacher*, Vol. 15, No. 3, 78–80.

Collier, J. (1995 [1975]) 'Photography and Visual Anthropology', in P. Hockings (ed.), *Principles of Visual Anthropology* (Berlin and New York: Mouton de Gruyter), 235–54.

Croft, J. (1997) 'Youth Culture and Style', in M. Storry and P. Childs (eds.), *British Cultural Identities* (London: Routledge), 139–74.

Crowe, N. and Bradford, S. (2007) 'Identity and Structure in Online Gaming: Young People's Symbolic and Virtual Extensions of Self', in P. Hodkinson and W. Deicke (eds.), *Youth Cultures: Scenes, Subcultures and Tribes* (London: Routledge), 217–30.

Danesi, M. (1994) *Cool: The Signs and Meanings of Adolescence* (Toronto: University of Toronto Press).

Dant, T. (1999) *Material Culture in the Social World: Values, Activities, Lifestyles* (Buckingham: Open University Press).

Delamont, S. (1992) *Fieldwork in Educational Settings: Methods, Pitfalls and Perspectives* (London: Routledge Falmer).

Delamont, S. (2004) 'Ethnography and Participant Observation', in C. Seale, G. Gobo, J. F. Gubrium and D. Silverman (eds.), *Qualitative Research Practice* (London: Sage), 205–17.

DeNora, T. (2000) *Music in Everyday Life* (Cambridge: Cambridge University Press).

Dickinson, R., Murcott, A., Eldridge, J. and Leader, S. (2001) 'Breakfast, Time and "Breakfast Time": Television, Food and the Household Organisation of Consumption', *Television and New Media*, Vol. 2, No. 3, 235–56.

Dicks, B., Flewitt, R., Lancaster, L. and Pahl, K. (2011) 'Multimodality and Ethnography: Working at the Intersection', *Qualitative Research*, Vol. 11, No. 3, 227–37.

Dittmar, H. (1992) *The Social Psychology of Material Possessions: To Have is to Be* (Hemel Hempstead: Harvester Wheatsheaf).

Dodman, D. R. (2003) 'Shooting in the City: An Autophotographic Exploration of the Urban Environment in Kingston, Jamaica', *Area*, Vol. 35, No. 3, 293–304.

Doherty, T. (2002) *Teenagers and Teenpics: The Juvenilization of American Movies in the 1950s* (2nd edn., Philadelphia: Temple University Press).

Drotner, K. (2000) 'Difference and Diversity: Trends in Young Danes' Media Use', *Media Culture & Society*, Vol. 22, No. 2, 149–66.

Druits, L. (2008) *Multi-Girl-Culture: An Ethnography of Doing Identity* (Amsterdam: University of Amsterdam Press).

Epstein, J. S. (1998) *Youth Culture: Identity in a Postmodern World* (Oxford: Blackwell).

Erikson, E. H. (1968) *Identity: Youth and Crisis* (New York: Norton).

Fetterman, D. M. (2010) *Ethnography Step by Step* (3rd edn., London: Sage).

France, A. (2004) 'Young People', in S. Fraser, V. Lewis, S. Ding, M. Kellett and C. Robinson (eds.), *Doing Research with Children and Young People* (London: Sage), 175–90.

France, A. (2007) *Understanding Youth in Late Modernity* (Maidenhead: Open University Press).

Frith, S. (1984) *The Sociology of Youth* (Ormskirk: Causeway).

Frith, S. (1996) *Performing Rites: On the Value of Popular Music* (Cambridge: MA: Harvard University Press).

Furlong, A. and Cartmel, F. (2006) *Young People and Social Change: New Perspectives* (Buckingham: Open University Press).

Gauntlett, D. (2007) *Creative Explorations: New Approaches to Identities and Audiences* (London: Routledge).

Geertz, C. (1973) *The Interpretation of Cultures* (New York: Fontana Books).

Giddens, A. (1991) *Modernity and Self-Identity: Self and Society in the Late Modern Age* (California: Stanford University Press).

Gilbert, N. (1993) *Researching Social Life* (London: Sage).

Glevarec, H. (2009) *La Culture de la Chambre: Préadolescence et Culture Contemporaine dans l'espace Familial* (Paris: La Documentation Française).

Goffman, I. (1959) *The Presentation of Self in Everyday Life* (London: Penguin).

Griffin, C. (1993) *Representations of Youth* (Cambridge: Polity Press).

Griffiths, V. (1995) *Adolescent Girls and their Friends: A Feminist Ethnography* (Aldershot: Avebury).

Hall, S. and Jefferson, T. (eds.) (1975) *Resistance through Rituals: Youth Subcultures in Post War Britain* (London: Hutchinson and Co).

Hammersley, M. and Atkinson, P. (1995) *Ethnography: Principles in Practice* (London: Routledge).

Hammersley, M. and Atkinson, P. (2007) *Ethnography: Principles in Practice* (3rd edn., London: Routledge).

Harris, A. (2004a) *Future Girl: Young Women in the Twenty-First Century* (London: Routledge).

Harris, A. (ed.) (2004b) *All About the Girl: Culture, Power and Identity* (London: Routledge).

Heath, S. (1999) 'Young Adults and Household Formation in the 1990s', *British Journal of Sociology of Education*, Vol. 20, No. 4, 545–61.

Heath, S. (2004) 'Peer-Shared Households, Quasi-Communes and Neo-Tribes', *Current Sociology*, Vol. 52, No. 2, 161–79.

Heath, S. and Kenyon, L. (2001) 'Single Young Professionals and Shared Household Living', *Journal of Youth Studies*, Vol. 4, No. 1, 83–100.

Heath, S., Brooks, R., Clever, E. and Ireland, E. (2009) *Researching Young People's Lives* (London: Sage).

Hebdige, D. (1979) *Subculture: The Meaning of Style* (London: Methuen).

Henderson, S., Holland, J., McGrellis, S., Sharpe, S. and Thomson, R. (2007) *Inventing Adulthoods: A Biographical Approach to Youth Transitions* (London: Sage).

Hendry, L. B. (1983) *Growing Up and Going Out: Adolescents and Leisure* (Aberdeen: Aberdeen University Press).

Hendry, L. B. (ed.) (1993) *Young People's Leisure and Lifestyles* (London: Routledge).

Hetherington, K. (1998) *Expressions of Identity: Space, Performance, Politics* (London: Sage).

Hey, V. (1997) *The Company She Keeps: An Ethnography of Girls' Friendships* (Buckingham: Open University Press).

Hodkinson, P. (2002) *Goth: Identity, Style and Subculture* (Oxford: Berg).

Hodkinson, P (2003) '"Net.Goth" Internet Communications and (Sub) Cultural Boundaries', in D. Muggleton and R. Weinzierl (eds.), *The Post-Subcultures Reader* (Oxford: Berg), 285–98.

Hodkinson, P. (2007) 'Interactive Online Journals and Individualisation', *New Media and Society*, Vol. 9, No. 4, 625–50.

Hodkinson, P. and Lincoln, S. (2008) 'Online Journals as Virtual Bedrooms? Young People, Identity and Personal Space', *YOUNG: The Nordic Journal of Youth Research*, Vol. 16, No. 4, 625–50.

Hollands, R. (1995) *Friday Night, Saturday Night* (Newcastle-upon-Tyne: University of Newcastle Press).

Hollands, R. and Chatterton, P. (2001) *Changing Our 'Toon': Youth, Nightlife and Urban Change in Newcastle* (Newcastle-upon-Tyne: University of Newcastle Press).

Hollows, J. (2008) *Domestic Cultures* (Maidenhead: Open University Press).

Hopkins, P. (2010) *Young People, Place and Identity* (London: Routledge).

Horsley, R. (2005) 'Men's Lifestyle Magazines and the Construction of Male Identity', unpublished PhD thesis (London: University of Westminster).

Howard, S. (1998) *Wired-Up: Young People and Electronic Media* (London: UCL Press).

Hulme, M. (2009) 'Life Support: Young People's Needs in a Digital Age', www.youthnet.org (accessed 14/10/09).

James, K. A. (2001) '"I just gotta have my own space!": The Bedroom as a Leisure Site for Adolescent Girls', *Journal of Leisure Research*, Vol. 33, No. 1, 71–90.

Jenkins, H. (2006) *Convergence Culture: Where Old and New Media Collide* (New York: New York University Press).

Jones, G. and Wallace, C. (1992) *Youth, Family and Citizenship* (Buckingham: Open University Press).

Kearney, M. C. (2007) 'Productive Spaces: Girls' Bedrooms as Sites of Cultural Production', *Journal of Children and Media*, Vol. 1 No. 2, 126–41.

Kehily, M. J. (2008) 'Taking Centre Stage? Girlhood and the Contradictions of Femininity across Three Generations', *Girlhood Studies*, Vol. 1, No. 2, 51–71.

Kenyon, L. (1999) 'A Home from Home: Students' Transitional Experiences of Home', in T. Chapman and J. Hockey (eds.), *Ideal Homes: Social Change and Domestic Life* (London: Routledge), 84–95.

Kenyon, L. and Heath, S. (2001) 'Choosing this Life: Narratives of Choice amongst House Sharers', *Housing Studies*, Vol. 16, No. 5, 619–35.

Knowles, C. and Sweetman, P. (eds.) (2004) *Picturing the Social Landscape: Visual Methods and the Sociological Imagination* (London: Routledge).

Lahelma, E. and Gordon, T. (2003) 'Home as a Physical, Social and Mental Space: Young People's Reflections on Leaving Home', *Journal of Youth Studies*, Vol. 6, No. 4, 377–90.

Largey, G. P. and Watson, D. R. (1973) 'The Sociology of Odors', *American Journal of Sociology*, Vol. 77, No. 6, 1021–34.

Larson, R. (1995) 'Secrets in the Bedroom: Adolescents' Private Use of Media', *Journal of Youth and Adolescence*, Vol. 24, No. 5, 535–50.

Leccardi, C. and Ruspini, E. (2006) *A New Youth? Young People, Generations and Family Life* (Aldershot: Ashgate).

Lefebvre, H. (1971) *Everyday Life in the Modern World* (London: Allen Gate).

Lefebvre, H. (1987) 'The Everyday and Everydayness', *Yale French Studies*, No. 73, 7–11.

Lefebvre, H. (1991) *The Production of Space* (Oxford: Blackwell).

Lenhart, A. and Madden, M. (2007) 'Teens, Privacy and Online Social Networks', Pew Internet and American Life Project, http://www.pewinternet.org/Reports/2007/Teens-Privacy-and-Online-Social-Networks.aspx (accessed 06/11/10).

Lincoln, S. (2004) 'Teenage Girls' Bedroom Culture: Codes versus Zones', in A. Bennett and K. Kahn-Harris (eds.), *After Subculture: Critical Studies in Contemporary Youth Culture* (Basingstoke: Palgrave Macmillan), 94–106.

Lincoln, S. (2005) 'Feeling the Noise: Teenagers, Bedrooms and Music', *Leisure Studies*, Vol. 24, No. 4, 399–414.

Lincoln, S. (2006) 'Beyond Bedrooms? Revising "Subculture" for Teenage Private Spaces', in T. Palmaerts (ed.), *Talkie Walkie [Jongerensubcultuur] 4 believers/non-believers* (Leuven: ACCO), 18–30.

Livingstone, S. (2002) *Young People and New Media: Childhood and the Changing Media Environment* (London: Sage).

Livingstone, S. (2005) 'In Defence of Privacy: Mediating the Public/Private Boundary at Home', London. LSE Research Online, http://eprints.lse.ac.uk/archive/00000505 (accessed 09/11/08).

Livingstone, S. (2006) 'Children's Privacy Online: Experimenting with Boundaries within and beyond the Family', in R. Kraut, M. Brynin and S. Kiesler (eds.), *Computers, Phones, and the Internet: Domesticating Information Technologies* (Oxford: Oxford University Press), 128–44.

Livingstone, S. (2007) 'From Family Television to Bedroom Culture: Young People's Media at Home', in E. Devereux (ed.), *Media Studies: Key Issues and Debates* (London: Sage), 302–21.

Livingstone, S. (2009) *Children and the Internet: Great Expectations, Challenging Realities* (Cambridge: Polity Press).

Livingstone, S. and Bovill, M. (1999) *Young People, New Media: Summary Report of the Research Project 'Children, Young People and the Changing Media Environment'* (London: Media@LSE).

Machin, D. (2002) *Ethnographic Research for Media Studies* (London: Arnold).

Malbon, B. (1998) 'The Club: Clubbing, Consumption, Identity and the Spatial Practices of Every-Night Life', in T. Skelton and G. Valentine (eds.), *Cool Places: Geographies of Youth Cultures* (London: Routledge), 266–86.

Mallan, K. (2009) 'Look at Me! Look at Me! Self-Representation and Self Exposure through Online Networks', *Digital Culture and Education*, Vol. 1, No. 2.

Marshall, S. and Borrill, C. (1984) 'Understanding the Invisibility of Young Women', *Youth and Policy*, No. 9, 36–9.

Matza, D. (1964) *Delinquency and Drift* (New York: John Wiley).

Mays, J. B. (1954) *Growing Up in the City: A Study of Juvenile Delinquency in an Urban Neighbourhood* (Liverpool: Liverpool University Press).

McNamee, S. (1998) 'The Home: Youth, Gender and Video Games: Power and Control in the Home', in T. Skelton and G. Valentine (eds.), *Cool Places: Geographies of Youth Cultures* (London: Routledge), 195–206.

McRobbie, A. (1990) 'Settling Accounts with Subcultures: A Feminist Critique', in S. Frith and A. Goodwin (eds.), *On the Record: Rock, Pop and the Written Word* (London: Routledge), 66–80.

McRobbie, A. (1991) *Feminism and Youth Culture: From Jackie to Just Seventeen* (Basingstoke: Macmillan).

McRobbie, A. (2000) *Feminism and Youth Culture* (2nd edn., Basingstoke: Palgrave Macmillan).

McRobbie, A. and Garber, J. (1975) 'Girls and Subcultures', in S. Hall and T. Jefferson (eds.), *Resistance Through Rituals: Youth Subcultures in Post-War Britain* (London: Hutchinson and Co), 209–23. Reprinted in A. McRobbie (ed.), *Feminism and Youth Culture from Jackie to Just Seventeen* (London: Macmillan, 1991), 12–25.

Miles, S. (2000) *Youth Lifestyles in a Changing World* (Buckingham: Open University Press).

Miller, B. M. (1958) 'Lower Class Culture as a Generating Milieu of Gang Delinquency', *Journal of Social Issues*, Vol. 14, No. 3, 5–20.

Miller, D. (2001) *Home Possessions: Material Culture behind Closed Doors* (Oxford: Berg).

Miller, D. (2008) *The Comfort of Things* (Cambridge: Polity Press).

Molgat, M. (n.d) 'The Challenges of Youth Transitions for Youth Policy Development: Reflections from the Canadian Context', *Forum 21* [research]. http://www.coe.int/t/dg4/youth/Source/Resources/Forum21/II_Issue_No4/II_No4_Canadian_context_en.pdf (accessed 20/06/10).

Molgat, M. (2007) 'Do Transitions and Social Structures Matter? How "Emerging Adults" Define Themselves as Adults', *Journal of Youth* Studies, Vol. 10, No. 5, 495–516.

Moore, K. (2003) 'E-heads versus Beer Monsters: Researching Young People's Music and Drug Consumption in Dance Club Settings', in A. Bennett, M. Cieslik and S. Miles (eds.), *Researching Youth* (Basingstoke: Palgrave Macmillan), 138–53.

Moran, J. (2004) 'History, Memory and the Everyday', *Rethinking History*, Vol. 8, No. 1, 51–68.

Moss, D. and Richter, I. (2010) 'Understanding Young People's Transitions in University Halls through Space and Time', *YOUNG: The Nordic Journal of Youth Research*, Vol. 18, No. 2, 157–76.

Muggleton, D. (1997) 'The Post-Subculturalist', in S. Redhead, D. Wynne and J. O'Connor (eds.), *The Clubcultures Reader: Readings in Popular Cultural Studies* (Oxford: Blackwell), 167–85.

Muggleton, D. (2000) *Inside Subculture: The Post-Modern Meaning of Style* (Oxford: Berg).

Muggleton, D. and Weinzierl, R. (eds.) (2003) *The Post-Subcultures Reader* (Oxford: Berg).

Mythen, G. and Walklate, S. (2006) *Beyond the Risk Society* (Buckingham: Open University Press).

Nayak, A. and Kehily, M. J. (2008) *Gender, Youth and Culture: Young Masculinities and Femininities* (Basingstoke: Palgrave Macmillan).

Nicholls, J. (2009) 'Young People, Alcohol and the News: Preliminary Findings for The Alcohol Education and Research Council', http://www.aerc.org.uk/insightPages/libraryIns0067.html (accessed 01/11/09).

Nilan, P. and Feixa, C. (2006) *Global Youth? Hybrid Identities, Plural Lives* (London: Routledge).

Nippert-Eng, C. E. (1996) *Home and Work: Negotiating Boundaries through Everyday Life* (Chicago: University of Chicago Press).

O'Reilly, K. (2005) *Ethnographic Methods* (London: Routledge).

Orlet, C. (2007) 'The Look at Me Generation', *The American Spectator*, http://spectator.org/archives/2007/03/02/the-look-at-me-generation (accessed 12/10/10).

Osgerby, B. (1998) *Youth in Britain since 1945* (Oxford: Blackwell).

Osgerby, B. (2002) 'A Caste, A Culture, A Market: Youth, Lifestyle and Marketing Practice in Postwar America', in R. Strickland (ed.), *Growing up Postmodern: Neoliberalism and the War on the Young* (Chicago: Rowman & Littlefield).

Osgerby, B. (2004) *Youth Media* (London: Routledge).

Pearson, E. (2009) 'All the World Wide Web's a Stage: The Performance of Identity in Online Social Networks', *First Monday*, Vol. 14, No. 3, http://firstmonday.org/htbin/cgiwrap/bin/ojs/index.php/fm/article/view/2162/2127 (accessed 30/01/12).

Piepmeier, A. (2009) *Girl Zines: Making Media, Doing Feminism* (New York: New York University Press).

Pink, S. (2004) *Home Truths: Gender, Domestic Objects and Everyday Life* (Oxford: Berg).

Pink, S. (2007) *Doing Visual Ethnography* (2nd edn., London: Sage).

Pink, S. (2009) *Doing Sensory Ethnography* (London: Sage).

Ponterotto, J. G. (2006) 'Brief Note on the Origins, Evolution and Meaning of the Qualitative Research Concept "Thick Description"', *The Qualitative Reporter*, Vol. 11, No. 3, 538–49.

Prosser, J. (ed.) (1998) *Image-Based Research* (London: Routledge/Falmer).

Proweller, A. (1998) *Constructing Female Identities: Meaning Making in an Upper Class Youth Culture* (Albany: State University of New York Press).

Redhead, S. (1997) *From Subcultures to Clubcultures: An Introduction to Popular Cultural Studies* (Oxford: Blackwell).

Redhead, S., Wynne, D. and O'Connor, J. (eds.) (1997) *The Clubcultures Reader: Readings in Popular Cultural Studies* (Oxford: Blackwell).

Reid-Walsh, J. and Mitchell, C. (2004) 'Girls' Websites: A Virtual "Room of One's Own?"' in A. Harris (ed.), *All About the Girl: Culture, Power and Identity* (Oxford: Routledge), 173–82.

Reimer, B. (1995) 'The Media in Public and Private Spheres', in J. Fornäs and G. Bolin (eds.), *Youth Culture in Late Modernity* (London: Sage), 58–71.

Reimer, S. and Leslie, D. (2004) 'Identity, Consumption and the Home', *Home Cultures*, Vol. 1, No. 3, 187–208.

Robards, B. (2010) 'Randoms in My Bedroom: Negotiating Privacy and Unsolicited Contact on Social Networking Sites', *Prism*, Vol. 7, No. 3, http://www.prismjournal.org/fileadmin/Social_media/Robards.pdf (accessed 30/01/12).

Robards, B. and Bennett, A. (2011) 'MyTribe: Manifestations of Belonging on Social Networking Sites', *Sociology*, Vol. 45, No. 2, 303–17.

Roberts, K. (2009) *Youth in Transition: Eastern Europe and the West* (Basingstoke: Palgrave Macmillan).

Rose, G. (2007) *Visual Methodologies: An Introduction to the Interpretation of Visual Materials* (2nd edn., London: Sage).

Rose, N. (1999) *Governing the Soul: The Shaping of the Private Self* (London: Free Associations Books).

Rubin, H. J. and Rubin, I. S. (2005) *Qualitative Interviewing: The Art of Hearing Data* (2nd edn., London: Sage).

Russell, R. and Tyler, M. (2002) 'Thank Heaven for Little Girls: "Girl Heaven" and the Commercial Context of Feminine Childhood', *Sociology*, Vol. 36, No. 3, 619–37.

Ryle, Gilbert (1971) *Collected Papers, Volume II, Collected Essays 1929–1968* (New York: Barnes and Noble).

Savage, J. (2007) *Teenage: The Creation of Youth 1975–1945* (London: Chatto & Windus).

Seiter, E. (1999) *Television and New Media Audiences* (New York: Oxford University Press).

Sessions, L. F. (2009) '"You Looked Better on MySpace": Deception and Authenticity on Web 2.0', *First Monday*, Vol. 14, No. 7, http://firstmonday.org/htbin/cgiwrap/bin/ojs/index.php/fm/article/view/2539/2242 (accessed 30/01/12).

Shildrick, T. and MacDonald, R. (2006) 'In Defence of Subculture: Young People, Leisure and Social Divisions', *Journal of Youth Studies*, Vol. 9, No. 2, 125–40.

Shildrick, T., Blackman, S. and MacDonald, R. (2009) 'Young People, Class and Place', *Journal of Youth Studies*, Vol. 12, No. 5, 457–65.

Sibley, D. (1995) *Geographies of Exclusion: Society and Difference in the West* (London: Routledge).

Skeggs, B. (1994) 'Situating the Production of Feminist Ethnography', in M. Maynard and J. Purvis (eds.), *Researching Women's Lives from a Feminist Perspective* (Abingdon: Taylor & Francis), 72–92.

Skelton, T. and Valentine, G. (eds.) (1998) *Cool Places: Geographies of Youth Cultures* (London: Routledge).

Spradley, J. P. (1979) *The Ethnographic Interview* (New York: Holt, Rinehart and Winston).

Stahl, G. (1999) 'Still "Winning Space?" Updating Subcultural Theory', *Invisible Culture: An Electronic Journal For Visual Studies*, Issue 2, http://www.rochester.edu/in_visible_culture/issue2/stahl.htm (accessed 30/01/12).

Steele, J. R. and Brown, J. D. (1995) 'Adolescent Room Culture: Studying Media in the Context of Everyday Life', *Journal of Youth and Adolescence*, Vol. 24, No. 5, 551–76.

Strickland, R. (ed.) (2002) *Growing up Postmodern: Neoliberalism and the War on the Young* (Chicago: Rowman & Littlefield).

Sveningsson, E. (2009) 'Exploring and Negotiating Femininity: Young Women's Creation of Style in a Swedish Internet Community', *YOUNG: The Nordic Journal of Youth Research*, Vol. 17, No. 3, 241–64.

Tapscott, D. (1998) *Growing Up Digital: The Rise of the Net Generation* (London: McGraw-Hill).

Tapscott, D. (2008) *Grown Up Digital: How the Net Generation is Changing Your World* (London: McGraw-Hill).

Thornton, S. (1995) *Club Cultures: Music, Media and Subcultural Capital* (Cambridge: Polity Press).

Turkle, S (1995) *Life on Screen: Identity in the Age of the Internet* (New York: Simon & Schuster).

Turkle, S. (ed.) (2007) *Evocative Objects: Things We Think With* (Cambridge, MA: MIT Press).

Tutt, D. (2005) 'Mobile Performances of a Teenager: A Study of Situated Mobile Phone Activity in the Living Room', *Convergence: The International Journal of Research into New Media Technologies*, Vol. 11, No. 2, 58–75.

Tzioumakis, Y. (2006) *American Independent Cinema: An Introduction* (Edinburgh: Edinburgh University Press).

Valentine, G. (1997) 'A Safe Place to Grow up? Parenting, Perceptions of Children's Safety and the Rural Idyll', *Journal of Rural Studies*, Vol. 3, No. 2, 137–48.

Valentine, G. (2004) *Public Space and the Culture of Childhood* (Aldershot: Ashgate).

Valentine, G. and McKendrick, J. (1997) 'Children's Outdoor Play: Exploring Parental Concerns about Children's Safety and the Changing Nature of Childhood', *Geoforum*, Vol. 28, No. 2, 219–35.

Van Zoonen, L. (1994) *Feminist Media Studies* (London: Sage).

Walker, C. (2000) '"Its difficult to hide it": The Presentation of Self on Internet Home Pages', *Qualitative Research*, Vol. 23, No. 1, 99–120.

Wallace, C. and Kovatcheva, S. (1998) *Youth in Society: The Construction and Deconstruction of Youth in East and West Europe* (Basingstoke: Macmillan).

Walsh, S. and White, K. (2006) 'Ring, Ring, Why Did I Make That Call?: Mobile Phone Beliefs and Behaviour Among Australian University Students', *Youth Studies Australia*, Vol. 25, No. 3, 49–57.

Waters, C. (1981) 'Badges of Half-formed Inarticulate Radicalism: A Critique of Recent Trends in the Study of Working Class Youth Culture', *International Labour and Working Class History*, Vol. 19, 23–37.

Watt, P. and Stenson, K. (1998) 'The Street: "It's a Bit Dodgy Around Here": Safety, Danger, Ethnicity and Young People's Use of Public Space', in T. Skelton and G. Valentine (eds.), *Cool Places: Geographies of Youth Cultures* (London: Routledge), 249–65.

Whyte, W. F. (1943) *Street Corner Society Street: The Social Structure of an Italian Slum* (Chicago: University of Chicago Press).

Willis, P. (1977) *Learning to Labour: How Working-Class Kids Get Working Class-Jobs* (Farnborough: Saxon House).

Willis, P. (1990) *Common Culture: Symbolic Work at Play in the Everyday Cultures of the Young* (Buckingham: Open University Press).

Woodman, D. (2009) 'The Mysterious Case of the Pervasive Choice Biography: Ulrich Beck, Structure/Agency and the Middling State of Theory in the Sociology of Youth', *Journal of Youth Studies*, Vol. 12, No. 3, 243–56.

Wyn, J. and White, R. (1997) *Rethinking Youth* (London: Sage).

Index

CPI Antony Rowe
Chippenham, UK
2016-12-20 21:20